CHAPTER 1

Wake-up Call

Sometimes the truth doesn't set you free. Sometimes the truth arrives like a suicide bomber with an explosive device attached to his chest, next to his heart, ready to obliterate your own. Although I had been running from this possibility for years, galloping through my days and nights like a mad woman pursued by a demon, the bomber was here to serve notice that any further attempts at resistance on my part were futile.

The early afternoon of August 6, 2015, was warm and unusually humid in the town of Huntsville, Utah, located on a 5,000-foot-high mountain valley surrounded by the towering peaks of the Wasatch Mountains. Despite the state's well-earned reputation as a bone-dry desert, a heavy summer rainstorm the night before had left behind a blanket of muggy air that settled around me. I sat on our log home's wraparound porch on an old, faded wicker bench, the cracked, tortuous sinews of bamboo long ago bent beyond their natural limits. I felt that same pain deep in my own bones—I knew what it was to be pushed beyond the limits of endurance and locked in a twisted agony of waiting. I stared at my cell phone and willed it to ring: it was the only remaining lifeline between our son, Eric,[1] and me. Beads of sweat ran down my back, and I pulled my shoulder-length hair off my neck in a vain attempt to cool down.

I had spent the morning frantically texting and calling our son, who had run away from home a few days ago after another failed attempt by his father and me to get him to return to an inpatient drug rehab program. We knew that he had a car, so at least he wasn't sleeping on the streets. But we were both terrified as to what lengths he might go to get his next heroin fix. The last time I'd talked to him, he had sounded more desperate than ever. He told me he would rather die than go back to rehab, and I was afraid his ultimatum might turn into a self-fulfilling prophecy.

My cell phone screen suddenly beeped to life with a text from him. My pulse pounded in my throat and forehead. Despite the humidity, my mouth suddenly felt so dry that I couldn't swallow. I opened the message.

"I hate my life. I just want to end this."

I'd heard this many times from him over the past three years. "Your life can be better," I texted back. "We love you and we want to help you fix this."

"You can't fix this. Nobody can."

My adrenaline was peaking, preparing me to protect my child at any cost from the predators that surrounded him. But there was nothing I could do. Rather than running from a pack of wolves, he was running from himself. "We love you! PLEASE CALL ME. Tell me where you are, and we will come get you."

No response. My lips and face were tingling, and I tried to slow my breathing in order to stop hyperventilating. I knew Eric didn't have much fight left in him, and I imagined him slumped over in his car on some back road in Salt Lake City, dying alone.

As this catastrophe was unfolding, my husband, Jason, was leading an appraiser through our home as we tried to complete a refinance. Jason knew that things with our son were grim, but he didn't know about the latest text messages we had exchanged. Enmeshed in the details of refinancing, he had temporarily surrounded himself with a protective Teflon coating that removed him from the pivotal moment playing out. It was all I could do not to snarl when the real-estate appraiser made the mistake of approaching me on the front porch. "How are you doing, Mrs. Taylor?" he asked pleasantly.

My clipped response told him that I was *not* doing well

at all. It wasn't his fault—he didn't know about the life-and-death scenario that was unfolding at that instant. When he finally left, I sharply motioned my husband to come toward me and lashed out at him in an agony born of despair. "While you were showing our house to a total stranger, our son told me he is going to kill himself!" I quickly read him the series of text messages that we had just exchanged.

Jason's face drained of color. I knew that he completely loved both of our children and would do anything for them, but as a retired United States Navy submarine officer, he was much better at compartmentalizing all the disparate parts of his life that seemed inextricably tangled in my own. He sank onto the bench beside me and dropped his head into his hands. "What can we do? There's nothing we can do."

"I don't know where he is!" My hands shaking, I texted our son again: "Where are you? We will come pick you up and bring you home and then take you to rehab."

This time, our son answered. "I'm not going to tell you where I am." This back and forth went on for another hour. I was growing more frantic by the minute. He had been depressed before, but this time it felt more ominous.

Finally, Eric texted and told me that he was sitting in his car in the Salt Lake Behavioral Health Clinic parking lot in south Salt Lake City. He had been there in March 2015 for four days of inpatient drug rehab before our insurance company had decided that the treatment was no longer medically necessary. I knew that if I could get him to walk into the hospital, they could commit him and keep him safe.

Then my cell phone buzzed with a new message. When I read it, my fear only deepened: "Don't worry Mom. Everything's going to be OK, and so am I." This sudden shift of tone alarmed me more than the previous series of hopeless messages. When I told this to one of my therapist friends later, she confirmed that before committing suicide, some people experience a sense of respite and peace when they believe that the end is near.

"Don't do anything to hurt yourself!" I wrote back. "PLEASE CALL ME!"

No answer.

"Are you still in the hospital parking lot?"

No answer.

I had to make a quick decision. Did I believe his life was in danger? I knew without a doubt that the answer was yes. I dialed the behavioral clinic and told them that my son, a former patient, was sitting in their parking lot and that I was terrified that he was going to hurt himself. My voice trembling, I asked the nurse, "Can you please go out to the parking lot and bring him in?"

"How old is he?" she asked. "If he's over the age of eighteen, it's against the law for us to force him inside."

"He's twenty-four."

She was exceptionally kind but apologetic. "If you can just convince him to walk through the front door and *tell* us that he needs help, we can keep him here under observation until we deem him to be safe."

"But he won't do that!" I cried. "And I can't drive there fast enough to drag him inside." I explained that we lived at least an hour away from the hospital; and *that* was only if Interstate 15, the state's main north-south corridor, wasn't backlogged with traffic, road construction, or multiple wrecks, which it often was.

"I'm so sorry, ma'am," she said softly. I could hear the regret in her voice. "We are legally prohibited from committing an adult to a mental health facility unless the person walks in voluntarily."

"So there's *nothing* you can do?"

"Mrs. Taylor, I want you to hang up and dial 911. Tell the police that you think your son is a suicide risk and give them our address. Then, please call your son again and try to get him to walk in."

I quickly dialed 911 and spoke to a dispatcher. "I believe my son is going to commit suicide—we just exchanged some terrifying text messages." When the person on the other end asked me why I believed this, I explained that our son was battling a drug addiction and had recently been kicked out of our home. "Can you please go look for him?" I pleaded. Then I started to weep. I gave them my son's name and a description of his car. The operator repeated everything I had said and then hung up.

I was suddenly, completely exhausted; the act of pulling air into my lungs and pushing it out again required too much effort. Total silence enveloped my husband and me as we sat unmoving, unspeaking. There was nothing left to do or say. A sense of unreality slid over me as silently as a bat's wing. I felt curiously detached, as if I were two people: one of them was about to lose her only son; the other stood a distance away, a silent witness.

As we waited for the phone call that would forever change our lives, I felt disoriented. How had we arrived at this particular juncture? I thought back to my idyllic, small-town childhood and adolescent years spent in Farmington, Utah. I had done my best to follow the rules passed down by my *Mormon*[2] pioneer ancestors and had believed that I was protecting myself and later my children from the destructive forces in the world, but obviously something had gone wrong —terribly, inescapably wrong.

CHAPTER 2

Pioneer Children

I grew up watching the hit TV series *The Andy Griffith Show*, which ran from 1960 to 1968 and later morphed into a spin-off called *Mayberry, RFD*. To this day, I love the nostalgic, black-and-white images and the gentle brand of small-town humor. Sheriff Andy's all-knowing wisdom, young Opie's wide-eyed wonder, and Aunt Bea's home cooking and grandmotherly advice all soothed my childhood soul. When I heard the familiar whistling during the opening credits, I knew that all was well in the world, both Andy Griffith's and my own. It wasn't until I was an adult that I realized why I loved the show so much: it perfectly captures the essence of the community that I grew up in.

Visitors who see the ever-expanding commercial development throughout Utah or the encroachment of housing developments up the sides of what was once pristine mountain terrain might be surprised to learn of the state's historically empty vistas and wide, open valleys. On July 24, 1847, when Brigham Young reached Salt Lake after a serious two-week illness that had left him bedridden in the back of a wagon, he supposedly rose up from his sickbed, pointed down at the landscape before him, and uttered, "This is the right place."[3] Although the region had long been settled by Indigenous Americans and was nominally under the control of Mexico until 1848, the Mormon pioneers were the first sizeable group of white descendants of European immigrants to set up permanent residence. Shortly after his arrival, Brigham Young instructed families to establish neighboring towns and to begin the herculean task of preparing for the many thousands of immigrants who would arrive over the next twenty years.

Generations of Mormon youth have rightly been taught to revere their pioneer ancestors, who left behind home, family, and most of their belongings to slog their way through a dangerous, ill-equipped journey. The settlers' final destination was so far removed from the established population centers in the country that only a group seeking total isolation would have found it an attractive option. And for a church that was running from its polygamist past in Nauvoo, Illinois, a practice that had stirred up the surrounding non-Mormon communities like a hornets' nest, Utah was as good a place as any to settle and continue to follow this peculiar doctrine.

Farmington, Utah, was one of the first towns settled in 1847 when a few families set up a small community and began to grow crops and establish permanent homes for the others who would soon follow. The early *Saints*[4] in Utah were assured that the Biblical promise in Isaiah applied directly to their arid home: "The wilderness and the solitary place shall be glad for them; and the desert shall rejoice, and blossom as the rose. . . . For in the wilderness shall waters break out, and streams in the desert" (Isa. 35:1, 6). These words were preached from the pulpit throughout my youth, and we all believed that this prophecy was one that foretold the building up of the Lord's modern-day Zion in the latter days.

Farmington grew to sleepy adulthood in long, luxurious stretches. The settlers worked hard, and very few outside influences disturbed their peace. The evils of the world that Brigham Young and successive Mormon leaders preached against were largely kept at bay for decades, and when I grew up there in the 1960s and '70s, it was still a small, conservative town settled by a few prominent pioneer families. Those families produced lots of children and grandchildren, most of whom stayed, and the cycle repeated itself for the next 120 years.

Although horses and buggies were the original means of transportation for the new arrivals, the Bamberger Railroad, built in the 1890s as a steam-powered railway and later converted to an electric line, served for decades as an essential means of transportation. The railroad reached Farmington in 1895 and was used for years to shuttle residents around the northern, more populous parts of the state. Although the train was eventually rendered obsolete in 1952 by improved highways and faster driving vehicles, the old train tracks stood for years in the foothills of Farmington.[5] My friends and I used to play along the abandoned rails, throwing rocks at the rattlesnakes that sometimes startled us as they sunned themselves along the same paths we played on.

My growing-up years were idyllic in the way common to all small towns. In our cozy, close-knit community, most of us knew everybody's business, but in a congenial, grandmotherly way that has long since disappeared as many of Utah's small towns have grown into fully mature cities. The Mormon Church was the only church in town, and, for all we knew back then, in the world. I grew up in the comforting embrace of stories passed down by my pioneer ancestors about how God loved us so much that he led us to this barren mountain desert to protect us from those who would have destroyed our way of life and our faith. I loved the scripture in Psalms 91:4 that told us He would "cover . . . [us] . . . with his feathers," and keep us safe "under his wings." We must have been very beloved of God to gain this kind of promise!

When my parents moved to Farmington in 1966, I was entering kindergarten. The neighborhood consisted of old brick homes that were strung up and down Main Street like so many mismatched beads. Our town was nestled up close to the western side of the Wasatch Mountains, which acted as a handy, built-in compass for those who were directionally challenged. "If you get lost, just remember that the mountains are east" was a common refrain.

My parents paid $10,000 for their modest house, an

oddly shaped, toffee-colored brick structure that squatted just a few feet back from U.S. Route 89. Now known as an official "Utah Heritage Highway," the route serves as a nostalgic reminder of slower, simpler times, and often beckons to tourists who want to experience the local flavor of the state. Back when I was growing up, however, Highway 89 was the main road in town and meandered through the state like a confused, elderly uncle who couldn't decide where he wanted to go. It wasn't until the 1960s that Interstate 15 (I-15) was started in Utah, and the freeway that now links much of southern and northern Utah wasn't completed until the early 1990s.[6]

We grew up as carefree as the windswept, desert land itself. We were surrounded by seemingly endless miles of undeveloped land, acres of waist-high wild grass, and thousands of grasshoppers that clicked as they leapt from the slender green stalks and attached themselves to our bare arms and legs. Corn silos and cow pastures dotted the rural landscape. All of my friends owned secondhand bikes, and our legs pumped up and down like smoothly oiled pistons anytime we needed to find an adventure.

Our only childhood rules were "Stay together and come home when it starts to get dark." That was it. There were no cell phones to check in with and no reason to check in, anyway. People rarely locked their doors. Our parents knew we'd survive in neighborhood packs the same way they had —by keeping each other in line and tattling on each other when necessary. There was no Internet to distract us from hours of outdoor play. We hunted down wasp nests; giant anthills; pale-blue, speckled birds' eggs; and old, sloughed-off rattlesnake skins. We played hide-and-seek and tag and kick-the-can. We built forts out of scavenged lumber, put on talent shows for our parents, and swung from dangerously frayed ropes tied to dead tree limbs to drop into the local swimming hole, Farmington Pond. Our childhoods were as different from those of today's children as an old record player is from a smartphone. We started neighborhood clubs that dissolved and re-formed as frequently as childhood squabbles. If any of us ever dared to complain that we were bored, our mothers would arch their eyebrows and tell us to go clean our bedrooms. This suggestion almost instantly and miraculously banished boredom; we usually found ways to escape within seconds before the bedroom-cleaning threat could materialize.

We biked everywhere in packs. None of us wore helmets or sunblock. My knees were routinely bloodied and skinned as I ran around the black asphalt playground at our elementary school. All girls were required to wear dresses at school, something which seemed completely ordinary, if nonetheless inconvenient. In the dead of Utah's freezing winters, we were allowed to wear a pair of pants, but only underneath the required dresses. When we entered fifth grade, my best friend and I started a petition to allow girls to wear pants to school; our principal relented only when the parents complained about their daughters' knees repeatedly getting scraped during recess.

The entire neighborhood attended religious services in a tiny, red-brick church that perched atop a gently sloping hill in North Farmington. Finished in 1919, it was the second church built in Farmington to meet the needs of the rapidly increasing population.[7] The building has long since been razed, but it served as the heart of the community for decades: weddings, baby showers, Christmas programs, cooking demonstrations, choir practices, and, of course, funerals were all held there.

Funerals have always been viewed as an opportunity for believing Mormons to proselyte any unbelievers who might be in attendance. I have attended more than one service where earnest and often teary speakers have spent more time calling upon the mourners in the audience to repent and turn to Jesus Christ than they have in memorializing the dead. But funerals were more than a chance to preach the gospel; they were also for socializing and eating. Several of the women in the *ward*[8] would be asked to provide platters of baked ham, cheesy funeral potatoes, freshly baked rolls, desserts, and odd mixtures of Jell-O salads with fruits, nuts, vegetables, cottage cheese, and sometimes even tuna. The men were asked to set up the folding chairs and long, plastic tables with folding legs in the church gymnasium. Then the family and friends of the deceased swarmed the gym and ate as many heaping plates of food as they could. After the food was gone and the conversations had ceased, the entire group pitched in for cleanup.

And, of course, we all scrubbed ourselves clean each Sunday morning to attend a series of nearly all-day church meetings. The men attended an early morning *priesthood*[9] session that usually ran for about an hour. Families attended ninety-minute-long *Sunday School*[10] meetings in the early afternoon that were segregated by age and then went home to eat a midday meal. The whole family returned later in the afternoon or early evening for a ninety-minute to two-hour *sacrament meeting* in which all members congregated together and partook of the sacrament in remembrance of Christ's atonement. Members of the ward also took turns offering prayers and giving talks. Whenever a long-winded speaker stood up with only a few minutes left in the meeting, everyone held their breath in the fruitless hope that the meeting wouldn't run overtime. We knew we were in trouble if the final talk started with "I know we're running out of time, but I feel inspired to speak about . . ." Despite some exaggerated yawns, deep sighs, and notable eye rolls from the audience, the earnest speaker was usually so carried away by the spirit that he or she was completely oblivious to the aroma of apathy wafting from the captive congregation.

With meetings this lengthy, toddlers squirmed, children and teenagers collapsed into boredom, and senior citizens fell asleep with their mouths wide open, snoring as they sat on the hard-backed church pews. Sometimes we were lucky enough to witness a member of the *bishopric*[11] fall asleep while sitting on the pulpit in front of the entire congregation. We eagerly watched to see which man's head would tip forth only to bounce back up into an upright position with eyes opened wide in an exaggerated pantomime of shocked alertness before dropping back down to his chest again.

Ward choirs were another source of great entertainment for youngsters held hostage on Sundays. The choirs were composed of diligent members—some of them musically gifted and others who were tone-deaf but more than willing to develop their talents in the service of the Lord. Choir conductors used a small, wooden-handled baton that magically bestowed legitimacy upon them. When my mother served as the choir director, I was amazed to see the baton transform her from my familiar, occasionally frazzled parent into a competent music leader, one who was able to corral the musical mayhem that confronted her into a respectable sound.

Sister[12] Conrad was one of our favorite choir singers to watch. She was short and shaped like a barrel, yet she was impeccably groomed in matching beads, bracelets, and earrings; her small, alert eyes peered out from behind bejeweled cat eye glasses as she waited for the conductor's baton to be raised. Then from her lungs issued forth a miraculous and deafening vibrato that echoed throughout the chapel, bouncing off the walls and completely drowning out every other singer. Sister Conrad took the scriptural admonition to raise a "joyful noise unto the Lord" to its logical, albeit extreme, conclusion. As the choir conductor frantically signaled the other choir members to increase their volume in an attempt to match Sister Conrad's, soon the entire group was shouting.

We sat in small, stuffy classrooms. The building was completed long before air conditioning had become common, and even after that, it was considered a wasteful luxury. The wooden floors in the basement of the building were scuffed by the shoes of generations of children who had sat in those same rooms and heard the same lessons recited: "We believe in God, the Eternal Father, and in His Son, Jesus Christ, and in the Holy Ghost. We believe that men will be punished for their own sins, and not for Adam's transgression. We believe that through the Atonement of Christ, all mankind may be saved, by obedience to the laws and *ordinances*[13] of the Gospel." These are the first three of the *Thirteen Articles of Faith,*[14] and all thirteen of them are burned into the deepest part of my brain. My guess is that long after old age has stripped away my short-term memories, these precepts will still be preserved in an ancient keepsake box in my frontal lobes, an eternal part of my childhood.

In addition to attending local church meetings, twice a year members gathered (either in person, or, in modern times, usually in front of their television sets) to listen to the church's semiannual *general conferences*. General conferences consist of five two-hour meetings that occur over two days and are broadcast around the globe. During these meetings, members receive spiritual guidance and counsel from the highest-ranking leaders. In one of the televised general conferences near the end of David O. McKay's lengthy presidency (1951-1970), when I was about eight years old, several groups of *Primary*[15] children from my *stake*[16] were invited to attend and sing in person. We had been warned repeatedly to be on our best behavior and were awestruck as we sat in the official Mormon Tabernacle Choir chairs in front of the imposing Salt Lake Tabernacle organ and saw the television cameras pointing towards us. Several of my relatives had gathered at my grandmother's house to watch the session on television; when they spotted me, there was a collision as some of them ran toward the screen to point at me.

Located on *Temple Square*,[17] the *Salt Lake Tabernacle* is a spacious, circular building that was finished in 1867, ten years before Brigham Young's death. The church website reports that architect and builder Henry Grow used a "lattice truss design so the Tabernacle roof was able to span its 150-foot-width without center supports." Both the exterior and interior of the Tabernacle are impressively beautiful, and the famed acoustics inside the building are such that a pin drop can be heard from "170 feet away," one of Young's requirements so that speakers could be heard by the entire audience decades before the invention of electronic microphones.[18] Tours are still given, and the public can attend rehearsals of the famed Mormon Tabernacle Choir and also hear live organ recitals played on one of the largest pipe organs in the world. The Tabernacle housed general conferences for over 130 years before it was replaced in 2000 by the Conference Center, a new, larger building that is located directly north of the Salt Lake Temple.

Throughout my youth, families babysat for each other, dated each other, and married each other. Neighbors ministered to one another in childbirth, sickness, poverty, and death. Bodies were embalmed and prepared for burial by the town mortician, but before the funeral, local ward leaders met to clothe their deceased neighbors and family members in their *temple clothing*.[19] It wasn't until I was a young adult and had been married in the Salt Lake Temple that I realized that the clothing I had seen in open-casket funerals—the white dresses and suits, the white veil for the women, the white hat for the men, and the green aprons patterned with embroidered fig leaves—were all symbolic of covenants made in the Mormon temples. In her job as our ward's *Relief Society president*,[20] my own mother helped dress several women in their official temple clothing before burial.

It is impossible to overstate the uniformity of religious beliefs that bound our small town and others throughout the state in a tight embrace. Back then, and for decades afterwards, we viewed the world in two categories: Mormons and *non-Mormons*. The arrogance in this distinction was unnoticeable because it was invisible, just like the clean, mountain air that we took for granted. But now I see a danger in it, a rendering of all things into two separate categories: insiders and outsiders, believers and non-believers, us and them. Most Mormons would be offended to be called a non-Catholic by their Catholic neighbors, but it never occurred to us that the label of non-Mormon was ethnocentric and hurtful. Mormonism's almost fanatical desire to enfold the entire world within its loving, if somewhat restrictive, grasp has ensured that one of the key tenets of church doctrine is missionary work. Generally, Mormons are hard-working, loving, generous people who desperately want everybody to join their club. For those who reject that invitation, members will oftentimes perform temple ordinances for people after they pass away. Their motives are good: doesn't everybody want to live in heaven, after all?

But the mindset that these motives produced was a skewed way of looking at the world. Everybody I knew growing up (myself included) believed that Mormons were right, and the rest of the world was wrong. I thought about this idea endlessly as a kid, trying to figure out how it would all play out in heaven when the Catholics, Baptists, and other "non-Mormons" arrived and were greeted by a Mormon messenger at the gates of heaven:

I imagined an elderly man shuffling up to pearly gates, nervously smoothing back his thinning hair. "Hello. I was told to report here for entrance into paradise."

The heavenly messenger squints his pale gray eyes while carefully perusing a long scroll of parchment paper rolled up on a pair of ornately carved sticks. "But aren't you Catholic?"

"Well, yes, and a good one at that. I had a shrine to the blessed Virgin Mary in my living room and had all my infants baptized by the priest."

The heavenly messenger frowns. "Apparently, you haven't been informed that the Mormon God is the one who's actually in charge up here."

The deceased man draws back in protest. "What? But I lived a good life, I helped my neighbors, I confessed every month to the priest!"

"Well, that does speak to your good intentions, but you also turned away a pair of Mormon missionaries, two young men who came knocking at your door back in—" He checks the scroll. "I believe it was 1964 while you were living in Baltimore. Let's see, it seems that one of them kept clearing his throat, and the other offered his hand multiple times in greeting, but you refused to take it."

The postmortem Catholic gasps in shock. "But I always thought Mormonism was a nontrinitarian cult! How could I have known that—"

The messenger cuts him off neatly, but not unkindly: "Please step to the left. You'll be assigned to spirit prison until you can rectify your mistaken beliefs."

As the poor deceased man stumbles to the left, mouth hanging open, heavenly Mormon missionaries dressed in white shirts and navy blue suits with their name tags pinned to their coat jackets escort him gently to a large waiting room. "It's really not as bad as you think," one of them says soothingly, tugging the man by the elbow. "There are lots of good Jell-O casseroles and funeral potatoes here, and in about a thousand years or so, you will most likely be paroled and get on with your heavenly adventure."

I pictured the looks of disbelief as the recently departed realized that the Mormon Church really was the *"only true and living church upon the face of the whole earth"* (D&C 1:30)[21] and that they should have listened to the young missionaries who knocked on their doors. I pictured them weeping, wailing, and gnashing their teeth. But my youthful innocence could not condemn anyone to hell, and luckily, our theology backed me up. We were explicitly taught that after a non-Mormon's death, ghostly missionaries would swoop in, preach the true gospel, and save those who finally believed. Then the new, albeit deceased, converts would get the Monopoly equivalent of a "Get out of Jail Free" card and go directly to the highest degree of heaven. And as for those who still didn't believe? Well, they would be assigned to a lesser kingdom where they would receive at least some blessings, sort of like an afterworld consolation prize for those who messed up.

All of the puzzle pieces in my life fit together perfectly back in that magical time. I knew that I was loved by God, my church, my family, and my friends. If a question crossed my mind, my mother could easily answer it, and I could get back to the serious business of climbing the large Queen Anne cherry tree in our backyard with my younger sisters as we hunted for the first fruits to show their yellowish-pink faces to the sun. We spent hours devouring the barely ripe cherries and spitting the seeds onto the ground. When we were satiated, we'd climb down to the lowest branch of the tree, swing back and forth a few times to prove our fearlessness, and drop eight feet to the ground. My life was perfect and whole; my happiness was complete. Unbeknownst to me, however, a dangerous passage named adolescence loomed on the horizon; once it arrived, cracks began to appear in my orderly world, gradually at first, and then with a rapidity that left me dazed.

CHAPTER 3

Paradise Lost

The old, red-brick church from my childhood made frequent appearances in my dreams throughout adolescence and for decades afterwards. Oftentimes I was running through the building laughing with friends, finding secret passages to explore or pilfering leftover cookies and cakes from the church kitchen. Other times my girlfriends and I were checking our hair and lip gloss in the mirrors that adorned the women's small restroom. Sometimes, however, the dreams took on a more menacing tone. Those were the dreams in which I was pursued by a tall, skeletal, nightmarish figure who was dressed completely in black. He had unnaturally long, disjointed limbs stretching out like spiders' legs from his tiny, misshapen body. His head was unnaturally large and balanced upon a slender stalk of a neck that looked like it might snap at any minute. With his deranged grin, he would chase me up and down a seemingly endless series of narrow staircases that crisscrossed and formed intricate *X* patterns hidden behind the church's white plaster walls. All the while, his teeth clacked like castanets as he repeatedly lunged at my ankles, just missing me by inches.

My other recurring nightmare was one where the church parking lot was covered in a thick sheet of ice. Despite my stomping on the brake pedal repeatedly and frantically, I always careened out of control. I had scores of dreams where my car bashed into limousines, ambulances, groups of small children, pedestrians, glass doors, brick walls, and anything else that was hapless enough to be in the way of my sliding vehicle. A complete sense of terror always enveloped me, but I had to preserve the appearance of normalcy as my automobile slipped and skidded its way into multiple vehicular manslaughter charges.

As to why these dreams continued throughout my forties, my best guess is that the building served as a focal point for much of my early life. I attended Primary there and gave my first public church talks as a young child. The school bus would unload the elementary school students at the red-brick church on Wednesday afternoons, and there we would be taught gospel lessons and participate in group activities up through our twelfth birthday. I sang my first duet as a child in that building; I also appeared as an angel in a ward Christmas program where I was dressed in a white robe with resplendent, white gauzy wings attached to metal coat hangers and pinned to the back of my robe. When the stage lights turned on and temporarily blinded me as I recited my memorized lines, I felt euphoric and ethereal, as if I were a real angel. And I was *confirmed*[22] by my father to be a member of the church in the chapel when I was eight years old.

But perhaps most importantly, I spent time with all of my best friends there as we trekked through girlhood and into the uncharted wilderness of puberty together. Adolescence is the age where parental figures are suddenly revealed to be distinctly embarrassing, so we turned to our peers as a matter of psychological survival. After we turned twelve, we transitioned together into what is now called the *Young Women program*, the church curriculum for female teenagers up through age eighteen.

None of us considered shaving our legs or experimenting with makeup in elementary school. It wasn't until I was a seventh grader in junior high that my best friend sneaked some bright blue eyeshadow into the girls' bathroom during lunch and offered to help me put it on. She had several older sisters, so she had a distinct advantage when it came to understanding the ways of the world.

"Are you sure this is OK?" I asked nervously.

"Of course." She leaned forward and stared at herself in the mirror while applying the powder in amateurish streaks to her eyes. "It's not against the school rules to wear makeup, you know."

"But our moms might not like it."

"And how will they find out? We can remove it after school." She continued with the eyeshadow and tossed her blonde hair over her shoulders.

"I guess they won't." I leaned forward and attempted to copy her technique. Her eyes were a pale, silver-blue and looked notably better surrounded by garish blue than did my golden-brown eyes. Nonetheless, I convinced myself that this was a required rite of passage into womanhood and soldiered bravely onward. We imagined that we looked mature and sophisticated as we sauntered back to our afternoon classes and affected casual expressions when the other students stared in surprise at the bright blue half-moons above our eyes.

This was the same friend who demonstrated how to kiss a boy using a soft-serve vanilla ice-cream cone as a stand-in for the boyfriend. Although neither of us had ever kissed a boy, I took her for an expert because of her older sisters and studied her technique with a singular focus. She also counseled me on the finer points of using a tampon because she started her period before I did. We went to her older female cousin's house for the express purpose of having privacy for this critical undertaking; my friend stood outside the bathroom door and yelled through words of instruction and encouragement like an athletic coach. Midway through my attempts, I broke out in a cold sweat and was convinced that either something was defective with my body or that I had damaged myself in some irreparable way. Neither was true: like most of my girlfriends, I was just woefully ignorant about the structures of the female reproductive anatomy. After success was finally achieved, my friend and I both cheered and high-fived each other as if we had just won the puberty championship game.

But there was one thing she was unable to help me with. That same year, as I perched on the cusp of womanhood, my male *Junior Sunday School*[23] teacher announced that our founder and prophet, Joseph Smith, had been a *polygamist*.[24] None of us knew what that meant, so he explained it in detail: it meant that the prophet was married to more than one woman because God commanded him to do it. He told us that any person who hoped to make it to the *celestial kingdom* (the most exalted place in Mormon heaven), where God himself dwelt, would be required to be in polygamous marriages. There was a stunned silence, and then the boys began snickering and making jokes about "doing it" with more than one wife. Our teacher had the decency to glare at the boys: "If you think about it too much, it's the same thing as fornicating." His face turned bright red, and the beads of sweat that formed on his forehead were mopped away by the white handkerchief tucked into his blue polyester suit coat pocket.

But how could something that was commanded by God be sin? Did God make mistakes? Could He have somehow made a cosmic error in the calculation of the universe? Had he forgotten that men and women were equals? If one man could have multiple wives, it suggested to me that one man was worth five, ten, twenty, or more women. I performed the math problem in my head and was disturbed by the lopsidedness of it. Things weren't looking too good for Mormon women if this was indeed true.

For the first time in my life, I was completely horrified by something I had learned at church. It was as if the bottom had fallen out of my world: not only was I apparently going to be turning into a woman, but I was also going to be relegated to being a broodmare for some exalted stallion for all eternity. The fact that God had commanded it made it so much worse; this was God telling me in no uncertain terms that I was a second-class citizen because I was female. Although everybody around me at the time seemed to accept this with no qualms, for me it still remains one of the most disturbing revelations of my entire life. My physical, emotional, and religious lives were spiraling out of control, yet I never discussed it with my parents or any of my friends. A small, voracious beetle began gnawing its way into my previously unblemished heart; in order to protect myself, I encased the insect inside an impenetrable shell and pretended that it wasn't there. I didn't realize it then, but the first fault line in my religious belief system had just occurred.

As the dreaded time of menstruation arrived, I was mortified by everything occurring in my body: changes were being thrust upon me against my will. Puberty was a cruel goddess, but even though I despised her, she forced me to kneel at her altar, nonetheless. I was barely keeping up with the fact that I had started to menstruate and develop breasts. The humiliation was extreme when the boys would stare openly at my chest, fixated on those tiny bumps that were sending out a secret signal to them. I wanted the bumps and the boys to go away. I wanted to still be *me*, the kid version of myself I had become so comfortable with, the one who could run faster, climb higher, and play tetherball better than any boy in the neighborhood. But my hypothalamus gland had other plans for me. I decided I would give no outward show of emotion, no bloom of shame as the boys tittered about me. I would stare them down mercilessly and beat them at their own game. If they insulted me, I would return a worse insult; if they laughed at me, I would laugh back in their faces; if they chased me, I would outrun them.

And I had one final trick up my sleeve—I stopped eating. If my body was going to start poking out in odd places, I would choke off its supply at the source—the calories I needed to grow. This was in 1971, long before the term *anorexia nervosa* had become so widely known. (Karen Carpenter's tragic death from the disease in 1983 helped spread awareness of the condition.) At first, my parents had no idea what I was doing or why I was doing it. Neither did I. I just knew that I felt so much better—*so much more in control*—if I counted every bit of food, limiting myself to a few bites of apples, some water, a few soda crackers, and tiny morsels of vegetables for months on end. I don't remember feeling hungry. I do remember being inordinately proud of my self-control and being filled with a silent fury anytime somebody tried to sabotage my intense discipline system by coaxing me to eat.

From the middle of sixth grade through the beginning of seventh grade, my weight dropped from 105 pounds (on a five-foot-five frame) to 75 pounds. I secretly took my measurements every week and was beyond elated when I saw that my waist was down to twenty inches, the same size it had been in my baby book during first grade. None of this seemed unusual to me. I was not aware of trying to gain control over a body and life that seemed to have transformed without my permission. I was not aware of how sick I was; neither were my parents. There were no counselor's appointments, no visits to special doctors. This was small-town Utah, 1971, and about the only time we went to the doctor was to get our vaccinations or to get an antibiotic if we came down with strep throat.

As my weight loss became more extreme, however, my parents (and others) finally did notice that I was shrinking before their eyes. My mom took me to our family doctor, who told me, "You need to start eating more, young lady!" His statement surely qualifies as one of the most useless pieces of medical advice ever given to an anorexic teen. My dad offered to pay me one dollar for every pound I gained, which was a lot of money back then for a thirteen-year-old. That didn't work either. My parents were *not* uncaring—they were simply broadsided by something that nobody at that time knew anything about. Looking back on this now, it is glaringly obvious that I desperately needed some help. Back then, not so much.

After starving myself for almost two years, I somehow was able to reason my way out of the behavior. The turning point occurred when I had gone camping with my maternal grandparents. My grandfather had taken a few pictures of me standing near the edge of a lake, looking out at the water in my swimsuit. When I saw the pictures later, I remember drawing in a shocked breath at the skeletal figure that stood near the lake: *she* was monstrously thin—skin and bones. In another close-up picture, *she* had dark, sunken circles under her eyes and looked like a concentration camp survivor. I was stunned! This shrunken creature could *not* be me, but somehow, she *was!* This was the first time I was able to look at myself through an outsider's neutral gaze: the girl in those pictures did *not* look good.

When my grandparents first gave the pictures to my mom, I was resentful because I thought that my family was trying to control my eating habits again. But as time passed and I secretly studied the pictures (which my mom had put into a scrapbook), I concluded that my obsession with not looking "fat" had led me far afield of my original goal. It was time to make a change. I told my mom what I had noticed about myself; she was smart enough to realize that I might finally be open to some nonconfrontational conversations with her, and that was the beginning of my gradually eating myself back to a normal weight. I wish I still had the pictures, but in a fit of adolescent self-loathing, I went through all of our old scrapbooks and tore up most of the pictures taken of me at that time.

About that same time, a series of unanswerable questions arose unbidden: What if one member of your family didn't make it to heaven? Would it still be heaven? Who would want to live in a heaven that didn't include every family member anyway? Why would God only give such a small group of people his true church? Why would we be living in Utah? What about people on the other side of the globe who were born into bone-crushing poverty and despair? Were we really that much better than everybody else? One of the Mormon doctrines that was openly preached for decades was that the more righteous the spirit in heaven, the more favorable the circumstances on earth. That way, if people were barely surviving in China or Africa, you didn't have to feel guilty about having more than them because you had earned it according to some pre-earth, holy arithmetic.

I started to question if the Gospel was really the good news of Christ. Instead, it seemed like a bait-and-switch scheme, hawked by a snake oil salesman: "Ladies and Gentlemen! Step right up and drink from the waters of a Mormon baptism! The good news is your family can be together forever!" Once you purchased the potion and drank it, you turned the bottle over and saw the small print on the back on the label: "This guarantee only applies to righteous, tithe-paying, strictly obedient, temple-going Mormons."

One Sunday, I had an argument with my dad in the church foyer. Very few of our relatives on either side of the family had ever been to the temple or had their marriages sealed[25] there. I asked my dad if he thought he would be happy living forever apart from most of his relatives or his parents. He said nothing in reply, but I felt ashamed of myself when I saw the sadness in his eyes. I decided to never broach the topic again because I loved my parents. I had always known beyond a doubt that my parents loved me, too, but based on all the questions that now confronted me, I was starting to wonder if God really did.

CHAPTER 4

Polygamy Pie

For better or for worse, for richer or for poorer, in sickness and in health, the Mormon Church will forever be associated with polygamy. After learning about polygamy at the age of twelve, I secretly despised it with an intensity that most adults would have thought impossible in one so young. I am convinced that we underestimate children's emotional and intellectual lives, not only at their peril, but also our own. My horror only increased as I learned during the years that followed that ancestors on both sides of my family had been polygamists, which is actually quite common for anyone whose Mormon ancestors immigrated to Utah between the years of 1847 and 1900.

The church's teachings on assorted topics have become more mainstream over the years, and while they have officially disavowed polygamy on earth, it is still enshrined as an eternal principle that Mormons believe will be practiced in the heavens by some members. Because of the gradual evolution of this belief, many people are unaware of the shifts that have occurred in both the preaching and practicing of this doctrine.

A few years after the church was founded in 1830 in Fayette, New York, Joseph Smith introduced and practiced polygamy. Although the official revelation about polygamy was not written down until 1843 (*D&C* 132),[26] multiple sources suggest that as early as the mid-1830s, Joseph took his first plural wife, Fanny Alger, in Kirtland, Ohio. The teenaged girl had been working as a domestic helper in the Smith household and as such, had been close to both

Joseph and his only legal wife, Emma Hale Smith. The "marriage" was performed without Emma's knowledge, and once she learned of it, she furiously insisted that the girl leave their home immediately. Despite some controversy as to what level of intimacy the relationship entailed, several historical documents support the idea that this marriage and many of Smith's other plural marriages were consummated. A complete study of this topic is far beyond the scope of this chapter, but one definitive source is Todd Compton's 1997 seminal work, *In Sacred Loneliness: The Plural Wives of Joseph Smith.* Compton began researching polygamy when he realized that no verifiable list of the plural wives of Joseph Smith existed; according to Compton, there is evidence that Smith had at least thirty-three plural wives, ranging in age from fourteen to fifty-four. In some cases, Smith married sisters, mother-and-daughter pairs, and women who were already married to other living men although some of these marriages were thought to be for "eternity only" and may not have involved conjugal relations. It is worth noting that others historians have disagreed about the number of wives that Smith took. Fawn Brodie counted forty-eight wives; D. Michael Quinn believed that there were forty-six.[27]

Smith introduced polygamy to other church leaders, including the man who would eventually become the church's second president, Brigham Young. Young preached that "the only men who become Gods, even the Sons of God, are those who enter into polygamy." However, he added the caveat that if for some reason members were currently unable to practice polygamy, they had to "be polygamists at least in . . . faith," in order to dwell "in the presence of the Father and the Son, in celestial glory."[28] According to church sources, Young became a "strong advocate for the practice of plural marriage," and was eventually sealed to over fifty women.[29] During Young's thirty-three years of authoritarian rule in the Utah Territory, polygamy went from being a well-known secret that was hidden from the outside world to an openly preached doctrine that spread throughout many families and profoundly affected the lives of all who practiced it, especially the women. According to many of the primary and secondary sources, the women often suffered "acute neglect,"[30] both emotionally and financially, as they scrambled to support themselves and their growing broods of children. Their lives were difficult at best and often included lifelong "isolation and insecurity"; in addition, "depression, despair, anxiety, helplessness, abandonment, anger, psychosomatic symptoms, and low self-esteem" also afflicted many of the women.[31]

According to my ancestors' personal diaries, letters, and oral histories,[32] polygamy led to much unhappiness and marital discord in their own lives. My great-great-grandmother, who emigrated from Denmark in 1877, was one of many young women who was convinced to enter into a polygamous marriage almost as soon as she had arrived in Utah. Boletta Andersen was twenty-two years old when she and her mother completed their arduous pilgrimage to the United States via multiple ships, wagons, and trains; the last leg of their journey consisted of boarding a train in Salt Lake City that carried them south to a small Mormon settlement named Nephi. Although Boletta already had a Danish fiancé who had traveled in advance of her and was expecting her arrival, she and her mother were briefly housed with Niels Jensen Christensen, a Danish immigrant who had arrived in 1859 and who was serving as the first Mormon *bishop*[33] in the small town of Levan, Utah. One of Bishop Christensen's duties was to meet the new arrivals at the train station in Salt Lake City and help them get settled since none of them spoke English. It was aboard the train from Salt Lake to Nephi where Niels first spotted Boletta and was instantly impressed with her beauty and poise. As a bishop, he had been under repeated pressure from his priesthood leaders to embrace polygamy and take a second wife, but he had resisted for some time. His first marriage to Serena Andersdatter, which occurred in 1866, had remained childless, and it was considered the sacred duty of men and women at that time (and for decades afterwards) to produce as many offspring as possible so that God's spirit children might gain "tabernacles of flesh and bones" in righteous homes.[34] Serena was opposed to Niels's taking a second wife, but eventually relented under one condition: the second wife would be required to "relinquish" the first two children that might eventually be born to Serena's own care.

There are questions as to whether Bishop Niels Christensen communicated this prerequisite to the young Boletta before their marriage, but at least one ancestral source speculates that the young woman never would have agreed to such a marriage if she had known about the sacrifice that she would be required to make. Although the records are silent as to how Boletta was convinced to break off her engagement with her fiancé and accept a polygamous marriage, there must have been considerable pressure put upon her in order for her to accept such a proposal. It was a common tactic under both Joseph Smith's and later Brigham Young's leadership for women "and their families" to be promised either "rewards . . . [and] promises of salvation"[35] for submitting to the practice of polygamy or to "suffer [eternal] condemnation" for resisting.[36] Most women, such as sixteen-year-old Lucy Walker, who became "nearly suicidal" when presented with this choice; and fourteen-year-old Helen Mar Kimball, who wept at the loss of her "teenage dreams," eventually succumbed to the demands of their prophet.[37] Whatever happened in Boletta's case, she married the forty-two-year-old Niels only two months after she had arrived in Utah. Her heartbroken fiancé left the area shortly thereafter, journeyed south to Sanpete County, and became a school teacher. She never saw him again, and he never married.

Niels and Boletta's marriage produced five children. The first child, a daughter named Anna, died in infancy. The first wife, Serena, told Niels that since the first child had died, she "didn't count" as one of the two children that Boletta needed to give her. Accordingly, the next two children born, Mary and

Niels, were eventually turned over to Serena to be raised by her. There were reports of Serena's vicious jealousy over Boletta's ability to bear children, and Boletta's life was permanently scarred by the older woman's deep bitterness. Boletta later had two more sons, James and Oliver, who were permitted to remain with her.

As the first wife, Serena was the only woman with a legal claim to marriage, and as a result, she had more social standing in the community. She spent her days living in a large, red-brick home that Niels had built for her along with her two "adopted" children. Boletta, as the second wife, was housed a short distance away in a two-room log home with her two youngest children. While Serena's adopted children lived quite comfortably and received an education at the high school in Provo, Utah, Boletta's two younger sons regularly missed school in the fall and again in the spring because they were herding livestock to help support their mother. The youngest son, Oliver (my great-grandfather), was able to finish only the fourth grade before he permanently dropped out and became a manual laborer. Rather than complain about her lot, my great-great-grandmother Boletta worked hard to support herself, raising her own sheep, carding the wool, spinning it into cloth on a hand loom, dying it with homemade dyes, and then, finally, sewing her children's clothes. She wove carpets and sold eggs, milk, and butter when she could spare it. She raised chickens and sold apples from her trees.

During their marriage, both Niels and Boletta had to go into hiding on multiple occasions so that Niels would not be arrested for bigamy. After the passage of the Edmunds Anti-Polygamy Act in 1882, which declared polygamy to be a felony in the federal territories, Boletta hid out in the local *"tithing[38] granary"* for several months, only coming out after dark in order to help Niels evade arrest. During her last pregnancy, Boletta was moved to the northernmost county in Utah, Cache County, in order to protect her husband. She lived separately from him for most of the next two-and-one-half years, giving birth to their final son, Oliver, just a few months after she arrived there.

Eventually, Niels surrendered to the authorities and received a very lenient sentence of fifty days in jail and a fifty dollar fine. When he died in 1892 at the age of fifty-seven, he left behind two wives and four children. Boletta was forced to take Serena to court in order to keep her home or receive any of Niels's estate; eventually she received one-third of the property because of her children. Boletta died eighteen years later in 1910 at the age of fifty-four, and Serena outlived them both, dying in 1927 at the age of eighty-five. Her longevity may very well have been due to her inability to become pregnant since pregnancy and childbirth were two of the most hazardous undertakings in a woman's life in the nineteenth century.

When I went to visit their burial sites in Levan, I noticed something very telling. As the last surviving wife, Serena made sure that her own tombstone was placed very close to that of Niels, just a few inches away, while Boletta's tombstone was placed about ten yards distant. It seems that the bitterness she felt toward her husband's second wife never dissipated, even after the younger woman's death. One descendant's diary puts it succinctly: "Boletta had a hard life and endured many trials. Serena made her life miserable." In fairness to Serena, however, it must be mentioned that her life, too, was made very difficult because of polygamy. Her two adopted children grew to love her, as did all of the grandchildren that eventually came from Neils and Boletta's offspring. They affectionately called her "Mot," short for mother, and there is no doubt that she sincerely loved them and had a positive influence on them.[39]

In 1885, church president John Taylor, along with his two counselors, George Q. Cannon and Joseph F. Smith, all of whom were polygamists, went underground in order to escape being convicted of "unlawful cohabitation under the Edmunds Act." They still believed that the institution of polygamy was "divinely inspired," but attempted to hide the practice so that Utah could gain statehood.[40] Some of those who fled the United States to escape prosecution for entering into plural marriages traveled to Mexico and set up colonies there, although most eventually returned to the United States.

Finally in 1890, under pressure from the federal government, newly sustained prophet Wilford Woodruff announced that polygamy would be officially disavowed as an earthly practice, although it continued in a clandestine fashion for years. Because of Woodruff's statement, which is known as the *Manifesto*, Utah was granted statehood in 1896 after being denied entry to the union for four decades. However, it wasn't until the so-called *Second Manifesto* of 1904 when the sixth church president, Joseph F. Smith, emphasized that any member entering into a polygamous marriage would be "excommunicated" that the practice officially stopped within the church.[41] (Interestingly enough, Joseph F. Smith had been one of the church leaders who had earlier believed that polygamy would be *required* in order to enter the celestial kingdom.)[42] Heber J. Grant, the seventh president of the church from 1918 to 1945 (and, coincidentally, my great-great-great uncle on my mother's side), was the last prophet to have practiced polygamy in his lifetime although by the time he became prophet, he had only one surviving wife.

Current doctrine states that in the celestial kingdom there will be both monogamous and polygamous marriages in heaven. Thus, men whose wives have died can be eternally sealed to another living woman as long as that woman has never been sealed to a former husband. Current prophet Russell M. Nelson, who was a renowned cardiovascular surgeon before his calling to church leadership, married (and was sealed to) his first wife, Dantzel White, in 1945. After her death in 2005, Nelson married (and was sealed to) his second wife, Wendy L. Watson, in 2006. Likewise, Apostle Dallin H. Oaks, a lawyer and justice of the Utah Supreme Court before his apostolic calling, has also been sealed to two women. After his first wife, June Dixon, died in 1998, he married (and was sealed to) Kristen M. McMain in 2000 in the Salt Lake Temple. Of course, there is nothing wrong with anyone remarrying after the death of a spouse, but according to currently enshrined Mormon doctrine, Nelson and Oaks will both be eternally married to two different wives in the next life.

Mormon women who lose a spouse, on the other hand, *cannot* be sealed to another man if they were previously sealed to their first husband. This double standard has led to painful decisions for women and their families. At one of my summer college jobs, I met an older woman who had been married in the temple decades earlier and then widowed when she and her husband were both in their twenties. She had never remarried and bitterly told me it was because all of the Mormon men she dated considered her "damaged goods" since they couldn't be sealed to her.

One of our adult friends still resents his mother's decision to get a *temple divorce*[43] from his deceased father so that she could be sealed to another man. To this day, our friend feels bitter about how his mother threw away his birth father to gain a more respectable temple marriage to a second man in a predominantly Mormon community.

Another friend of mine lost her husband decades ago in a tragic accident. When she remarried, she was unable to be sealed to her second husband because she had already been sealed to her first husband. Even though her second husband was divorced from his first wife, he was heartbroken because he could not be sealed to his second, beloved wife—my friend. Because my friend never wanted to cancel her sealing to her first husband, she was left in a position where it was impossible for her to be sealed to her second husband, whom she also loved.

In my own mother's case, after my father passed away at age sixty due to a brain hemorrhage, she remarried ten years later; however, since she had already been sealed to my father, and since she had no desire to ever cancel their sealing, she was unable to be sealed to her second husband. Instead, they married with the understanding that they would only be together during their time on earth; this is most likely what led her second husband's daughter to insist aloud on more than one occasion that their marriage "was *not* a real marriage."

When Mormons are confronted with these kinds of difficulties, a common refrain is "It will all work out on the other side."[44] While this handy catchphrase can be comforting, it ignores the strange and often convoluted family bonds that are being set up in this life and supposedly in the life beyond. There are cases where children have been sealed to one parent and not the other, spouses have been temple divorced after death or infidelities, children have remained sealed to both of their birth parents despite divorces occurring on earth, and men have been sealed to multiple women.

The repeated insistence that nobody knows the exact details of how things will be set up on the other side seems disingenuous when one sees how much time, effort, and money the church spends to join family members together during mortality and to keep detailed records of such temple ordinances. Everything I was taught about the hereafter is expressed in this scripture: "Whatsoever ye shall bind on earth shall be bound in heaven: and whatsoever ye shall loose on earth shall be loosed in heaven" (Matt. 18:18). I see no other way to explain the church's intense focus on scrupulously documenting all official church ordinances, especially temple ordinances.

The main problem with polygamy lies in something that women have always recognized—the inequality inherent in it. In the past, the "Polygamy Pie Café" had a secret menu, available exclusively to the male members of Joseph Smith's inner circle. A woman could only gain entrance upon being invited by a man. Under Brigham Young, the menu was eventually opened up to more members, but it was still controlled by men, and its existence was denied abroad, including to the early European converts who sacrificed everything to journey to Utah. After Apostle Orson

Pratt officially announced and read the revelation about polygamy[45] on August 29, 1852, in a special conference session, the doctrine was met with shock and repulsion worldwide.[46] When statehood became a thorny issue, the café was supposedly shut down in 1890, but this was merely a superficial compliance meant to appease the federal government. Finally, when polygamists were threatened with excommunication in 1904, the earthly practice was officially discontinued in the main church although multiple splinter groups broke away and have continued the practice to this day. But even though the Polygamy Pie Café is currently closed in the Mormon Church, it remains open in the eternities. There the men may help themselves to as many pieces of pie as they choose, but the women are strictly, and forever, limited to one serving apiece.

CHAPTER 5

Mormonism for Dummies

Historians have questioned whether Brigham Young ever actually said "This is the place," but it is firmly entrenched in the annals of Mormon folklore.[47] Whether he said it or not doesn't matter in practical terms because Utah has become, for better or for worse, the epicenter of the Mormon Church and its hierarchical power structure. Worldwide edicts are issued from within the halls of the twenty-eight-story Church Office Building, which was officially dedicated on July 24, 1975. The building is only a block away from the historic Salt Lake Temple, which serves as both the literal and figurative center of the downtown portion of the city. When the pioneers arrived, they staked out the temple's location first in a ten-acre square, and every road that came afterward was laid out in precisely measured blocks that surrounded the temple site. Out-of-state visitors comment that it's relatively easy to find their way around Utah's largest city because of this.

Since its inception, Mormonism has been a high-demand religion that demands strict obedience from its adherents. While members are told to rely on the spirit and that each member can receive revelation from God, no revelation that runs counter to official church doctrine will be given credence. In fact, members who claim to have received personal insights that are not in agreement with the correlated teachings of the *First Presidency*[48] or the *Quorum of the Twelve Apostles*[49] often face *excommunication*.[50] The official public relations arm of the church claims that members are not excommunicated for having differing opinions, but rather for sharing those opinions publicly.

One well-known excommunication is that of Dr. John Dehlin, who received his Ph.D. in Clinical and Counseling Psychology from Utah State University in 2015. He was excommunicated that same year for advocating for marriage equality for LGBT members on his popular Mormon Stories podcast although the church says he was removed for criticizing church leaders and doctrines.[51]

Another example is former Mormon bishop and returned *LDS missionary*,[52] Sam Young. Young was excommunicated in 2018 in Texas after opposing the common practice of closed-door, one-on-one *worthiness interviews* between youths and their bishops.[53] Such interviews, while culturally acceptable for decades, have often included inappropriate questions about "sexual sins" (including masturbation, petting, and orgasm during sexual relations between unmarried persons) and have induced a deep sense of shame in many of the underage interviewees. Young started the "Protect LDS Children" movement in 2017 with the stated goal of ending all private interviews between underaged children and adult men after learning that several of his own daughters had been asked embarrassingly intimate questions by their male church leaders. I, myself, experienced numerous interviews like this, as did all of my Mormon friends.

Like all cohesive groups, Mormonism has unique ways of perceiving the world and interacting with it. If I were to approach a stranger in an airport, I am confident that within a very short time of conversing with them, I would be able to guess if they were Mormon. There are subtle clues, many at the subconscious level, that a member would instantly recognize in a fellow member. Years ago, the first Mormon contestant appeared on the TV program *Survivor: Marquesas*. A Utah native, Neleh Dennis's constant refrain of "Oh, my heck!" on the program quickly became noted as a peculiar way of speaking that most in her generation would *not* have adopted. Everybody who was raised Mormon (especially in Utah) instantly recognized that phrase as a long-standing method of avoiding swearing while still expressing displeasure and shock.[54]

Officially known as The Church of Jesus Christ of Latter-day Saints since four years after its founding in 1830, the "Mormon Church" and the "LDS Church" are the more familiar names which are commonly used in colloquial speech. After President Russell M. Nelson took leadership in January 2018, he told members during the October 2018 general conference that Jesus Christ had revealed to him the importance of no longer using the term "Mormon" to refer to the church. Nelson explained that "the name of the Church is not negotiable. When the Savior clearly states what the name of His Church should be, and even precedes His declaration with, 'Thus shall my church be called,' He is serious. And if we allow nicknames to be used and adopt or even sponsor those nicknames ourselves, He is offended."[55] Those of us who had spent decades in the church remember the global "I'm a Mormon" ad campaign started by Nelson's predecessor, President Thomas S. Monson, in 2010. Scores of videos were produced that included both well-known and everyday members speaking about their lives in positive, relatable ways.[56] There has been some confusion (and more than a few jokes) as to how the previously "inspired" campaign suddenly transformed into a "major victory for Satan."[57] I have purposely chosen to use the terms "Mormon" and "Mormonism" because of their continued cultural and historical relevance.

Some scholars say Mormonism deserves to be classified as an ethnic group, with unique customs of worshipping, praying, marrying, dressing, eating, and even speaking.[58] Some in the church have only half-jokingly referred to their Mormon vocabulary as *Mormonese*. Think of it as a specialized dialect that takes years to master. In addition to having a distinct vocabulary, the group has similar ways of seeing, thinking, believing, and behaving. Being Mormon is much more than attending church on Sundays. It is about sharing common worldviews, long-term marriage and family goals, and beliefs about the hereafter.

So-called "Mormon culture" dominates everything, from whether or not bikinis are acceptable swimsuit apparel for young women (they are *not*) to whether or not white shirts are the preferred color for young men to wear to church (they *are*). A sleeveless top that would be considered modest by almost any standards would be frowned upon by most *active*[59] Mormons. The term "porn shoulders" originated as a flippant response to Elder Dallin H. Oaks's statement in one of the general conferences that young women who "dress immodestly" are "becoming pornography to some of the men who see you."[60] Shorts are supposed to come down to slightly above the knee; cleavage is a no-no. Brigham Young University (BYU) in Provo, Utah, which is funded by millions of dollars of tithing donations paid by faithful members, didn't start selling caffeinated sodas within the hallowed halls of its student cafeterias until 2017. Some students literally capitalized on this caffeine ban for decades by buying Coke, Pepsi, and Mountain Dew products off campus, storing them in coolers in their dorm rooms, and selling the contraband caffeine products to their fellow students.

Today, Mormonism can boast of being the religious affiliation of many highly successful individuals. Mitt Romney, former governor of Massachusetts and the Republican nominee for the 2012 presidential election, is a fifth-generation member of the Mormon Church. The founder of the multi-billion-dollar Marriott Hotels franchise, J. Willard Marriott, was a lifelong Mormon. Singer and songwriter Gladys Knight joined the church in 1997 after two of her children were baptized. National Football League quarterback Steve Young, great-great-great-grandson of Brigham Young, spent fifteen seasons in the NFL and was inducted into the Pro Football Hall of Fame in 2005. And the list goes on. Mormons have created successful communities and families throughout the world and are rightly honored for their work ethic and their commitment to family.

Despite what I would argue have been serious shortcomings—such as a lack of authenticity about the church's history, and social policies that have hurt racial and sexual-orientation minorities—to claim that Mormonism's impact has been only negative would be shortsighted and unfair. Dancer and actress Julianne Hough, best known for her role in ABC's hit show *Dancing with the Stars*, grew up in Orem, Utah, and was raised in the Mormon Church. Although she has since left the church, she told the *New York Post* in 2013, "I'm so glad I was raised Mormon."[61] She has expressed what many adults who have left the church have thought about their upbringing. Good family values? Check. Avoiding drugs and promiscuity? Check. Weird doctrines? Check. Offensive attitudes toward women? Check. It's a double-edged sword to be raised Mormon: on the one hand, young people are given a good start in life as they learn about the importance of practicing self-control and respecting the divinity in those around them. On the other hand, they're taught that heaven practices eternal polygamy, that leading a gay "lifestyle" is a choice, and that anyone who doesn't follow strict codes of conduct (orthopraxy) or subscribe to a narrow set of beliefs (orthodoxy) is doomed to spend eternity without beloved family members.

This dichotomy points to an important contradiction in Mormonism: the gap between official doctrines and the things that members actually consider relevant in their lives. Some have bridged this gap by focusing on what brings them happiness and ignoring the rest. This tendency has drawn criticism from church leaders, such as current church president Russell M. Nelson, who warned members in a 2011 general conference talk that they would "encounter people who pick which commandments they will keep and ignore others that they choose to break. I call this the cafeteria approach to obedience. This practice of picking and choosing will not work. It will lead to misery. To prepare to meet God, one keeps *all* of His commandments."[62]

And while I have sympathy for the cafeteria Mormons among us, I do agree with the leaders in one regard: Mormonism is not for the faint of heart. It doesn't invite members to be part in, part out, part undecided. In Mormonism, once people are in, they're *all* in, and if—heaven forbid—any of them stumble upon a disturbing doctrine or historical fact, they're in the deep end without a life jacket. Mormonism demands total obedience from its believers. They can't waffle, wander, or wiggle. They are fully committed to prophets and apostles receiving revelation from God, the prophet never leading the members astray, and members following every commandment and point of doctrine.

The fear of not being good or faithful enough to obtain *exaltation*, or living with God, Jesus Christ, and one's family in heaven, has always been a serious concern for church members. When my daughter was five years old, she attended a weekly church class for young children called Primary. The children were being noisy and talkative during the singing practice time, so the Primary president, a grimly determined woman, turned off the lights in the room to get the children's attention. When a hushed silence fell, she told this group of children aged three to twelve that unless they were more reverent, they would be cast into *outer darkness*, a particularly nightmarish place in Mormon teachings where a person lives desolate and forever condemned, with no family and no hope of redemption (D&C 19:36-38).

Our impressionable daughter came home crying and having nightmares. After a few days of prodding her for information, I found out what the leader had told the children. I explained my concerns to our local bishop, and he released the leader from her church *calling* (unpaid church job) within two weeks. The fact that this woman felt entirely justified in discussing outer darkness with a group of young children, and that none of the other adults in the room (there were about ten —teachers and counselors) felt the need to correct her, speaks volumes about how deeply these beliefs are entrenched in the average member's mind.

The church's emphasis on sealing families together for eternity sounds comforting until one scratches the surface; then one finds many disturbing sentiments beneath the veneer. During the church's semi-annual general conference on Sunday, April 7, 2019, President Russell M. Nelson made troubling remarks about *earning* the "high privilege of exaltation." He said that unless the people in the world accept the sealing ordinances provided by the Mormon Church, they will not be bound to their families in the hereafter.[63] Many saw this as a direct assault on part-member families or families with gay members.

In the October 2023 conference, Nelson said that those who *"unwisely* choose to live *telestial* laws now . . . are choosing *not* to live with [their] families forever" [emphasis in original].[64] Mormon doctrine teaches that those who commit serious sins, such as adultery, or who reject the gospel of Jesus Christ will eventually be assigned to the *telestial* kingdom, or the lowest kingdom of "glory" in the afterlife. First, however, they must suffer in hell for one thousand years during the *Millennium*, which Mormon doctrine teaches will be the "1,000 years following the Savior's Second Coming" to the earth.[65] The inhabitants of the Telestial Kingdom will be visited by the Holy Ghost, but not by the Father or the Son. It is also important to note that the church has taught that no families will be living together in this lowest kingdom, although they may be visited by relatives who have been assigned to one of the higher kingdoms (See D&C 76).

In the most recent April 2024 conference, Nelson said that "many other organizations *can* and *do* make your life better here in mortality. But no other organization *can* and *will* influence your life after death" [emphasis in original].[66] This echoes many similar teachings since the church's founding that although *other* churches might help their members during their earthly lives, *only* the Mormon Church contains the necessary priesthood ordinances that can lead people and their families toward complete exaltation and happiness in the eternities. The claim that Mormonism possesses an inherent superiority is one that other systems of belief find offensive, yet the idea persists.

Of course, none of this is obvious to the child's mind as he/she is thinking and growing up in *Mormondom*, another interesting word that means what it sounds like: the kingdom (or community) of Mormons. Many lifelong members are completely unaware that they view the world through a pair of peculiarly fashioned spectacles; it is as if every raw experience must be filtered through their Mormon lens to be correctly understood.

Once members reach age twelve, they can travel to their local Mormon temple (there are many around the world) to perform *proxy baptisms* (baptisms on behalf of deceased persons, usually ancestors). And, to the chagrin of many, to baptize everybody from Anne Frank and Albert Einstein to all the deceased United States presidents. Inside the Salt Lake Temple in the baptismal font room, there is an imposing, circular, stone bowl, filled with waist-high water and raised upon the backs of twelve large, sculpted oxen (representing the Biblical Twelve Tribes of Israel). When my friends and I turned twelve, and after we had donned our white baptismal suits in one of the temple dressing rooms, we were completely immersed in the water multiple times by authorized male priesthood holders who recited a script to help those who had passed away without a Mormon baptism continue in their eternal progression.

The women attend weekly *Relief Society*[67] meetings where they study church doctrine, learn how to be effective homemakers and parents, discuss the importance of keeping all the commandments of God, and analyze how to best support church leaders. During the decades I attended, we were taught each week that in a world full of complexity, hilarity, confusion, and endless puzzlement, we, alone, had been gifted with the complete truth. The sheer hubris of it would be laughable if it weren't taken in such deadly seriousness.

Yet it wasn't for lack of an education that we believed such things. I was raised by an educated mother and father in a community that prized education. My mother was one of the very few women of her generation who received a college degree. I read voraciously growing up. I questioned, I searched, I wondered, I rebelled, and, finally, I conformed. Before I graduated from high school, I had experienced a genuine crisis of faith and had removed myself from activity in the church for a while. I knew about several of the older doctrines, including *blood atonement*, or Brigham Young's belief that some sins were so serious that instead of being covered by Christ's atonement, the sinner himself had to make recompense for his sins by voluntarily giving up his life. In addition, I knew about the *patriarchal order*, or the submission of women to their husbands in the temple ceremony and in their daily lives. The church has recently changed the wording of the temple ceremony to make such feminine submission less pronounced, but female compliance remains a major cultural force nonetheless and is still reflected in the all-male priesthood. Women are told they can access the power and blessings of the priesthood through their husbands and male leaders, but they cannot officially hold it.

As an English literature major at Brigham Young University, I vicariously experienced numerous belief systems and lifestyles by reading novels from around the world and from every time period. Yet even this was not enough to pull me out of the Mormon vortex completely. The social pressure to conform was too strong. My friends, family, ancestors, fellow students, teachers, doctors, and community were all Mormon. When I came of age in the 1970s, Utah was vastly, predominantly Mormon. A non-Mormon was an oddity, a spectacle as amazing as a peacock appearing in a field of pheasants. There were just a handful of non-Mormons in my high school in Kaysville, Utah. I dated one of them throughout high school and beyond. Two of the others became some of my best friends.

Looking back now, from the vantage point of the Internet and the astonishing ability one has to gain instant access to information, it is almost incomprehensible that educated, well-traveled, well-meaning people could have had almost no idea of their religion's convoluted history. Yet the only version of Mormonism that we were familiar with was the correlated, sanitized version that had been published or approved by the church. Any hints of scandalous behavior on the part of our founder, the Prophet Joseph Smith, were explained away as vicious lies and anti-Mormon sentiment on the part of the *Gentiles*, or non-Mormons. Our local library wasn't much help because the book selections were influenced by the community standards. There might have been a handful of books critical of the Mormon Church on the shelves, but I never found any of them.

Yet even in Farmington, Utah, sheltered from the outside world by the majestic Wasatch Mountains, we heard rumors of a dangerous type of person who was to be avoided at any cost: the *anti-Mormon*, or someone who preached against the church's divinity. We were warned against the evils of books such as Fawn M. Brodie's groundbreaking biography of Mormonism's founder, *No Man Knows My History: The Life of Joseph Smith*. Published in 1945, Brodie's book was an unprecedented, scholarly study of the first prophet's life. Unlike official church materials, which universally revere Joseph Smith as a righteous man inspired by God, Brodie takes a more complex view of his motives and portrays him as a brilliant, charismatic man nonetheless beset by serious frailties and failures. Although she had grown up in an orthodox Mormon home, Brodie began to drift away from her family's faith once she left her hometown of Huntsville, Utah.[68]

Her uncle, President David O. McKay, was one of the

most prominent and beloved of all of the Mormon prophets, partly because of his long tenure in the church's governing body. In 1906, at the age of thirty-two, he was called to serve in the Quorum of the Twelve Apostles, a group outranked only by the First Presidency itself. Then in 1951, he became the president of the church until his death in 1970. He was the prophet who served during the first eleven years of my life, and I have vivid memories of learning and singing about him as a child in Primary. A tall, strong, and physically imposing man, McKay maintained a punishing work schedule until his ninth decade. His full head of luxuriant white hair set him apart from most men his age, and when he died at the age of ninety-six, the entire church mourned his passing.

Naturally, the McKay family was extremely distressed when Brodie's biography of Joseph Smith was published. Although her book was hailed in the mainstream press and is still considered a foundational work of scholarship, the church's official response was one of revulsion and condemnation. Brodie was seen as having tarnished the family name, and in 1946, while pregnant with her second child, she was excommunicated from the church. Many believe that her uncle David O. McKay, then serving as an apostle, was the force behind her excommunication. He stated, "She found the poison grain of unbelief and now languishes in spiritual apathy and decay." I remember hearing her denounced from the pulpit and being warned to stay away from her "scurrilous work" and "ghoulish act."[69]

Other authors like Jerald and Sandra Tanner were also infamous among church members as former, fifth-generation Mormons who had apostatized. The Tanners spent decades writing books critical of the church's history even though Sandra Tanner was a great-great-granddaughter of Brigham Young. Their 1964 book, *Mormonism—Shadow or Reality?*, is considered by many to be one of the most important books written on Mormon history in the first 150 years of the church's founding (1830–1980).[70] Yet we were routinely admonished to stay away from anything written by the Tanners since their words were likened to veritable stepping stones to hell.

To impressionable young minds, these were heady lessons, woven into our cells like the food we ate and the water we drank. To be Mormon was not to be merely a member of a religious group. It was to be part of a monolithic, unquestioned worldview that ruled everything from how we dressed and what we drank to whom we married and where our souls would spend eternity. This, then, is the backdrop against which our early lives played out. To the best of our efforts, my peers and I followed the rules that our parents, church, and community had instilled in us, never suspecting that there was a much larger world outside the confines of our small hometown that would eventually intrude upon our temporary shelter.

And this is where the wicket gets sticky. By speaking out about the church's problems, historical controversies, and questionable doctrines, one is not only sinning against his/her parents, heritage, and culture, but also risking eternal damnation. My writing this book, for example, will forever brand me as an apostate, one who has lost the light of Christ in her life. It is hard to explain to non-Mormons how these consequences can be devastating and lifelong: friendships have been ruined, livelihoods have been lost, social circles have been destroyed, marriages have been terminated, and relationships with relatives have been severed over simply stating one's personal beliefs publicly.

CHAPTER 6

All is Well!

One of the most iconic Mormon pioneer hymns, "Come, Come, Ye Saints," contains these words:

Come, come, ye Saints, no toil nor labor fear;
But with joy wend your way.
Though hard to you this journey may appear,
Grace shall be as your day.
'Tis better far for us to strive
Our useless cares from us to drive;
Do this, and joy your hearts will swell—
All is well! All is well!

The appeal of this sentiment neatly coincided with my mother's desire to find a stable mooring amidst a sea of family troubles as she was growing up. Her mother (my grandmother) was married at the age of fifteen to my twenty-two-year-old grandfather. Their first child, a boy named Grant,[71] was born when my grandmother was sixteen. I have seen one of the few photos that was taken of Grant when he was an infant. It is a black-and-white photo that has been colorized. He is sitting outside in a red Scout Boy wagon, a plump, healthy baby in a diaper, a grin on his face as the early afternoon sunshine slants over his fair skin. His light-brown hair is neatly combed to one side, and he rests one of his small hands on the side of the wagon. He was born in 1934, right in the middle of the Great Depression. Money was tight, times were hard, and jobs were scarce. To help make ends meet, my grandparents lived for a while in the home of my grandmother's parents.

Although a whooping cough vaccine had been licensed in the United States as early as 1914, it wasn't until the development of the diphtheria-tetanus-pertussis (DTP) vaccine in 1948 that access became widely available.[72] Tragically, shortly after his first birthday in 1935, the little boy caught whooping cough and passed away at home despite frantic attempts to save his life. While my seventeen-year-old grandmother and her own mother watched in what must have been unbearable agony, the one-year-old baby took his final breath. The devastation of that loss rippled through the family for years and left a permanent scar: my grandmother was unable to speak about his death for decades.

This, alone, would have been enough to unhinge an adult with twenty additional years of life experience. As it was, at the time of her son's death, my grandmother was also seven and one-half months pregnant with her second child, my mother. When my mother was born, she was loved and coddled with infinite care, and she recorded in her life history that "because I was the first baby born after Grant died, I can never remember a time in my life when I didn't know that my mom and dad loved me with all of their hearts. I never felt unwanted or unloved."[73] In the next seven years, my mom gained three additional siblings, which meant that by the time my grandmother was twenty-four, she had given birth to five children and buried one of them.

Although my mom doesn't say a word in her life history about what happened during those extremely stressful years, my grandmother became addicted to alcohol. It happened when the children were quite young. I know from overhearing bits and pieces of stories that the adults discussed through the years. My grandfather began to drink heavily, too. When my grandmother was twenty-nine, she and my grandfather bought a café in a nearby small town and turned it into a financial success, working long, arduous hours serving the locals and many of the truckers who passed through. Somehow, my grandmother managed to run the café's grill alone from the early morning hours until the early afternoon when my grandfather showed up and took over until the lunch crowd was done. My mom and her younger sister eventually worked as waitresses there. Although their family life was heavily impacted by alcoholism for decades, my grandparents' work ethic and pure grit helped pull them out of poverty. To their credit, they stayed married and raised four intelligent, successful children.

My mom almost never mentioned the negative details of her childhood. Instead, she often told us entertaining and humorous anecdotes about her adventures growing up with her younger sister, Karla, and her two younger brothers, Lewis and David. One of our favorite stories was how she and Lewis would walk to one of the nearby movie theatres in Layton, Utah, every Saturday. They would head out to the weekly serial (or chapter) movie featuring evil villains, hapless heroines, and fearless he-men who would brave any danger to save the damsel in distress. With one quarter in their pockets, which was enough to buy two entrance tickets, a bag of popcorn to share, and some candy, they felt rich.

One Saturday they saw a new sign posted that said, "Babe in arms. . . free admittance." They decided to buy only one ticket, which my mother carefully explained to the woman who ran the theatre.

"But there's two of you."

"I know," my mom said. "But if I hold my brother on my lap for the whole movie, he would count as a 'babe in arms,' right?"

"I guess if you want to do that, it's OK by me."

"That way we'll have twenty-five cents to spend on candy." My mom beamed down at her little brother, who watched this exchange hopefully.

"OK, you kids. Go find your seats." She smiled down at them as they skipped together toward the theatre with victorious grins on their faces.

The woman happened to know my grandmother, so she called her using the theatre phone and could barely stop laughing long enough to tell my grandma about her kids' brilliant money-saving scheme. And sure enough, every time the manager walked into the theatre to check on them, there they were with my mom's younger brother dutifully sitting on her lap even though he weighed more than her. They watched all of the features sitting like that—surrounded by rows and rows of empty seats.

My mom and her siblings walked to and from school every day; picked cherries to make extra spending money; roasted hot dogs and baking potatoes in a big firepit in their backyard; played hide-and-go-seek in the weed-choked, undeveloped fields that surrounded the homes on their street; and enacted countless variations of Tarzan and Jane: Tarzan would save Jane from certain death, then Jane would save Tarzan from certain death, then Tarzan and Jane would save Boy and Girl from certain death, then Boy and Girl would save Tarzan and Jane from certain death, and so on. The only set rule was that my mom was always Jane, and her brother Lewis was always Tarzan. Once, Karla dared to complain that it wasn't fair that *she* always got stuck playing Girl: my mom's cool response was that since she was older than her sister by four years, it was only natural that the more mature role would fall to her.

Thus, fingers interlaced, the siblings meandered through their growing-up years cushioned by the luxurious haze of youth, sipping every bit of nectar from the endless experiences that surrounded them. And even though the angel of innocence hovered over them with her generous wings aloft to soften the blows of life, the time came when the magic of childhood passed, and the darker tones that had been hidden behind a gauzy screen seeped into their lives.

When I was in my forties, my mom let slip a single remark that encompassed a world of hidden pain. She told me about nervously hurrying home from elementary school each day, unsure of what state her mother would be in: "Lots of times when I came home from school, my mom would be passed out drunk in the kitchen or on the living room floor. Sometimes I had to change her sanitary pad because she had bled onto the floor. I was afraid to invite friends over because I never knew what I'd find when I got home." I was stunned at her confession. I could only imagine how, as the oldest daughter of four children, she must have felt it her duty to protect her siblings from the embarrassing details of life with an alcoholic mother. In no way do I share these stories to shame my grandparents, who have long since passed away. Rather, I share them to make a point about my mother's coping mechanisms.

When my mother was eventually taken to the Mormon Church by her maternal grandmother (my great-grandmother), she clung to it like a shipwreck survivor. Today, it is understood that adult children of alcoholics have experienced severe trauma and have been forced to find ways to organize and interpret their world. During my mother's formative years, however, no families talked openly about their dysfunctionality. Nobody went to therapy. It was unseemly. It was disconcerting. It was better to smile and sing "All is Well!" each week with your friends at church.

My mother thus mastered the fine art of denial and took this to extremes. Everything was *always* good. *Nothing* ever made her worry. She had *never* been depressed for a day in her life! *Every* cloud had a silver lining, and so on and so forth. As kids, my three younger siblings and I naturally believed her fairy-tale version of the world for quite a few years. But as time passed and the eyes of my younger self were replaced by the eyes of my emerging adult self, I realized that my mom was living in a sunny world without shadows because she had learned that was what it took to survive.

By the time I was a junior in high school, I had begun to seriously question many church doctrines, but I still hesitated to completely discard my religious heritage. My non-Mormon, high school boyfriend had begged me to see reason and admit that the church I had been raised in was a man-made organization that seemed to receive revelations only when it was expedient to do so. He challenged me about the 1890 Manifesto that disavowed polygamy (at least officially) around the same time Utah was seeking statehood. Even after the Manifesto, however, Mormon leaders and members continued to secretly practice polygamy, and rumors to this effect eventually reached the nation's capital. In response, the Senator Reed Smoot Congressional hearings began in 1904 to consider whether the duly elected Smoot should be seated because of his membership in the Mormon Church. (He retained his seat after three years of hearings.[74]) As a result of these hearings, the Second Manifesto was issued in 1904, in which then-prophet Joseph F. Smith (the nephew of Mormonism's founder, Joseph Smith) announced that any members who continued practicing polygamy would be excommunicated.[75]

In 1978, the year I graduated from Davis High School in Kaysville, Utah, there was another "miraculous" revelation allowing black men to hold the Mormon priesthood and black families to be sealed in the temple. My boyfriend again pointed out that it seemed quite convenient that the church had made such a dramatic change to its doctrine just as social pressures were ratcheting up on the church to modernize its racial policies. I had always been bothered by that issue, too. "I don't know about that one," I faltered. Some older church members who had grown up during the period of segregation before the Civil Rights Act of 1964 were disturbed by the revelation granting the priesthood to all worthy male members, and racism continued to be a thorn (and, according to some, still is) in the church's side for decades. I believe, however, that there were far more members who welcomed the change with open arms than not. All of my friends and I were relieved because we were old enough to recognize the embarrassment of being associated with an organization that promoted racist policies. (It is worth pointing out that the Mormon Church was by no means exclusive in their racially tinged policies at that time and that as of 2016, 86 percent of American churches were still largely segregated.[76])

Yet despite my unease about the church's past and then-current practices, the tenuous thread that bound me to the organization never snapped. I carried the burden of being the oldest daughter, though without any of the trauma that my mother had experienced years earlier. I was the one who babysat my youngest sister and brother and cajoled them into completing their chores. I broke up fights between my two sisters, and my mother assigned me a permanent spot in between them during every car ride we took as a family. Finally, I had no desire to hurt my parents: I knew they depended on me, and I knew they loved me.

The same year I turned sixteen, my forty-year-old father was diagnosed with Parkinson's disease. Throughout my father's twenty-year illness, my mother continued to insist that all was well; in fact, it was the standard sign-off phrase that she used in every phone conversation with my siblings and me. How could all be well, we discussed amongst ourselves, when her beloved husband and our beloved father was slowly losing his ability to dress himself, walk, and eventually talk? One of the medications that was commonly prescribed to treat Parkinson's caused permanent neurological damage, so our dad spent the last twelve years of his life writhing in uncontrolled muscular spasms which overtook his face, arms, torso, and legs. He was dancing to a silent rhythm that only he could hear.

A conversation with him was a frustrating series of Morse code dots and dashes. He would try to say a word—pause—try again, stutter—pause—repeat a syllable several times so rapidly that the listener had no idea of what he was talking about—pause—and eventually drop silent. As a young adult, I desperately wanted to talk to him about real problems in the world; I wanted to talk to somebody who could consider the notion that the world was not a perfect place. I wanted to talk to somebody who would give it to me straight and admit that things were never going to be as tidy and perfect as my mom seemed to believe they were. My mom was figuratively deaf because she could only hear a limited range of happy, cheerful tones. My dad, on the other hand, was actually mute, locked away in a silent prison cell where his words were never able to force themselves out from behind his clenched teeth and spasming tongue.

All of this was taking place inside the monolithic Mormon worldview that buttressed our beliefs, directed our decisions, and funneled our future choices into those that the church deemed worthy. The Book of Mormon taught us that "wickedness never was happiness" (Alma 41:10); in corollary, those who were *not* happy were certainly doing something against the will of God. We believed that our best chance of living happily ever after was by embracing every word that came forth from the mouth of God or from his mouthpieces, the Mormon prophets and apostles. After our father's death at age sixty due to an experimental Parkinson's surgery that led to a cascade of devastating and irreversible complications, we all held tightly to the hope that we would see him again someday. My mother picked up the pieces of her broken heart and plucked along bravely as she always had. We four siblings followed her example, doing the best we could with our mortal limitations and lives.

CHAPTER 7

BYU Blues

As an inquisitive child and teen, I developed a sense of cognitive dissonance early on as I compared the church's teachings about women's roles to my internal vision of who I wanted to be. I longed to experience things outside the narrow walls of my upbringing; the richness of the unexplored world was just beyond my reach, and I continually stretched toward it. But I had no idea where to go for any kind of support in my mental peregrinations. As the oldest child in my family, I had no trusted older confidante to turn to about the riddles of life and faith. When I asked two of my bishops, I was told to read my scriptures more diligently and pray more fervently. The problem wasn't the church, they hinted. The problem was me.

Although the women's liberation movement had burst upon the national scene in the late 1960s, eventually spreading around the globe throughout the '70s and '80s, there was almost no sign of it on the Brigham Young University (BYU) campus when I started attending as a new student in the fall of 1978. Brigham Young University has always been a bastion of religious and political conservatism. Although I was a diligent student and took my studies seriously, I was repeatedly told at church (and in a few of my classes) that any career aspirations I might have were only temporary distractions from my real calling—to be a wife and a mother. Luckily, one of the most forward-thinking departments on campus was the English Department, which was where I eventually ended up. It was there that I found room to question and explore with professors who cared about the intellectual development of all of their students—whether they were male or female.

When the proposed Equal Rights Amendment (ERA) to the United States Constitution was passed in 1972 by the Senate and the House, the states were given ten years to endorse the amendment. When the 1982 deadline arrived, however, the proposed amendment was scuttled because not enough states had ratified it. Coincidentally, that was the same year I finished my undergraduate degree. During my time at the university, the ERA came up frequently in discussions, not only on campus, but also in church meetings. During one Sunday worship service, the speaker spent an hour railing against the evils of the Equal Rights Amendment: he reminded the young men and women in the audience that God had already revealed everything we needed to know about a woman's divine role. Although I had mixed feelings about the amendment, I was bothered that a speaker would use a church meeting as a platform to discuss political issues and tell those listening exactly what their opinion should be. Since that time, it has remained a controversial and divisive issue. Interestingly enough, although Utah was one of the states that did *not* ratify the amendment by the 1982 deadline, the territory of Utah had led the way in women's suffrage, albeit for complex and often contradictory reasons. Utah women gained the right to vote in 1870, then lost it in 1887 due to anti-polygamy sentiments in the nation's capital, then regained it (along with the right to hold office) when the territory officially became a state in 1896.[77]

I mention this history only to point to the prevailing climate at BYU when it came to women's rights and roles. One of my clearest memories from BYU is having a long, heated argument with one of the young men in my *student ward* (Mormon church unit for university students). He argued that my role as a woman was to submit to my future husband and follow his patriarchal leadership. I told him to take his patriarchy and shove it up his rear end as far as it would go. Some people overheard and were offended, and my dorm mother admonished me to watch my language. I was angry and defiant on the one hand, yet eager to please and not to cause problems on the other. The box of my Mormon upbringing was starting to suffocate me, yet I had no idea what to do about it other than break some of the rules that I considered to be ridiculous. What was wrong with me? Why couldn't I just go along and get along? Why did I always have to kick against the pricks?

One of my university religion professors loved to use the term "kick against the pricks" to describe our faithless and self-absorbed generation (Acts 9:5). This particular phrase is mentioned only twice in the King James Version but is a well-known metaphor for uselessly protesting against something incontestable or inescapable. This professor reminded us that the truly faithful would gratefully accept the pricks and prods that God provided along the way to guide his people through the strait gate and onto the narrow path that led back to heaven.

This same professor told us one day that only men could become *sons of perdition*, or the worst category of heretics who were cast into an eternal hell. This phrase occurs in the New Testament, the Book of Mormon, and the Doctrine and Covenants; and its description was enough to strike terror into my heart for years. According to the Book of Mormon, those who "transgress and go contrary" to the truths they have been taught will suffer "guilt, and pain, and anguish, which is like an unquenchable fire, whose flame ascendeth up forever and ever" (Mos. 2:36-39). The idea that my final doom might be to endure a never-ending torment was reminiscent of the famous sermon preached by Jonathan Edwards in July 1741 in Enfield, Connecticut. In that sermon, the exquisite tortures of God's wrath "burn against . . . [the sinners], their damnation does not slumber; the pit is prepared, the fire is made ready, the furnace is now hot, ready to receive them; the flames do now rage and glow. The glittering sword is whetted, and held over them, and the pit hath opened its mouth under them."[78] To someone raised in an authoritarian church that claimed to contain the full, ultimate word of God, turning against such teachings conjured up a fate worse than death.

But when my religion professor said that only *men* could become sons of perdition, he explained that it was because only *they* held the power of the Mormon priesthood and had enough mature knowledge and the spiritual capacity to fall so far. As an eager college student trying to come to grips with my religious heritage and my intellectual questions, I raised my hand.

"Yes?" He looked at me with piercing eyes.

"So, are you saying women can't become sons of perdition?"

"Yes." He continued to stare at me with his heavy eyebrows knit in a straight line across his broad forehead.

"But that means you're saying that women aren't spiritually advanced enough to fall—" My voice tapered off in uncertainty. I didn't want to appear stupid or overly confrontational.

"Yes," he said again, this time more firmly.

"But that means that you're saying that women are second-class citizens when it comes to spiritual maturity," I persisted once more, knowing full well that I was on thin ice. Total silence fell over the classroom.

"What?" he bellowed suddenly. "Are you telling me that you are offended because you can't go to hell like a man can?" A look of condescension crossed his face as he played to his conservative audience: "What do you think, boys? Do we need to make sure our women can go to hell as surely as our men? Do you think *that's* a good idea?" He spread his arms out to his sides, palms up, as if to ask the students in the classroom if they had ever heard something so preposterous. Several students tittered nervously, a few shot me looks of disgust, and I silently fumed. I never asked another question again in my four years of required religion classes at BYU because I had learned an important lesson. Although the religion professors and Mormon bishops and even the young men in my student ward might try to shut me up in public, they would never be able to control what I thought about privately.

The longer I stayed at BYU, the lonelier my struggles became. During the 1970s and '80s, there was no Internet and no way for a person to find support from anyone outside his or her geographical boundaries. Today people say that the Internet has created a mirage of connectedness that masks the gaping loneliness from which this generation suffers. Back then, I would have given anything to find somebody to discuss my questions with me. I remember standing outside the office of another one of my BYU professors, a popular English instructor. I stood there multiple times over a few semesters, waiting silently, hoping against hope that he would open the door and ask me if I wanted to talk. I was too timid to knock for fear that I might inconvenience him. But still I stood, frozen, my knuckles held a few inches from his closed door, as the seconds ticked by. He never opened the door; I never asked. It was only years later that I learned that this professor, Dr. Eugene England, has come to be considered one of the most open-minded, enlightened educators in BYU history.

The conversations I couldn't safely have with anybody echoed inside my head. I remember feeling unhappy and guilty almost all the time for every stray thought that crossed my mind. I thought I was probably going to be consigned to hell for my gross sins. Actually, I was just a normal teenage girl who hadn't done much of anything too serious. I'd drunk a few beers (which I could barely gag down), smoked two or three marijuana cigarettes (which made me feel panicky and dizzy), and kissed only one boy. Yet I was surrounded by a sea of young, Mormon, college students, all of them leading seemingly perfect lives of virtue. (Later I learned this wasn't exactly true.) I berated myself for my inability to comply perfectly with the rigid requirements of my faith and wondered what negative consequences might unfold in the future due to my lack of unwavering faith.

CHAPTER 8

On Board

Despite my challenges at BYU, one very fortunate thing occurred: I met my husband, Jason, during my sophomore year. He went out of his way to pursue me, for I was skittish when it came to dating. After we had been going out for only six months, his five roommates ganged up on him one night and told him to dump me because I obviously wasn't committed to the relationship. Thus were the dating customs at BYU. It wasn't uncommon for couples to marry after dating for only a few months. A high school friend of mine got married just a few weeks into the first semester and got pregnant on her honeymoon. Two of my roommates got engaged after three months; in fact, of the six roommates I started my freshmen year with in one of the student dorms, only two of us completed our degrees. Students joked about women getting their "bachelor's" degree when they snagged an eligible young man who had just returned from his two-year *LDS mission.*[79] If an engagement and marriage occurred, the coeds were said to have earned their "M.R.S." degree. Many new brides dropped out of school to earn their advanced "Ph.T.," or "Putting Hubby Through" degree.

Quick engagements were the norm, most likely because of the church's insistence that no sexual relations occur outside of marriage. Sometimes quick divorces happened, too. Years after I had left BYU, I heard a few stories about couples driving to Las Vegas, getting married in a two-minute ceremony, having sex for a couple of days, and then getting divorced before returning to campus. There were other

BYU workarounds when it came to maintaining at least the appearance of chastity. One of the most famous was "Levi loving," or the practice of gyrating against someone else's private parts while fully clothed. As one person wryly reported on a discussmormonism.com board post, "Levi Strauss® was the official blue full-length condom of BYU and UVU [Utah Valley University] back in my day. Levi loving or dry humping was not considered sex." At least one graduate student from BYU verified that during her time at the school, the slogan "Stay moral, go oral" was popular among a certain portion of the students.[80] And I remember being told multiple times as a young woman by both my male and female church leaders, "Don't ever find yourself in a horizontal position with a member of the opposite sex. Make sure both of your feet are firmly on the floor at all times."

Most of the students I knew personally tried their best to follow the no-sex rule on campus; and although some found creative ways to get as close to the line as they could without crossing over into forbidden territory, sometimes there were well-publicized mishaps. One of the most popular, charismatic young men in my first student ward was within one week of leaving for his mission when he and his steady girlfriend suddenly disappeared. Someone saw them holding hands a few weeks later at a *married student ward*[81] and waved to him. He reportedly frowned, lowered his eyes, and turned his head away without responding. A few students eagerly spread the gossip far and wide. I have often wondered if the shame they endured because of their familial and religious conditioning damaged what could have been a happy marriage; I truly hope it didn't. During my second year at school, a returned missionary in another student ward impregnated the adopted granddaughter of then-current prophet of the church, Spencer W. Kimball. A hasty marriage was arranged. The young man had hung out a few times in our apartment and confessed to me shortly before the wedding that he had no desire to marry the girl. I was shocked and felt sorry for them both but believed that there was no other way for them to escape their predicament. Mormons have always been counseled to seek abortions only as a last resort under a very narrow set of circumstances, and the easiest way "out" back then was for the couple to marry quickly and quietly. It wasn't until several years later that I realized the great injustice that had been done to both of them in coercing them to marry.

College is a place where people enter as teenagers and leave as adults, and oftentimes things get messy. Somehow, in the midst of all the physical, emotional, spiritual, and academic pressures, Jason and I maintained our balance. Because of his patience and persistence, I came to realize that I cared for him deeply. Before I consented to marriage, we had many long, frank discussions about polygamy and its accompanying patriarchal structure in the church. I told him that I completely despised both doctrines, so much so that I was unsure if I wanted to be married in the temple.

In one of my college classes, the instructor had lectured us about the "Locus of Control," a theory developed by researcher Julian B. Rotter in 1954. The term still maintains its importance in all branches of psychology because it explains the widely differing opinions people have about how much control they have over the outcomes in their lives. Do people generally believe that they have a high degree of control in shaping the course of their lives? If so, they have an *"internal* locus of control."* Or do they generally believe that outside forces, such as luck or fate, determine their future? If so, they have an *"external* locus of control." Psychologically healthy adults most likely move back and forth on this continuum throughout their lives, depending upon their circumstances. However, those who consistently feel that they lack control may get stuck relying on outside authority figures to tell them the "correct" way to lead their lives. Instead of achieving psychological adulthood and emotional independence, they forever seek the approval and permission of outside authority figures before doing anything.[82]

This can sometimes occur with Mormon women, who are indoctrinated from childhood to trust in the divine authority of their male leaders, fathers, and husbands. In some cases, especially during past decades, this set them up for a lifetime of spiritual and emotional dependence—a prolonged childhood of sorts. When Jason and I were dating in the early 1980s, women who married in the temple had to promise to "obey" their *husbands* during the ceremony, while the men had to promise to "obey" the *Lord*. The lopsided power dynamic in this anachronistic pledge was one that I and many of my female friends found personally offensive.[83] While Jason and I discussed this before our marriage and deliberately chose *not* to follow this formula for feminine obedience, many couples accepted the asymmetry and still do. I have heard many "faith-promoting" stories where good Mormon women have explained how they have wrestled with this dilemma, which usually ends with them submitting to their husband's wishes and receiving blessings from God for their obedience.

Then in 1990, changes were made to the temple ceremony. The revised pledge called for a woman to "hearken" to her husband's counsel as he hearkened to the Lord's counsel. Feminists saw this as a step in the right direction, but it was not enough. As one of my lifelong friends quipped, "How is 'hearken' anything but a synonym for 'obey'?" Finally, in 2019, the church again revised the ceremony, completely eliminating the women's covenant to "hearken" to their husbands and putting them on an equal footing with men in the temple ceremony. As Mormon writer Jana Riess explains, "Gender equality [now exists] in the language of the sealing ceremony, where the bride and groom now apparently make the same promises to each other."[84] However, it is important to note that although women have been edging closer to spiritual independence in Mormonism, they still are explicitly denied authority to receive the priesthood, or a man's ability to act in the name of God. And they are still expected to respect the authority of their priesthood leaders, who are always male.

No woman has ever served in the First Presidency, the Quorum of the Twelve, or the quorums of the Seventy, which are the highest governing bodies of the church.

I told Jason point-blank during our engagement that if the church ever reinstituted polygamy on earth, I would leave the church and never look back. I believed in full disclosure before a commitment as important as marriage; I wanted him to know exactly how I felt. He agreed with me. He, too, had been skeptical about the apologists' explanations for polygamy; and as for patriarchy, he said he had never believed that men had any more spiritual aptitude or insight than women. He also said that he thought any man who tried to pull "patriarchal rank" on his wife was most likely delusional about his own righteousness, not to say lacking in the basic understanding of what it took to make a partnership of equals work. Even though Jason was a returned missionary, he was flexible enough in his attitudes to believe that while some things the church preached were important, others bordered on the ridiculous.

We married in the historic Salt Lake Temple in 1981 after dating for eighteen months, which was an almost unheard-of, lengthy engagement for a couple at BYU. Now, I look back at the time of our marriage (I was nearly twenty-two; Jason was twenty-three) as an underripe age to make such a monumental commitment. Luckily, we seem to have chosen well. We married with the explicit understanding that I would finish my senior year and complete my bachelor's degree in English literature. There was no way I was going to sacrifice my education as I had seen many young women do at the university. We also agreed to put off having children for several years so that I could complete my master's degree in the same field of study. Both of these decisions put us in a very tiny minority of young, married, Mormon couples at that time.

After Jason's graduation in mechanical engineering, he was recruited by both the Marines and the Navy. He chose to join the United States Naval Submarine Force.

Under Ronald Reagan's presidency (1981-1989), with its heavy focus on containment of the Soviet Union and other communist countries, there occurred a massive increase in defense spending. While historians still debate whether or not Reagan's leadership contributed to the ending of the Cold War, it is certain that the military buildup incentivized an immense number of young people to join the armed forces at that time.[85]

Jason's twenty-year Naval submarine career started with a series of highly demanding training programs. We moved almost every six months for the first two years of our military career, which began two years after we got married. We started in Newport, Rhode Island, for six months at the Naval Officer Candidate School. Jason drove out by himself in our only car to find us an apartment, and I flew out about a month later. Having grown up in Utah, I had never understood why people referred to our mountainous state as a "desert" climate. We had trees and grass, after all! As the plane began its descent into the Providence, Rhode Island airport, however, I stared out the window in amazement. I had never seen so many trees in my life! Beneath me was a solid sea of green that rolled on in unbroken waves as far as I could see in every direction. On land, navigating the narrow, winding roads with no view other than walls of thick, green trees was completely disorienting; I was never really sure which direction we were traveling or how to get from one place to another.

Jason was only able to leave school on the weekends, so we rented a very small, unfurnished apartment. We were too poor to afford much, so our meager furnishings consisted of a double-sized, blow-up mattress; a microwave oven; two foldable, metal chairs; and a used TV with rabbit-eared antennas that produced only fuzzy reception at best. We usually sat on the carpet to eat our simple dinners together. Sometimes we drove around Newport to gawk at the magnificent mansions built during the last half of the nineteenth century by tycoons who needed summer "cottages" in which to entertain their wealthy families. Comparing the glorious splendor of the past accommodations of the rich to our own tiny apartment gave me an economic perspective that I had never attained during my younger years. As a kid growing up in Utah, I thought we were well-to-do because my parents owned a very old, three-bedroom home with a big backyard. It wasn't until years later that I understood how frugal both of my parents were and how carefully they had managed their middle-class income to give us the best life they could.

During the long weeks while my husband was away, I amused myself by taking lengthy walks through the surrounding areas, always being very careful to pay attention to any twists or turns in the landscape that might disorient me. I experienced terrible homesickness for the first time in my life. I spent much of my solitary time reading classical literature and two of Mormonism's most sacred standard works, the Book of Mormon and the Doctrine and Covenants. I memorized multiple scriptures that were soothing to my soul as I grappled with intense loneliness, and I spent many hours in deep, serious reflection about my religious beliefs.

Throughout our twenty-year career, Jason was often gone. The lifestyle was adventurous on some levels, but highly stressful on others; and the wives, girlfriends, and children left behind banded together to offer each other the high levels of moral support that were absolutely essential to maintaining sanity. Because the location of each submarine was classified as top secret during its operation, family members almost never had any idea where their submariner was. This was before the cell phone and Internet eras, which meant that the only way to contact one's sailor was through a weekly "family gram," or a forty-word telegram that that was transmitted to the submarine via morse code. Sometimes submariners received abrupt notifications that their spouse or girlfriend was tired of being left alone and had decided to terminate the relationship. (And sometimes they didn't find out until the submarine pulled into port and nobody came to welcome them home.) In between each sea duty assignment, the men were rotated to shore duty assignments to help lessen the intense pressures that were put upon them and their families.

Being a member of a worldwide religious organization that provided instant friendship, solace, and socialization was a lifesaver. Despite what I eventually came to see as serious shortcomings within the Mormon Church, I don't think I could have navigated the strenuous decades in the Navy without the aid and comfort that I drew from my religious network. It was a common saying that the submarine service produced two kinds of families: those who broke apart and those who grew closer. From the beginning, Jason and I were determined to be totally committed to our marriage and our family, and the church was a big part of that commitment. However, one of the drawbacks of that same spiritual commitment was that many hours were spent attending perfunctory, and usually boring, church trainings for adults (which neither one of us enjoyed); church-sponsored service projects (which were sometimes worthwhile, but oftentimes simply obligatory); and Sunday worship services (which we always attended together as a family, but which effectively canceled any family recreation on Sundays).

Differing interpretations of what it meant to keep the Sabbath day holy led to varying degrees of strictness within families. I knew a few families who insisted that their children wear Sunday clothes (dresses, suits, ties) throughout the entire day, even at home. I knew (and still know) others who didn't allow TV or watching football on Sunday. Once we had our two children, Jason and I let them wear regular clothes as soon as church was over, but we didn't allow them to have friends over on Sundays. We tried to focus on activities like writing letters to grandparents, drawing pictures, discussing whatever challenges our children were facing, baking cookies or treats, and playing board games as a family. A company named Living Scriptures produced a series of thirteen animated VHS tapes from 1987 through 1992 about the events in the Book of Mormon which supposedly occurred between 600 B.C. and A.D. 400. The videos were quite expensive to purchase when they were first released, but we viewed them as an investment in our children's religious education. We eventually bought them all, and we watched them with our kids repeatedly on Sundays since we didn't allow them to watch regular movies on that day. On rare occasions, we took them out to parks on Sunday, but I always felt guilty about letting the rules slide even that little bit.

During the hundreds of Sundays we spent with our children, we dutifully told them, "It's time to get ready for church" instead of asking them, "Where do *you* want to go today, and what do *you* want our family to do?" Since our Navy retirement over twenty years ago, Jason has told me repeatedly that he wishes he could get back all the hours he spent at church meetings and invest them into our children's early, blossoming lives. Like all fantastical and regretful wishes, however, this one certainly won't come true unless time travel becomes a reality.

CHAPTER 9

Parenthood May Result
in Serious Injury

Who was this Mormon God? From what I had been taught in church, I pictured him as a white, bearded, slightly disapproving father figure; one who could be benevolent on the one hand, yet intimidating on the other. He would smile upon his children kindly if we followed all the household rules, such as no swearing, no smoking or drinking, and absolutely no sex before marriage. Yet He would also reprimand us if we broke any of the rules, some of them as serious as murder, and some as minor as disagreeing with a church leader or drinking coffee.

All of my Mormon friends and I grew up thinking that God was omnipotent, omniscient, and omnipresent. That meant He knew if we had ever inhaled a single cigarette or indulged in a French kiss in the back seat of a car. Later on, after I married and had my two children, I wondered how a male god could possibly understand what it felt like for a woman to carry newly burgeoning life in her womb or to be turned inside out as the baby pushed its way into the world. Would Heavenly Father understand that as the baby's first, thin cry pierced the air, it shattered the woman's soul with the certainty that her heart was no longer hers alone? Being a mother was a double-edged sword: loving a child and possibly losing a child were now forged together in terrifying brightness, two halves of a whole, two inescapable realities that could either create or destroy.

My pre-motherhood life was severed in an instant at the

birth of my daughter, Leah. The possibility of losing her or later her younger brother hung over my head like the sword of Damocles. As my babies sighed their milk-soft breaths against my chest, I knew what all parents, and especially women, instinctively know: to lose a child would leave a laceration that would never heal. For the first two months of our daughter's life, I was too exhausted to be cognizant of anything other than a deep, imperative duty to guard the delicate infant in my arms. I went through the motions of feeding and holding her instinctively: at any cost I must feed, nurture, and protect. No one had to tell me to do this. Instead, something ancient and primeval had stirred to life and whispered to me from the dark recesses of my *Homo sapiens* past: "Take care, take care. This child is *everything*." My prehistoric grandmother had encoded her message in the DNA of my female ancestors and had passed it down from mother to daughter through the millennia.

I talked to one of my good friends who had given birth a few months before me. She told me that as time passed, I would start to notice that I had fallen in love with my baby. She called it *bonding*. I couldn't understand how anything could be more intense than the genetic mandate that drove my every waking moment. At about the three-month point, however, I noticed that in addition to caring for my daughter's physical well-being, I was unable to look away from her. I could stare for hours at her dainty fingers, the tiny, pearlescent fingernails like miniature gemstones; the pale-pink blush and heart-shaped pucker of her lips; the delicate upturn of her perfectly shaped nose; the serious, unblinking gaze with which she began to regard me in return. My love for her grew from an instinctual thing to an all-encompassing thing. Is my daughter healthy? Is my daughter happy? Is my daughter dreaming of maternal heartbeats and the deep, ancient rhythms of her origin? Something new blossomed inside me, and I found that I had more room in my heart.

Our firstborn child confirmed to me that coming back to the fold and raising my children inside the belief system of Mormonism was an inspired choice. She was an intelligent, obedient, deeply reflective child. She possessed a preternatural quietude for one so young. She understood the concept of consequences years before most kids did, and she seemed to sail along on a smooth, unruffled ocean—her hazel-colored eyes taking in everything around her with the solemnity and maturity of a sailor who knows the depths of the water and has already plotted her course using the stars in the night sky.

The pregnancy with my son nearly three years later was intense. I was in premature labor for the last six weeks and was put on medication to stop the contractions. My husband was on new-construction duty for a fast-attack submarine being built in Groton, Connecticut, the USS Springfield (SSN-761), and his time was *not* his own. When a new submarine is manufactured, the assigned contractor fabricates the individual components: everything from the exterior hull and the propeller to the periscopes and the nuclear reactor that powers the ship. Once each component is finished, the contractor turns it over to the submarine crew for exceptionally stringent testing and inspection. Even a single flaw could potentially jeopardize the lives of the crew once the submarine is operational. New-construction duty is exhausting. Jason was working twelve- to fourteen-hour days, rotating shifts, and barely dragging himself home every few days to collapse and get a few hours of sleep. This was no time for a premature baby to be born.

My doctor put me on medication and ordered me to go on bed rest, and I managed to lie around for a few weeks, nearly driven crazy by the fact that I wasn't supposed to move, stand up, or do anything that remotely resembled living. My biggest adventures were the ten-yard shuffles to the bathroom several times a day, and I tried to put those off as long as I could for fear that it would start up my labor again. Jason was given one week of emergency leave, and we cobbled together a few babysitters while we arranged to have my sister and my mother-in-law fly out for two weeks each. One day after the babysitter had left, but before Jason had come home for the evening, I discovered our nearly three-year-old daughter sitting on the kitchen floor surrounded by popsicle wrappers, grinning up at me, her teeth, lips, and tongue dyed a bright orangish-red. I couldn't get mad at her. She had discovered that while I was confined to the living room couch, it was an excellent opportunity for her to pull a kitchen chair over to the refrigerator, climb on top of the chair, and help herself to the big bag of popsicles inside the freezer.

Finally, the day arrived when my doctor gave me permission to start moving again. I was overjoyed; so Jason, his mother, Leah, and I piled into our car for a short drive to a nearby beach. No sooner had we parked and started to move slowly towards the beach than I felt what can only be described as a bowling ball dropping at full force from high underneath my ribs into my pelvic girdle. Jason and his mother each took an arm, helping me back to the car, and we returned home. I laid around resting all day, but the next morning I was awakened early by the unmistakable signs of labor. Hurrah! I thought. Let's get this baby here! Jason drove me to the nearby Lawrence + Memorial Hospital in New London, Connecticut, while his mother stayed home to watch Leah.

Luckily, our son Eric was a perfectly healthy baby. I had already learned what this love felt like; I already knew what it was like to be overwhelmed by the certainty that if this new person were to disappear, my life would be over. At the nanosecond that a sperm and an egg joined in an ancient, mindless dance, a tiny being who now ruled my world had blinked into existence. As my infant son began to return my gaze with an increasingly earnest focus, my mother's heart unquestioningly gave itself over to him. As he grew older, he developed little rolls of baby fat; curly, blonde ringlets sprouted out from his scalp in charming disarray; and his gray eyes turned light-blue, fringed by a curtain of blonde lashes. He truly was a beautiful child. For the longest time, his hair smelled like a fresh spring meadow, sprinkled with sunlight and breezes. During his younger years, whenever I felt sad, I gathered him into my arms, buried my nose in his curls, and breathed in deeply, overcome by an ancient joy that began in some primitive past and threaded its way through my bones and into my heart.

But we should have suspected that our son's refusal to follow our suggested deadlines when it came to his birth was a harbinger of things to come. He was in a hurry—to be born, to experience life, and to resist boundaries. His first words showed an independent naughtiness that was charming in a toddler but foreshadowed some worrisome behaviors that occurred later. This energetic, miniature person and his mercurial moods became an integral part of our family dynamic.

In many ways, Eric was our daughter's antithesis. Somehow, these two very different children had come from the same set of parents, which has never ceased to amaze Jason and me. While our daughter's first sentence recorded in her baby book was a polite "More apple juice, please," our son's first sentence recorded was "I no wanna-a-a-a-a-a!" He said this while kicking his block-shaped toddler feet as I attempted to wrestle his shoes onto him. Although our daughter was perfectly suited to spend her formative years in an authoritarian religious environment, our son would chafe against its restrictions almost from the beginning.

Our perfect family was complete: a hazel-eyed, strawberry-blonde girl with a smattering of freckles on her nose and cheeks; and a blue-eyed boy with blonde curls and an infectiously naughty grin. I decided that my former concerns about the Mormon Church didn't matter; Jason and I were going to invest our whole hearts and souls into raising this family exactly like our church said we should. And so we did, reading scriptures together, holding *family home evenings* (weekly family religious instruction and activities), attending church, paying *tithing*,[86] and doing everything that we were asked to do by our religious leaders. I still remembered my old doubts, my old concerns about polygamy and women's places in the modern church, but I stuffed all those thoughts down like an unwelcome intruder, and continued on the best I could, full of happiness and hope for our family.

Through the years that followed in our military career, every time we packed up and headed off into the unknown, our daughter and son were each other's support system. They braved the first days of marching into a new school together and the first timid attempts at making friends in a new neighborhood. It wasn't easy for them, but wherever we went, they had each other. As their mother I plugged along, always putting my family first, above any career I might pursue or anything else that would take me away from my children. Although I had been taught in my church that becoming a mother was a woman's highest achievement, I had resisted that teaching for years because of my tendency to distrust any external advice, especially when it was given by a male church leader. In addition, my early exposure to the doctrine of polygamy had left behind a bitter taste that I had mistakenly equated with bearing and raising children. However, much to my joy, motherhood was an unexpected revelation: it taught me that my imperfections could be transformed into something hallowed as I loved and nurtured my children. My old concerns about becoming a broodmare in a polygamous heaven disappeared.

There is a secret that every parent knows, but that no child knows until he or she becomes a parent; it is usually not discussed openly, but it lies at the center of the loss that every parent experiences. It is that children and parents love each other in different ways. There is no doubt that children love their parents, rely on them, appreciate them, and depend on them. Sometimes they even emulate them. To survive childhood, children must gain and maintain their parents' attention for years. Eventually, however, children wander the world in ever-widening circles, sensing that their attachment to the center must become more tenuous if their own adulthood is to proceed normally.

For parents, the opposite is true. Parents never outgrow their children. They will never stop reminiscing about their children's formative years and the joys and challenges of guiding them to a state of independence. Parents will always need their kids—need them in ways that they don't want to admit. Children find their parents' love invaluable. Parents find their love for their children all-encompassing. When a parent dies, it is a time of profound mourning for the children left behind. When a child dies, however, it is a lifetime of sackcloth and ashes, a fatal frost that destroys the harvest and leaves only emptiness behind. If a parent dies prematurely, their children will always miss them. But if a child is taken prematurely, a pall settles over the family like a burial shroud.

Even after a child grows up, mothers will always remember the delicate heartbeat that once tapped inside their body. I will never forget the first time I experienced my daughter's movement inside my womb, often referred to as "quickening." I was working as a legal secretary in a Seattle law firm, and as I stood up to move from my desk to the drinking fountain, I felt a sudden trembling inside, like the fluttering of so many gossamer butterfly wings. I was instantly and unexpectedly overtaken by the most intense feeling of joy I had ever experienced in my life. It were as if liquid sunlight had flooded into my body and was radiating from every single pore. I gasped aloud, and it was all I could do to not burst into tears. The same feeling occurred when I first realized my son was announcing his tiny presence. Bubbles of elation rose up inside of me, from the tips of my toes to my suddenly luminous heart.

When I was pregnant, I realized that I had been completely taken over by an alien presence. I knew that my life would never be my own again, and I rejoiced at the loss of freedom. There is no way to explain this to someone who doesn't have children, and fear of this loss has probably convinced more than a few couples to skip the parenthood plunge altogether. I can understand their reluctance because I shared it for many years. And *plunge* is the perfect word here—becoming a parent is like jumping off a plane with an untested parachute, eyes closed, fingers crossed. I know a few younger couples who have decided not to have children, an idea that would have been shocking only twenty years ago, nearly unheard of fifty years ago, and most likely impossible for any sexually active person before then. But once the parental leap occurs, there is no turning back.

Watching a child pass through the turmoil of adolescence and the buffetings of life with its inevitable heartbreak is daunting. If a child hurts, a parent hurts. When a daughter reaches the age of puberty and starts to deal with menstruation and a rapidly changing body, echoes of one's own turbulent rites of passage into womanhood sound again. When a son reaches the age of puberty and experiences the awkwardness and rapid hormone surges that accompany the transition from boyhood to manhood, his parents ache for him. It is natural for parents to want to protect their child from any harm, including the cruelty of rejection by peers. Children and teens are surrounded by groups of feckless friends and eager enemies, and sometimes the friends and enemies change camps without advance notification. Surviving adolescence and reaching adulthood is a brutal sport, and watching it from the sidelines is excruciating. Of course, parents know none of this when their new, perfectly formed baby arrives, which is probably for the best. If, however, there were somehow a warning tag attached to every baby that arrives on the planet, it would say this:

CAUTION! Parenthood May Result in Serious Injury.

CHAPTER 10

The Word of Wisdom

One of the most well-known Mormon dietary guidelines is referred to as the *Word of Wisdom*. Mormons are raised from childhood learning about these rules, which are classified as revelations received by the church's founder, Joseph Smith, and found in the Doctrine and Covenants, Section 89. Section 89 warns members to avoid the use of tobacco, alcohol, and "hot drinks." Modern-day prophets have explained that the avoidance of hot drinks now refers to coffee and tea, although that was not their original intent. In addition, members are commanded to eat grain, herbs, plants, and meat; in return, they are promised that they shall "find wisdom and great treasures of knowledge" and that they shall "run and not be weary, and shall walk and not faint" (D&C 89: 9, 10-20).

Many of the guidelines are common sense precautions that have stood the test of time when it comes to protecting one's health. Others, however, especially the rules about coffee and tea, have been challenged by modern medical research. There have been numerous studies linking the regular use of coffee to increased mental alertness, improved mood, and a decrease in the chance of developing dementia, Type-2 diabetes, and even heart disease.[87] High doses of caffeine can cause a temporary spike in a person's blood pressure and heart rate, but moderate use seems to be a healthy option. Nonetheless, drinking coffee is considered a serious breach of conduct by devout Mormons; yet those same Mormons guzzle down gallons of Diet Coke, Dr. Pepper, and Pepsi each day without feeling a shred of remorse. There's an old Utah joke that still rings true: the only difference between Mormons and non-Mormons is the temperature of the caffeine they drink.

Although drugs are not specifically mentioned in the Word of Wisdom, modern-day interpretations have expanded the guidelines to include anything that might harm someone's body. When our kids were growing up, we spent years teaching them about the dangers of drugs, alcohol, and tobacco. Almost every week, we had lessons during our family home evenings about how our children could protect their bodies from the contaminants of the world. Even iced tea was included in the list. Our children stared up at us, wide-eyed and trusting, as we reiterated how their bodies were temples and needed to be kept pure.

When our son was about twelve, he returned from spending the night at his cousin's house and shamefacedly confessed that he had mistakenly drunk some iced tea. It was labeled as "chai," and he didn't know that it was a form of tea.

"It's not that big of a deal," I told him. "Just try not to do it again." He nodded solemnly. Within three years, he'd started drinking and smoking pot. By age sixteen, he was using opioid pain pills. By age eighteen, he was smoking heroin and cocaine. After that, he started injecting them both, which I later learned was much more dangerous than smoking it.

Of course, we didn't know any of this at the time. I had seen firsthand the devastation wrought upon the lives of family members, friends, and students because of their drug and alcohol addictions. Nothing scared me more. When my kids reached their mid-teens, I told them, "I don't want you to start having sex anytime soon, but if you have to choose between drugs and sex—choose sex!"

"Oh, Mom!" they laughed, but I was completely serious. I had decided that sexual explorations were a natural outgrowth of adolescent development and that rarely did they end a person's life. But substance addiction? After watching some of the people I loved derail their lives and their relationships with alcoholism, drug use, and jail time, I was terrified about the havoc that addiction could wreak.

The cheery "Just Say No!" anti-drug campaign started by First Lady Nancy Reagan in the 1980s was an attempt to do the right thing, but it failed to address the real issues that led students to experiment with drugs. According to a 2016 article in the *Guardian*, "Much like abstinence-based sex education, Dare and 'Just Say No' spread fear and ignorance instead of information, placing all responsibility on the individual while denying them the tools they need to make key decisions." The end result was that many viewed drug addiction as a "moral rather than societal failure."[88]

Although there have been debates about whether or not drug addiction qualifies as an illness, the most current thinking is that "addiction has a neurobiological basis." Therefore, it should not be seen as a sure sign of an evil or corrupted nature. It strikes without discrimination and crosses all economic, geographic, and racial boundaries unimpeded in its disastrous march. In the 2021 publication of the medical journal *Neuropsychopharmacology,* Heilig et al. argue that viewing addiction merely as a weakness makes it more difficult for "people with substance use problems to access evidence-based treatments."

The authors also ask why post-traumatic stress disorder (PTSD) and depression, which are classified as diseases without any sense of controversy, should be treated differently than drug addiction. Oftentimes, these illnesses overlap, or co-occur, yet drug use alone is stigmatized and is still seen by some as "falling outside the scope of medicine and into that of morality." Heilig et al. write that it is "recognized throughout modern medicine that a host of biological and non-biological factors give rise to disease," and that nothing in this convergence would suggest that drug addiction is *not* a disease. It may very well be that "pre-existing vulnerabilities and persistent drug use lead to a vicious circle of substantive disruptions in the brain that impair and undermine choice capacities for adaptive behavior, but do not annihilate them."

All of this is to say that those with substance-abuse issues are not morally degenerate but are individuals in the throes of a serious, complex, life-threatening illness.[89]

The modern field of epigenetics has shown that there is a complex interaction between environmental, social, and genetic factors that can lead to gene expression being altered. For example, an infection caused by the tuberculosis bacterium could lead to changes in immune cells which result in a weakened immune system.[90] Likewise, a common neurodegenerative disorder such as Parkinson's disease can be triggered in people predisposed to such illnesses by external factors, such as exposure to chemical pollutants.[91] Most believe that drug addiction, like many other diseases, must somehow result from a complex interplay between inherited genomes and external environments.

Now add to this mix the increasingly available sources of opioids that began to flood the United States during the late 1980s and early '90s as opioid pain pills were prescribed for the treatment of "non-cancer related pain" with promises from "pharmaceutical companies and medical societies . . . that the risk of addiction to prescription opioids was very low."[92] For persons with a genetic predisposition to addiction, easy access to opioids could easily have been the switch that started them down a dangerous, often deadly, path.

A church acquaintance of mine from decades ago broke down in sobs as she tearfully confessed that she was addicted to Oxycontin. This woman, who was a married mother of four, was a respected member of the local church and community. After the birth of her fourth child via C-section, her obstetrician had given her a prescription for Oxycontin with multiple refills. Although she followed all of her doctor's instructions, she found that she was unable to cope once the Oxycontin was gone, so she began the dangerous and illegal practice of "doctor shopping," or seeking out many different healthcare providers in order to continue to receive prescriptions. Today, such behavior would be much more difficult to hide because of the interconnectivity of medical records and patients' prescriptions that have come about as a result of the Internet. However, during the early 1990s, it was quite easy for patients to deceive both the doctors and the significant others in their lives. Eventually, her husband found out. He gave her a *priesthood blessing*[93] and commanded her in the name of the Lord to stop using opioids, but to no avail. Then he took her to their local bishop who told her that she just needed to have more faith and pray more fervently to overcome her weakness. I was horrified at her story, and I told her that she was *not* weak or sinful. Instead, I told her she was addicted to opioids through no fault of her own. I begged her to find another doctor, explain what had happened, and take her husband with her so that *he* might learn humility and patience. We were transferred to a new area shortly after this conversation, so I never found out how her story ended.

As for our own son, we learned that he started his experimentation with opioids after his father was prescribed Percocet for recurring kidney stones. Once medical professionals began to understand the conflagration that they had inadvertently fueled, the prescriptions for opioid pain pills decreased substantially. However, those who were used to getting their daily fix from pills soon turned to heroin as a cheaper alternative, as did our son. According to a 2015 Centers for Disease Control and Prevention (CDC) report, heroin use skyrocketed a "staggering 63 percent" during the period from 2002 to 2013. Use also spread to new demographic groups that had previously been more resistant to addiction: notably, people with private insurance, who tend to have more disposable income, started moving to heroin once their prescriptions ran out.[94] According to the most recent CDC data, there was a "30% increase from . . . overdose deaths" between 2019 and 2020. In addition, drug overdoses are now "the *leading cause of injury-related death* in the United States" and have been influenced by the COVID-19 pandemic, among other things [emphasis added]. Deaths caused by "multiple drugs (i.e., polysubstance overdose deaths)" are also rapidly rising, as are deaths from fentanyl.

Understanding the seriousness of a problem doesn't solve it, but it's an important first step. The CDC suggests that a multi-pronged approach is needed, and one of the key components is the need for "private and public insurers . . . [to begin by] addressing gaps in coverage [and] removing barriers to treatment for substance use disorders." The CDC adds that collaboration between "employers, . . . the criminal justice system, . . . and community organizations" can provide the foundation that recovering users need to avoid relapse and recidivism.[95]

A childhood friend of mine suffered the agonizing loss of her teenaged son after he overdosed on heroin. She had spent weeks begging her insurance company for help, only to be told that his condition was not severe enough to warrant inpatient rehab. A few days after he died in his own bed, she called the company, told them her son had passed away, and asked if they still stood by their clinical decision that he didn't qualify for immediate hospitalization and help. The representative on the other end of the line was speechless for a moment, then sputtered out an apology. My friend never received any other acknowledgement from the company that their policies had contributed to his death.

I believe that the Mormon Church's emphasis on avoiding any sort of drug use has been one of its most beneficial teachings. My girlhood friends and I grew up believing that we should not experiment with anything that was outlawed in the rules. That belief gave us a firm foundation for building lives free of harmful, addictive substances.

From our son's first innocent drinking of chai tea to his full-blown addictions to both heroin and cocaine, there was a slow evolution to which Jason and I were completely oblivious. I now believe that it was a confluence of events, some inherited, some inflicted, that led him to risk his life on a daily basis for years. Unbeknownst to us, by embracing Mormonism we had invited a dangerous bedfellow into our home who would soon cast a deadly shadow over the life of our son. For the part that his religious upbringing contributed to his sense of brokenness, I will forever be profoundly sorrowful.

CHAPTER 11

A Question of Worthiness

From an early age, Eric disliked attending sacrament meetings on Sundays. Like many young children, he hated sitting on hardbacked benches and trying not to squirm as adults gave long, boring talks. We tried the standard parental diversion tactics of books, crayons, treats, and toys. When all else failed, we would take him out of the chapel and let him zoom around the carpeted halls for a while to burn off some of his excess energy. We were never alone in chasing our child; many other parents were having the same challenges as we were. Once Eric had gotten some of his wriggles out, we'd carry him back into the chapel and try again.

In 1999, when Leah was eleven and Eric was eight, they and most of their friends were seized by the Pokémon card craze. All of the neighborhood kids were buying and trading cards nonstop. They would gather in big groups outside in the common areas of our military-assigned housing units in Hawaii and try to one-up each other into making a bad trade. Both of our kids saved up their meager allowances to purchase cards whenever they could. Some of the most dramatic moments in our home were when the foil packets containing the cards were carefully opened to reveal either a highly sought-after card or a complete dud. Depending upon the value of the card, cheers or tears ensued (always on Eric's part—Leah was old enough to deal with the inevitable letdowns). One week I noticed Eric sitting much more quietly than usual in sacrament meeting; he was perched on the end of the bench that was closest to the aisle and was staring straight ahead with great focus. No sooner had I congratulated myself on finally helping him to enjoy church more than I thought I saw a quick flash as his hand rotated forward and then back down. I looked a few rows up and saw one of his friends also sitting by the aisle. As I watched, the friend also performed a quick wrist motion back towards Eric. As soon as I saw the easily recognizable Pokémon card design, I realized why Eric had been so willing to attend church that day. He and his friends were trading cards during sacrament meeting. Jason and I gave him a half-hearted reminder to be more reverent, but made no serious attempts to stop the high-stakes trading that continued for several weeks. To this day, we still laugh about how he solved his Sunday boredom dilemma.

After young men turn twelve, they receive the *Aaronic priesthood,* or the lower of the two levels of the priesthood that are held by all "worthy males" in the Mormon Church. As soon as a young man receives the priesthood, he can pass the *sacrament,* a weekly religious ordinance that consists of members partaking of bread and water in remembrance of Christ's sacrifice. After he turns sixteen, he is tasked with blessing the sacrament in front of the entire congregation. A special prayer is read; since members believe the prayer to be revealed, even a single slipup in the prayer means it must be repeated. I have seen numerous young men blushing bright red as a single mispronounced word, skipped word, or even a mumbled word has obligated them to start over and read the prayer again. Oftentimes it would take multiple tries before the young man got it right; by the time he finally did, the entire congregation would exhale in sympathetic relief that the embarrassment had ended.

After Eric reached adolescence, he absolutely despised any attention being focused on him and dreaded the times he had to perform this ritual. From age fifteen onward, he began to more frequently refuse to attend church with us. We cajoled and encouraged him but didn't force the issue. We figured he was going through a teenage phase that would work itself out.

One week when he was supposed to bless the sacrament, he got up and walked out of the chapel shortly before the service began. I followed him into the church lobby and found him staring out the large, glass, entryway doors that have become a hallmark of all Mormon churches built in the United States.

"What's up?" We had always had a good relationship, and I thought that he would feel comfortable talking to me about whatever was bothering him.

"I just can't do it," he said.

"You mean bless the sacrament?"

He nodded. "In fact, I won't do it anymore."

"Ok." I stood there silent for a moment, trying to guess what lay behind this open refusal. "Why don't you want to?"

He stood silent for a few moments. "Because I'm not worthy." He exhaled as if releasing something poisonous from his soul.

"Why do you think that? You know nobody's perfect, right? If only perfect people blessed and passed the sacrament, nobody would be doing it."

"I know." We stood without talking for a while.

"What's wrong?" I asked him. "Is there anything you want to talk to me about?"

He motioned me into one of the small classrooms that lined the hallways of the church and shut the door. After we both sat down, I waited. Finally he asked, "Why do *you* think I'm not worthy?"

I listed off a few possible things I could think of, including drinking alcohol, watching porn, or having sex. He shook his head no to all of them. Not sure what to do at that point, I asked him if he wanted to talk to our bishop about it.

"I guess so." He seemed to slump in his chair.

"Maybe you'll feel better after you do."

I felt reassured after our conversation. I knew our bishop was a decent, levelheaded man. He worked as a police officer in a nearby town, and he and his wife were busy raising their five

THE PRODIGAL MORMON MOTHER

young children. He didn't strike me as the type to overreact to anything a teenager might tell him. I called him later that day and told him that our son needed to meet with him.

In the Mormon Church, a bishop is an ecclesiastical leader equivalent to a parish priest. Such men are chosen from among the congregation and, with no special training, given the responsibility to watch over their flock and provide them with spiritual guidance. Bishops are almost always honored and revered by church members, and the duties they fulfill are heavy and unpaid. All conversations with a bishop are completely confidential, similar to any confessions that a Catholic priest might hear.

A couple of weeks later, the bishop pulled me aside after church. "You don't have anything to worry about," he said, while not revealing any specific details from his conversation with Eric. I felt relieved. "You wouldn't believe some of the things that teens are into these days," he continued. "Trust me —this is *not* that serious."

I wondered what those other, more serious things might be. I was glad our bishop had not taken the shaming route, which is what some ecclesiastical leaders have unfortunately done when members have approached them with questions or problems. I knew that shaming teens for normal developmental behaviors could be dangerous. I had heard horror stories of young men and women becoming suicidal when their bishops told them that *any* sexual explorations outside of marriage were just one step below murder, an openly taught Mormon doctrine for decades: "The doctrine of this Church is that sexual sin—the illicit sexual relations of men and women—stands, in its enormity, next to murder. The Lord has drawn no essential distinctions between fornication, adultery, and harlotry or prostitution. Each has fallen under His solemn and awful condemnation."[96] Every church president has reiterated the extreme seriousness of sexual transgressions in official statements of public doctrine. In 1988, the same year our daughter Leah was born, Brigham Young University president Jeffrey R. Holland gave a devotional speech entitled "Of Souls, Symbols, and Sacraments." He quoted a well-known scripture from the Book of Mormon which defines sexual sins as "most abominable above all sins save it be the shedding of innocent blood or denying the Holy Ghost" (Alma 39:5). Imagine being told as an impressionable teen that your furtive groping toward sexual maturity was just below murder in its seriousness.[97]

I had no idea why Eric's sense of unworthiness continued unabated, and I didn't want to pry. I chalked it up to teenage angst, something both Jason and I were well acquainted with after surviving our own passages through adolescence. But there was a reason that Eric had kept buried deep inside, something that he had been programmed to despise in himself since his first days of church attendance. For the moment, however, in our ignorance, the storm seemed to have passed.

CHAPTER 12

Coming Out

I thought I had prepared myself for every spiritual contingency. I was like the camper who takes a truckload of food, cooking utensils, sleeping bags, mosquito repellant, lanterns, toilet paper, and every conceivable camping necessity and then discovers that she has left the tent poles behind. I had received an excellent education at Brigham Young University; as part of that education, we were required to study the four standard works of the Mormon Church: the Holy Bible, the Book of Mormon, the Doctrine and Covenants, and the Pearl of Great Price. I read them multiple times. I knew the church's historical dilemmas (as far as I could in the pre-Internet 1970s and early '80s). I understood the concept of prophets being enlightened men who were, nonetheless, imperfect. I thought I understood the reasons behind and misconceptions surrounding the church's most controversial decisions, such as practicing polygamy for decades, officially opposing the Equal Rights Amendment in 1976, denying the priesthood to black members until 1978, and refusing to grant women the priesthood. All of these things still bothered me, but I was able to sublimate them for years by deciding that they did *not* apply to me. They were old, misunderstood things from another age and had nothing to do with the modern church and the way I was raising my family.

The one issue I was never able to understand or reconcile was the church's stance on homosexuality. I kept it at arm's length, like a pesky intruder who wouldn't shut up and wouldn't go away. I finally decided that it was another one of those unanswerable questions that would all make sense at some future point. Besides, like all those other religious riddles, it had *nothing* to do with my life.

I distinctly remember brushing my teeth in front of the bathroom mirror one Sunday evening after Eric had again refused to attend church. He also hated attending the church's official Boy Scout activities[98] and refused to participate in any of the church sports programs. In addition, he often skipped his church *seminary* classes.[99] Now that Eric was eighteen, Jason and I had begun to realize that our son would probably not want to serve a two-year Mormon mission. Although we believed that the decision was his to make, we still hoped he might change his mind since most of the young men we knew who had served missions had come home with a new sense of maturity and purpose. As I mulled over the events of the day, I began to compose a catalog of possibilities for Eric's continued religious reluctance. Is he truly a nonbeliever? Does he have a pregnant girlfriend? Is he an alcoholic? (It runs in my family on both sides.) And finally, just for kicks, is he gay?

As for same-sex orientation, I had been taught by my church for decades that it was a lifestyle choice, one acted upon in an attempt to come out in open rebellion against God or to hurt one's parents. Older church sources promised that homosexuality was "curable" as long as the those who suffered from the "malady" practiced appropriate "self mastery."[100] Other sources pointed to inept parenting or the lack of appropriate displays of "masculinity and femininity" to properly socialize the developing child.[101] I knew that Jason and I were not inept parents. We certainly weren't perfect, but our unconditional love for both of our children had always guided our decisions. As for the child purposely trying to inflict pain upon a parent, that, too, was impossible. Despite Eric's sometimes prickly exterior, I knew it was a protective shield that he had created to protect his particularly soft heart. I had never known him to purposely harm any type of living creature, let alone another human being. He definitely wasn't a bully; in fact, most of his anger seemed to be directed at himself whenever he fell short of achieving perfection. Eric just didn't fit the stereotypical definition of a gay person based upon the church teachings that both Jason and I had grown up with. I was glad to cross this possibility off my list: it was the one contingency I had not planned for, the one question I could not answer. As I drifted off to sleep that night, I resolved to speak to Eric openly in the weeks ahead and ask him if there were any chance that he might change his mind about serving a mission.

September 23, 2009, will forever be burned into my brain as the day my brave, new world arrived, bearing a shocking message in its outstretched hands. At first I didn't understand the full magnitude of the event; but as time has passed, I now see that it was the beginning of the end for me: the end of a lifelong belief system and the end of religious certainty. It was the day my eighteen-year-old son approached me and quietly said he needed to talk about something important.

I had decided earlier that day that I needed to stay home that night and skip a stake meeting scheduled for all relief society presidencies. I was two years in to my three-year church calling as the ward relief society president, the highest-ranking job for a woman in our local Mormon congregation. My counselors and I coordinated compassionate service needs for all the families who lived in our geographical area. We helped arrange meals for women with new babies, provide child care for ill mothers, cook and serve vast amounts of food at Mormon funerals, teach weekly Sunday lessons to the women in our ward, visit all of the *sisters* (a title of respect for adult women) in our boundaries even if they didn't currently attend church, prepare quarterly homemaking and craft workshops, and do anything else that was needed. But I just couldn't drag myself to another meeting when the thing I really wanted to do was stay home and talk to my son.

As Eric and I sat on the wicker bench on our large,

wraparound deck that evening, he started a conversation.

"Mom, I need to talk to you about something important."

"OK." I was nervous with the anticipation that something big was about to be revealed, but I had no idea what it might be. A gentle autumn breeze blew as we stared out at the leaves that had started to change colors.

"You might have noticed that I *really* hate going to church." His lips turned up into an apologetic smile.

"You're right—I have noticed that."

"And you're probably wondering why." He stared at me expectantly.

"I have to admit that I'm guessing you don't want to serve a mission." For young male members of the church, serving a mission is a cultural imperative and a religious duty.

"You're right."

We sat in silence for a few moments. "Do you want to tell me anything else?" He nodded his head but said nothing.

"What is it?" I finally asked.

"You take some guesses, and I'll tell you if you're close or not."

"So, you'll just answer yes or no?"

He nodded again in the affirmative.

"OK." I blew out a breath to calm myself. I started listing the things that I had wondered a few weeks ago when I was brushing my teeth.

"You got somebody pregnant." He smiled and shook his head to signify no.

"You've been smoking pot."

Another shake of the head. (He was lying about this, but I didn't know it yet.)

"You're drinking alcohol."

"No." (Another lie.)

"You've been shoplifting things from stores."

"No."

"You are a secret member of the Sicilian mafia and have been assassinating people for years," I added to lighten the mood. We both laughed.

"You think the Mormon Church is a complete farce, and you don't believe a word of what they say."

"Well, sort of," he admitted. "But that's not it."

"OK." I paused. "Well, there's only one thing left that I can think of, but I already know that it doesn't apply to you."

"Well, what do you think it *might* be?"

"You're gay," I said jokingly, positive that he would again shake his head to indicate no. But in the second before he answered, I saw something change in his expression. "You're *not* gay—are you?"

He turned to face me directly. "Mom, I'm gay."

I was completely stunned. I felt dizzy, almost as if I were going to faint. That single sentence instantly obliterated my reference point, and it was a physical reaction. I had always loved my daughter and son with an instinctive maternal ferocity. Never for a moment had it ever crossed my mind to reject either one of them for any reason. I distinctly remember the first words out of my mouth: "I love you completely and always will. Yet I also think the Mormon Church is God's true church."

As I look back on this moment now, with years of hindsight, I find it interesting that I so quickly articulated the unresolvable tension that would eventually send me into a psychological tailspin. This was cognitive dissonance raised to a new and terrifying level. I loved my son—I would take a bullet for him—yet the church that Jason and I had raised him in had always told us that he would be condemned to hell if he embraced a homosexual lifestyle. Spiritual and mental anguish engulfed me as I tried to make sense of this contradiction.

I now believe that at least part of the reason our son was susceptible to drug abuse was to numb himself to the unbearable pain of being a closeted gay Mormon. The weekly church lessons for teens, with their emphasis on the evils of masturbation and porn would have been disturbing enough to a straight kid. For a gay kid, the agony would have been exponentially increased. The straight kid knew he could eventually repent, get married, and have a church-approved relationship. The gay kid had no such promise—he was irreparably broken and needed to be fixed. There was no golden relationship waiting for him at the end of the rainbow—there was only despair and self-loathing.

I asked him when he had first realized that he was gay. He told me that it was a gradual thing, but that it had started very early.

"Did you know when you were fifteen?" I asked.

"Earlier."

"Twelve?"

"Before that."

"Ten?"

He sat silently for a moment. "Ever since I was about seven or eight, I noticed that something was different with me. All of the other boys were always talking about their crushes on girls, but I was much more fascinated with the boys themselves. For a long time, I had no idea what that meant."

I thought about the countless church lessons about the "unnatural" evils of homosexuality and what they must have done to his developing psyche. I felt sick to my stomach at what he had been unknowingly subjected to by his well-intentioned parents.

"Do you want to tell Dad?" I asked.

"You tell him whenever you want to."

I gave him a hug. "I love you."

"I know, Mom."

As we walked into the house together, I decided to wait a few weeks so that I could process the information before telling my husband. I'll wait until after the holidays, I thought. That way I won't spoil Jason's Thanksgiving or Christmas.

That night, however, after Jason and I went to bed, I lay awake tossing and turning into the wee morning hours. There was no way I could put off discussing this for a few weeks, let alone a few days. Finally at about two o'clock in the morning, I started tapping on his chest and woke him up from a deep sleep. "I have to tell you something important."

"Huh?" He was groggy and only half aware of his surroundings.

"I have to tell you something important," I said again, this time starting to sob.

"What's going on?" He sounded alarmed now.

"Give me a minute." I lay with my head resting on his shoulder, and he hugged me while I cried for over an hour. Each time I tried to talk, I couldn't bring myself to actually say the words.

"What's happening?" he asked again. "Please tell me."

Finally, I managed to say it aloud: "Eric told me tonight —" I paused and took in a gulp of air— "that he's gay."

"What?"

"Eric is gay."

"No, he's not," Jason said, fully awake now.

"Well, *he* thinks he is."

"He can't be gay. He's probably just confused. Remember when you told me he hinted on Facebook that he was looking for a girlfriend a few weeks ago? How could he be gay if he was doing *that*?"

"You're right!" I breathed out. I latched onto his statement like a swimmer clinging to a life jacket in a choppy ocean. "He's confused and going through a rebellious stage." My heartbeat began to slow. "He *did* say he was looking for a girlfriend—maybe his hormones are surging, and he's somehow got his wires crossed."

"I'll bet that's it," Jason said. "You know how crazy teenage boys can get."

"You sound like you're speaking from experience."

"Haha. Not funny."

As many ways as we twisted the object in front of us, the only way it made sense was if our son was confused. Although we considered ourselves open-minded, we had no other road map with which to navigate the rapidly changing landscape in front of us. I had known only one bisexual individual growing up, a very close male friend in high school. Although I loved him unconditionally, I had always wondered if his main goal in announcing his sexuality had been to inflict pain on his parents, for whatever reason. My husband had suspected that one of his BYU roommates decades ago might have been gay, but despite being good friends for years, they had never broached the topic. So with almost no personal experience, and with loads of preconditioning supplied by our church, we decided there was only one way this thing could play out: the next morning when we talked to Eric, we had to somehow convince him that *he wasn't really gay.*

CHAPTER 13

Delusional

The next morning, Jason and I were waiting for Eric in the kitchen. We had rehearsed what we were going to say because we did not want to be harsh or confrontational. But we knew we must convince him that any thoughts of experimenting with his same-sex impulses would lead him far astray of where God wanted him to be.

When Eric walked into the kitchen, he looked a bit surprised to see us both standing there. He was instantly on guard.

"Good morning, honey," I said in an artificially cheery voice. "Did you sleep well?"

"Umm, sort of." He remained standing and didn't sit down to eat the simple breakfast of toast, fruit, and juice that I had set out.

"Well, we need to talk to you about something." Jason cleared his throat. "Mom talked to me last night and told me what you said."

Eric dropped his gaze to the floor. "Okay."

"And we need to make sure that you know that we totally love you no matter what," I added quickly.

"Okay."

"But—we want you to know that what you're experiencing is probably an outgrowth of trying to figure out who you are and what you want in your life," Jason explained. "Everybody has to explore their identity when they're young, and this is probably an exploration phase for you. I had to figure out lots of things, too. We're not saying that you're a bad person or that we don't believe you, but we want you to really think about this."

Our son said nothing.

"Being a teenager is hard," I admitted. "I wouldn't want to redo those years for any reason because of how much I've learned since then. I remember lying awake at night trying to figure out how everything in my life would eventually play out —"

Eric interrupted me, his face reddening. "I thought you understood me last night, Mom. But it seems like you *didn't even listen.*"

"I *did* listen!" I moved closer to touch his arm. "And I understand why this is so difficult for you. I'm glad you trusted me enough to tell me what you were thinking, but a life decision as big as this shouldn't be made too quickly. Can you just give it some more time? You can discuss this with us anytime you want to, but we hope you'll also be willing to listen to our opinions and maybe go talk to a counselor. We're all trying to figure this out, you know."

"When you say I should listen to your 'opinions,' I'm guessing you don't believe that I know what I'm talking about, that I must be wrong about my sexual orientation." Eric's chest started to rise and fall as his breathing grew more labored.

"As time passes," Jason said, "we think you'll come to see this as a slightly confused, but genuine curiosity in figuring out who you really are. You know, the media rants about 'lifestyle choices' all the time now, and I can see that it would be hard to be growing up surrounded by that."

Our son pulled away from me. "I get this," he said, his voice rising. "I get what this is. I had a feeling you'd react like this. You don't know anything about who I am and what I want! I won't stay in this house if you won't even listen to what I have to say!"

"But we are listening—"

"Really?" Eric's face contracted into a scowl. "Dad, what if I told *you* when you were eighteen that your attraction to girls wasn't real? What if I told *you* that you were passing through a confusing teenage phase and that you would eventually see the light and become attracted to men? Huh? How would you like that?"

"I wouldn't like it," Jason admitted. "But that's because —"

"Why?" Eric asked. "Because you were attracted to the 'proper' sex, the one the Mormon Church *told* you that you were supposed to be attracted to? This isn't any different than when you realized you liked girls; the only difference is that I've realized that I like boys, and since we're Mormon you've got to find a way to convince me that I'm wrong. Well, I'm not wrong, and I'm *certain* about that. I'm not going to stay for one more minute and listen to anything else you have to say!" He stomped upstairs, grabbed a sleeping bag and a few clothing items, and then came back down and threw open the front door. "I don't live here anymore."

My heart dropped, and I felt like I might throw up. Jason looked at me with his eyebrows raised in a questioning glance as if to suggest that I might have a ready-made answer.

"You *do* live here," I said. "Please stay and talk to us." Tears had started to pool in my eyes. "Don't go, Eric. Please!"

"It's too late," he said in a clipped voice. "I'm not sure when you'll see me again."

As he walked out to the front porch, I followed him, trying to calm myself. I was coming undone, and I knew it. I valued our family's cohesiveness above all else, so public displays of embarrassing or negative family emotions had long been anathema to me. Yet I stood on our front porch crying out loud enough so that any curious neighbors would have been able to overhear me: "Don't leave! Don't leave, Eric! Please! Please!"

But it was too late. He bolted down the final few steps, threw his belongings into his car, and pulled out abruptly, sending up a shower of gravel from the rear tires.

My husband and I stood mute, gaping after him. I

was reminded of the trolls in Tolkien's *The Hobbit*, who had foolishly argued their way into permanent, stony silence when the dawn arrived unexpectedly and transformed them into statues. I prayed we hadn't just done the same thing with our son. We had to be able to talk to him again if we ever expected to make sense of any of this.

"Well, that didn't go as planned," Jason muttered. "I wonder when we'll see him again."

I couldn't speak at all due to the lump in my throat, and I struggled to catch my breath. Our son was gone, and we had no idea where he was going. I wondered what we could have done differently; I felt like a failure, not only as a mother, but also as a Mormon.

The next two days crawled by with no word from Eric. Then he sent a text message telling us that he was OK and would be home in a day or two. We still had no idea where he was, but we were so relieved when he finally returned that we decided not to raise the topic again in front of him unless he brought it up himself. We settled into an uneasy truce where we tiptoed around each other's feelings and blatantly ignored the elephant in the room.

During Eric's four-day absence, Jason told me that it would kill him to see Eric dating men.

"Well, you're going to *have* to see that," I said. "There's no way to avoid it."

"Actually, there is—" Something in his tone of voice scared me. "I could move out into an apartment."

My heart plummeted as I wondered if our marriage was about to implode. I stared at him with an expression midway between astonishment and rage. "If you think you're going to hide and let me deal with this on my own, you need to think again!" I knew that Jason's threat was an attempt to avoid seeing his son get hurt, but I also knew that he was going to have to accept our family's rapidly changing reality somehow.

As I waited for his reply, I suddenly realized that if Jason really did distance himself from our only son, then our marriage would end. I knew that I would choose my son's need for unconditional love over my husband's need for psychological comfort. This insight was deeply disturbing. Jason and I had never even talked about divorce because it simply wasn't an option. We had made a lifelong, eternal commitment to each other, and we both took that promise very seriously. I didn't say anything aloud at that point, but something shifted deep inside of me. I felt a seismic rumbling spring to life in the center of my chest and radiate outward until I trembled.

Thankfully, after a late-night, emergency conversation with our bishop that I initiated against Jason's wishes, he quickly realized that moving out would be a colossal blunder on his part. I later learned that the root of his dismay was that he had been programmed by the Mormon Church to believe that homosexuality was a *choice*. He couldn't understand why somebody would *choose* to take this path, one that would possibly bring pain to himself and others. In addition, both of us had been raised on a steady diet of extremely negative media portrayals of the "gay lifestyle" during the first forty years of our lives. Researchers who have focused on the media representation of LGBT individuals during that time period (the 1960s through the end of the 1990s) found that gay characters were stereotypically portrayed as "flaming queers, . . . villainous criminals, mental patients, child molesters, and vampires."[102] And the negative portrayals continued for at least another ten to fifteen years. A lifelong friend of mine who is a devout Mormon publicly confronted me in 2021 and asked how I could support my gay son's "choices" since homosexuality and pedophilia were inextricably linked in her mind. Although my experiences as an English teacher had taught me to be exceptionally tolerant of others' viewpoints, this display of gross ignorance hit my heart like a poisoned arrow, and our exchange became heated, to say the least.

It is important to note here that the word *homosexuality*

itself is outdated and has been considered offensive by the LGBT community for at least twenty years. While it's the word those of us now in our fifties, sixties, and seventies grew up using, it carries a "ring of disapproval and judgment" that is hard to ignore. The "H Word" has often been used to portray gays and lesbians as "deviant" in some essential way, most likely due to the classification of same-sex orientation as a subset of the "sociopathic personality disturbance" category in the first edition of the American Psychiatric Association's *Diagnostic and Statistical Manual: Mental Disorders-1* (DSM-1).[103] Although the DSM removed "homosexuality" as a form of "sexual deviation" in 1973, for many the linkage still persists. When the word is broken into its constituent parts, *homo* and *sexual*, more problems surface. *Homo* is an old derogatory term, and *sexual* suggests that same-sex orientation is all about sex, diminishing everything else that goes into creating and sustaining a bona fide relationship. Although the Associated Press (AP) stylebook now calls for restricted use of the "H Word,"[104] I have nonetheless used it throughout this book whenever quoting sources or when referring to historical usages of the word that occurred before, during, and after my youth.

While Jason and I were growing up during the 1960s, gay bars were illegal across the United States, but they stayed open in New York City because of the involvement of organized crime. The Mafia owned or ran most of the gay bars in the city and viewed them as a "gold mine"; bribery payments to the local police benefited everyone connected to the enterprise.[105] Jason and I had heard stories about frequent and violent police raids on gay bars; the stereotypes of promiscuous sex, group orgies, and bathroom stall encounters with strangers had been woven into our worldview of how such groups behaved. Although things like this did happen, it never occurred to us that they did *not* represent the norm and that most gay couples just wanted to be left alone and allowed to pursue romantic relationships in the same ways that straight couples did.

As embarrassing as it is to admit this fifteen years after the fact, in the beginning we wholeheartedly believed that our son was simply confused. But try as we might, Jason and I could not find a solution. We were spending hours every day for months on end discussing the issue whenever Eric wasn't around. We talked about it as we cooked, ate, and ran errands. We talked about it from the minute we woke up until the minute we went to bed. We cried more than we had in years. Even my husband, who has never been comfortable with public displays of emotion, wept as I had never seen him do before. We cried in the car as we drove to and from work each day and in our bedroom at night. We cried when we decorated our Christmas tree that year, reminiscing over each of our children's little childhood ornaments as we placed them on the tree. In the photo that Jason snapped of me standing near the tree, my eyes were red-rimmed and noticeably swollen as I tried to fake a smile. We cried whenever our son's name came up, which was a daily occurrence. I kept waiting for the spigot to run dry, but somehow the tears just kept coming from a bottomless well of sadness.

We soon realized that we needed an outsider's perspective to help us navigate the deep waters we found ourselves floundering in. We found a Mormon therapist who suggested that we read Elders[106] Dallin H. Oaks's and Lance B. Wickman's counsel to parents of gay children. These two senior-level church leaders sat down for an extended interview with the church's public affairs office in 2006. As I read through the article carefully, underlining and highlighting the things that I found relevant, a deep sense of unease crept over me. Although the article was carefully phrased and crafted, at the bottom it seemed like a call for parents to reject not only the sin, but the sinner as well.

Oaks began by clarifying that the "homosexual lifestyle" is "not normal." He continued that although the church "reach[es] out with understanding and respect for individuals who are attracted to those of the same gender," there are firm limits to what that understanding will look like. To parents, specifically, he suggested the following dialogue with a gay child: "Yes, come, but don't expect to stay overnight. Don't expect to be a lengthy house guest. Don't expect us to take you out and introduce you to our friends, or to deal with you in a public situation that would imply our approval of your 'partnership.'"

I tried to translate his advice: We love you, but don't spend too much time here. We love you, but we won't introduce you to anybody we know. We love you, but don't expect to be seen in public with us. I could never imagine myself saying this to my son. It struck me as rejection disguised as righteousness. If we truly loved our children (or so the argument went), we would reject them to help them come to their senses, forsake their sins, and return to the Mormon fold. Then they could look forward to a lifetime of solitude and, if they were righteous, receive the gift of being transformed in the hereafter into heterosexual individuals. Needless to say, this kind of eternal reward doesn't hold much attraction for gay Mormons.

In the same interview, Elder Wickman warned parents to "avoid a potential trap arising out of one's anguish over this situation." He's talking about me! I realized with a sick feeling. He added that we might "continue to open our homes and our hearts and our arms to our children, but that need not be with approval of their lifestyle." I tried to figure out what that would look like in real life. Could our son come to our home with his partner? Should we *not* be seen in restaurants with them? What might "condoning" the behavior look like? Could I hug my son? Hug his partner? Take them on family vacations? Or should we leave them home alone to teach them a lesson in proper sexual behavior while the rest of us went out and traveled without them?

The more I thought about it, the more ridiculous it became. I was reminded of the Biblical Pharisees who took the commandment to keep the Sabbath day holy to impractical extremes: there were "39 forbidden labors on the Sabbath, which included making two loops, weaving two threads, tying or untying [a knot], sewing two stitches, writing two letters, [and] extinguishing or lighting a flame." In addition, they needed to count the number of steps they took on the Sabbath to avoid offending God.[107] I couldn't see how to separate my love for my son from the practical realities of living with him without driving myself crazy over the minutiae of eternal do's and don'ts. Wickman ended with this warning: "There is no such thing in the Lord's eyes as something called same-gender marriage. Homosexual behavior is and will always remain before the Lord an abominable sin." So I could love my son, but only as long as I considered his behavior an abomination? And how in the world does that help me? I wondered.

When Oaks was asked if the church's insistence on marriage between a man and a woman was hypocritical given the church's polygamist past, he made a very telling remark: "In short, if you start with the assumption of continuing revelation, on which this Church is founded, then you can understand that there is no irony in this. *But if you don't start with that assumption, you see a profound irony* [emphasis added]."[108] This seemed like a sleight-of-hand trick: if Joseph Smith was a prophet and God still speaks to the church today, then whatever the leaders proclaim is divinely sanctioned. But if Smith wasn't a prophet, and God doesn't speak to the church today, then whatever the leaders proclaim is open to criticism. This frank admission from an apostle struck me with the force of a lightning bolt. Rather than answering my questions, this article had only raised more.

There was a disturbing dichotomy to the church's stance: on the one hand, the leaders kept assuring gay members that God loved them. On the other hand, they kept reminding them that their lifestyle was deviant and offensive to God. Was there a happy medium somewhere? Were there any answers that might lay out a blueprint for parents to follow other than shunning their children? I realized that continued ignorance on my part about such crucial matters was completely inexcusable, so I committed myself to plunge into some serious research about what the Mormon Church calls "same-gender attraction." To be cautious, I decided to start with church-approved sources only, never imagining that this journey would eventually lead me further afield than I had ever been before.

CHAPTER 14

Indoctrination 101, or
into the "God Box"

The people who raised us to be Mormon—our parents, relatives, and communities—had only the purest of motives when they lovingly enfolded us into the same religious system in which they had grown up. We all were taught that the spiritual community we had embraced was the *only one* that had God's full approval; therefore, raising a beloved child inside this religious structure was an act of love. Unfortunately, once someone is placed inside a culturally built, parentally approved, and divinely sanctioned structure, it is difficult, if not impossible, to extricate oneself from it. Hence a dilemma arises when children of any age attempt to escape the confines of their religious inheritance. Such attempts are viewed as rebellious, disloyal, heretical, selfish, and deluded. Those who leave behind their family's lifelong set of beliefs are not only betraying the sacred covenants they have made, but also rejecting the compass that their ancestors used to organize every facet of their lives. At least, such is the case in Mormonism.

I propose the shorthand term of the "god box" to explain the symbolic edifices that each religious community has created. All religions have specific rituals associated with induction into the god box, such as sacred rites or symbolic passages and requirements. In Mormonism, indoctrination into the god box begins early. Children are named and blessed shortly after birth and make baptismal covenants at age eight. Children are taught that from the moment they are baptized and blessed to receive the Holy Ghost, they are accountable for any sins that they might commit. This is a heavy burden to place on a slender pair of eight-year-old shoulders, especially for those children who are naturally inclined to obey and to please authority figures.

One Sunday afternoon, our five-year-old daughter came home from church crying. She was not the type of child to be overly emotional, so I pressed her to find out why. Finally, tearfully, she blurted out: "I am going to hell!"

"What?" I was shocked. Where could she have gotten this idea? She was a kind, inherently good-natured child. "You are *not* going to hell! We really don't know exactly what happens after we die, but trust me when I say that little kids will not be going to hell."

"Yes, I am," she repeated.

As we sat on the couch and I put my arms around her, she tearfully confessed that the last time we had gone to the gas station, she had grabbed a pack of candy from the display and put it into her coat pocket. I had to suppress a smile at her genuine innocence about what it took to be thrust down into the fires of hell, but I understood that for her, the fear was real.

"When you took it, did you think you were doing something bad?"

She thought for a moment, wiping her eyes. "I just wanted it. And I didn't think you would get it for me."

"Well, that seems like a normal thing for a kid to think. I stole some candy, too, from a small gas station near my house when I was about your age."

"You did?" She gazed up at me intently.

"Yes. And I was on my way home from Primary, which made it even worse!" She smiled a bit at this. "I'm pretty sure the owner saw me, and he was also the bishop in our ward, but he didn't say anything to me right then."

"Did you do it again?"

"No. I was embarrassed thinking that he might have told my parents."

"Well, my teacher told us today that stealing was a sin."

It wasn't until her primary teacher had explained the evils of stealing that our daughter had connected the idea of taking the candy and the idea of sin. When I explained to her that God would *not* consider this a sin, especially since she was so young, she was somewhat placated, but not entirely. She continued to worry about her "sin" for several more months, and this was three years *before* she would officially be held accountable in the church's eyes after her baptism.

In Mormonism, indoctrination into the god box is undertaken in utter seriousness. Families believe that those who do not wholly comply with the doctrines and their associated behavioral requirements will be punished unless they repent. The belief in eternal families comprising generations connected by holy temple ordinances is central to Mormonism, and many families have been comforted by this idea, such as when a young child or beloved parent passes away. Members believe that they will be linked in an afterlife where the bonds of familial love will be regenerated anew.

For others, however, such beliefs can cause despair. Some believe that any member of their family who diverges from the prescribed path will be cast out of the heavenly family reunion. What is a parent to do if a headstrong teen leaves the confines of the church? What is an older parent to do if an adult child decides to leave the fold? What is a parent to do if a child decides to marry outside the sacred Mormon temples, which members believe are the only places on earth where families can be eternally linked? And what, heaven forbid, is a parent to do if a child happens to be gay? In such cases, the idea of the broken family chain becomes a torment, a symbol of failure and of lost connections that will linger beyond the grave. This business of linking families is deadly serious, and those who attempt to leave their assigned god box will quickly discover how high the walls are and how bleak the outside world appears.

My husband's generation and mine were among the

last to be so fully enclosed in the Mormon god box. The information that I can now access in seconds on the Internet was completely unavailable during the decades in which Jason and I came of age, the 1960s through the early 1990s. Instead, the local libraries with their outdated books were our "Internet," and because I grew up in Utah, few of them would have contained anything that spoke negatively about the Mormon Church. The term *anti-Mormon* was commonly applied to any book, person, or belief that took a critical view of the church: the anti-Mormon label was damning, and members in good standing who feared God and prayed for their eternal salvation avoided those things at all costs. I know that I did.

Now that our son had come out, however, the old religious fractures that I had papered over decades ago began to reappear, and I wondered if the world was really as neatly organized as I had been led to believe. Mormons (and many other religious groups) tend to divide the world into two polarized factions: good versus evil. The two camps are separated by an impenetrable wall that reaches to the foot of God's throne, and there is no safe ground between the two. In addition, Mormons claim to know exactly which thoughts and actions will place a person on the wrong side of the wall. In Revelations 3:16, those with lukewarm faith are likened to lukewarm water, fit only to be spit out of the Lord's mouth. With our family's new reality came a new sense of urgency. I could no longer ignore all of my old questions about the faith tradition I had been born into: I absolutely *had to know* whether or not the Mormon Church really was what it had always claimed to be—the truest expression of God's voice on the earth.

I started my exploration of Mormonism's take on same-sex attraction by returning to a classic reference book that I had grown up with: *Mormon Doctrine*, first published in 1958 by high-ranking church leader Bruce R. McConkie. Most Mormon families kept his book in their homes right next to their four official *Standard Works*, or the four sacred volumes of scripture that the church endorses: the Holy Bible, the Book of Mormon, the Doctrine and Covenants, and the Pearl of Great Price. In fact, I still have a copy of McConkie's book that I purchased in 1979 sitting on one of the bookshelves in my living room. Although his opinions have fallen out of favor over the last two decades for being too harsh, for years they were considered to be on par with the prophet's words: they were preached from pulpits and included in numerous religious manuals for teenagers and adults. From 1958 until the early 2000s, McConkie's words and opinions reigned supreme. BYU students and returned missionaries used to jokingly refer to his treatise as *"McConkie* Doctrine" by "Bruce R. *McMormon.*" And they weren't too far off. However much the church might like to distance itself from his now embarrassing rhetoric (which it stopped printing in 2010 due to "low sales"),[109] it provided the ruler with which hundreds of thousands of young Mormons took their stature, most often to find that they were lacking.[110]

Nowhere is McConkie more forceful than when he is discussing one of the most "abominable" types of sin, or "sex immorality." In the 1966 edition, he lists homosexuality as one of the "whoredoms," like prostitution, adultery, and rape: "All these things, as well as many others, are condemned by divine edict and are among Lucifer's chief means of leading souls to hell." Those of us groping towards adulthood in Mormonism during those years knew exactly what the church's stance was on such matters. Although many younger or even middle-aged members today might have no recollection of McConkie's hardline stance on such "perversion[s]," it was an essential part of the church's teachings at the time.[111]

Mormonism is a religion of contrasts: it produces some of the kindest and most compassionate people in the world, along with some of the most judgmental. It produces teenagers of integrity and courage, along with teenagers who lie to hide their true lives from their parents. It produces members who believe that their church is the only true church on the planet, along with others who simply ignore the parts of church doctrine that don't sit well with them. It produces young missionaries who give up one to two years of their free time to preach the gospel and serve others around the world. And in Utah, it also produces serious depression among some of its most vulnerable members, contributing to one of the consistently highest suicide rates in the country.[112]

I have heard multiple theories about the causes behind the state's suicide epidemic. It has been linked to opioid addiction, social media influences, a high-demand religious environment, and even the altitude. (Utah's mean elevation is 6,100 feet above sea level, with its highest point reaching 13,534 feet.)[113] Yet at each of the suicide prevention trainings I attended during my twenty years of teaching at public schools in Utah, people with good motives have pointed to every possibility except the one that is so obvious that it is the two-ton elephant in the room: the Mormon Church's teachings are dangerously toxic for its gay members.

Imagine the plight of someone who has been programmed from birth to follow the counsel of church leaders. Both women and men have been taught to do so since the church's founding; in fact, to do otherwise would lead to a charge of apostasy and possibly expulsion. To complicate matters, throw in the monkey wrench of having a gay child. Mormon parents have already been conditioned to know how to deal with this issue: it's a temptation and a sin. They know that they are supposed to love the sinner but hate the sin. But this artificial dichotomy glosses over the fact that separating out such things with one's child is nearly impossible. Sometimes, parents decide the best way to solve the problem is to expel the errant child from their home; other times, they limit contact, especially if younger siblings who might be influenced by their gay brother or sister are still living at home.

No wonder gay members sometimes choose death: until quite recently, they have seen no chance of acceptance, either in heaven or on earth. National data shows that LGBT people experience an increased risk, not because of their sexual orientation per se, but because of "lower levels of acceptance and belonging in the broader community." This lack of acceptance can exacerbate mental illness and substance abuse problems, which further increases their risk. While suicide is admittedly a complex issue that affects all age groups and nationalities, in Utah "harmful gender norms" are also considered a risk factor.[114] According to the statewide 2019 Utah Student Health and Risk Prevention (SHARP) Survey, gay, lesbian, and bisexual students were over three times more likely to consider suicide than were their heterosexual peers. Indeed, a lack of "safe environments" for gay youth in their "religious and civic institutions" has created a dangerous mix for some of our most at-risk populations.

Another study published in 2020 by several universities across the country found that lifetime suicide attempts were 39.5% for sexual-minority youth compared to 10.6% for straight youth. In addition, suicide ideation, or thinking about committing suicide, is much higher for sexual-minority youth than it is for heterosexual youth, with a lifetime risk of 61.5% versus 21.2%, respectively.[115] While there are two types of suicide ideation—active (having a suicide plan) and passive (desiring to be dead but having no specific plan)—both are considered serious warning signs about a person's mental health.[116] Statistics aside, even a single death from suicide is one too many; the ripples of pain that spread out after a suicide are far-reaching, long-lasting, and often severely incapacitating for those left behind.

I watched two colleagues deal with the deaths by suicide of two of their children. One woman lost a son; the other lost a daughter. To say that they grieved is an understatement: instead, they became different people leading altered lives and presenting unrecognizable faces to the world. One woman carried such a deep burden of sorrow that I almost didn't recognize her when I saw her again a few years later. When

I asked her how she was doing, she sighed. "I get up in the morning. For a few seconds, I don't remember. Then I do. I shower, force myself to eat, and go to work just to have something to do other than watch the minutes tick by. I ask my daughter 'Why?' every second of every hour. That's all." After a few more awkward attempts at conversation on my part, I hugged her and promised to call. I never did.

Anything that increases a person's thoughts of suicide is unequivocally wrong. Yet the church has told gay members for decades that they are deceived, sinful, weak, evil, broken, unforgivable, and cursed. They have told them that they will never be able to have a marriage ordained of God, never be able to marry in any Mormon temple, and will only have a *possibility* of being accepted after death when their defective sexual orientation is sloughed off like a snake's skin. The old mantra of "pray the gay away" has led to the suicides of hundreds, and most likely thousands, of gay youths from numerous religious communities across the country. Furthermore, the Mormon Church still advises its gay members that their sexual orientation is just another temptation in the flesh that they can overcome if they have enough faith. This kind of advice has led some gay members to read scriptures for hours each day and to kneel in prayers so long and desperate that they have lost feeling in their legs and even bruised their kneecaps.

Dr. John Dehlin, a psychologist who lives in Utah and produces the popular Mormon Stories Podcast, has explained that religiosity is a type of religious OCD that has run amok among certain Mormons. Determined to prove their faith and overcome their perceived sins, they devote endless hours to praying, serving, reading scriptures, repenting, journal writing, attending church meetings, and so on until they have lost all sense of the normal rhythms of their lives, and instead are chained to increasingly frantic attempts to overcome the natural man. "For the natural man is an enemy to God," Mormon scriptures preach (Mosiah 3:19). If a straight man is offensive to God, imagine how despicable a *gay* man must be in God's sight. Ostracized by their religious and social communities, gay members sometimes choose to end their lives rather than live on hoping for positive change.

I'm not sure it's possible for young adults raised in this digital era to understand how completely we were marooned on our isolated, information-restricted islands. There were no other options, there were no other trusted sources, there were no other words than the ones that had been correlated in church headquarters and published in church manuals and taught to children and adults for decades in church buildings. Our children had trustingly followed our example when we placed them into the god box of our Mormon pioneer ancestors. It wasn't until our son took a sledgehammer to the walls that we realized we needed to find an exit.

CHAPTER 15

Cognitive Dissonance

Jason and I desperately wanted to help our son, and we needed a more updated resource than an old book that had fallen out of favor. The possibility of our son losing his life to suicide because he felt like "an enemy to God" terrified us. We decided to go talk to our Mormon therapist again, even though the interview with Dallin H. Oaks and Lance B. Wickman that he had given us had opened up more questions than answers. We still held on to the hope that he might be able to offer an alternative perspective.

Our therapist was a kind, nonjudgmental man who showed neither disgust nor shock at anything we said. He was supportive and gave us an essential sounding board at one of the most critical times in our lives. As we tried to explain the enormous impact of our son's announcement, I resorted to an analogy between our family's changing reality and the events that had occurred in the United States on September 11, 2001.

During the early morning hours of September 11, the Twin Towers in New York City's World Trade Center were destroyed by radical Islamic terrorists. At the time, our family was stationed in Pearl Harbor, Hawaii, for our final tour of duty, and we were living in a small military housing area located in Ewa Beach, Oahu. I had come out to sleep on the couch in the middle of the night as I sometimes did when Jason's snoring kept me awake. I had finally settled into a deep slumber when suddenly I was awakened by the TV being turned on with its volume up high and my husband standing over me saying something. I was confused. Why was he waking me up? Didn't he know how tired I was? Then his words finally penetrated my foggy brain.

"The Twin Towers have been hit by planes! They think it's terrorists!"

"What are you—" I tried to force the haze from my mind and focus on the surreal image before me: two skyscrapers with sinuous, black plumes of smoke snaking up into a flat blue sky. In the background, frantic-sounding TV announcers were breathlessly trying to keep up. I glanced at the clock in our front room and saw that it was about four o'clock in the morning local time.

"I'm telling you—the U.S. has been attacked by terrorists!" Jason explained that he had just received a phone call from one of our church friends who worked as an air traffic controller at the Honolulu International Airport. This friend told Jason that all flights had been grounded nationwide, an exceptionally rare move that highlighted the seriousness of the situation.

A rush of adrenaline hit me, and I sat up ramrod straight on the couch. This was not possible, and yet it had happened. Something that *could not be true* somehow *was true*—suddenly, irreversibly true! Terrorist attacks were things that happened overseas, in Israel, in Egypt, in Lebanon—not things that happened on U.S. soil. And in that instant, vertigo set in. I felt the magnetic poles shift in my brain: the United States was now a nation that was vulnerable to terrorists. Those of us who watched the images on TV remember the dizzying speed with which our previous worldview was turned upside down. Terrorism had come to roost in our country, our cities, and our hometowns. The disorientation was intense. All of us had to learn new ways of living in our new, terrifying world. This was a seismic event—a shifting of the tectonic plates to an extent that we had never believed possible.

Our therapist, who was listening carefully, nodded—he knew where this comparison was going. We explained that our son's recent coming out had impacted us in the same way as

9/11. We knew—*knew!*—that we would always love our son. And we also knew—*knew!*—that his being gay would mean that he was forever separated from our family in the afterlife. These two incontrovertible facts existed, and yet could *not* coexist. To contemplate an eternity shut off from our son, which we literally believed to be possible at that time, was unbearable. If we couldn't be together as a family, nothing else mattered. Existence itself was rendered meaningless if the love we had experienced as a family could be severed by a cold, eternal decree. If our son was going to hell, then God was *not* just. Cognitive dissonance set up a clanging in my head that only I could hear.

Coined in 1957 by psychologist Leon Festinger, "cognitive dissonance" is a term that describes the mental discord that occurs when deeply held beliefs collide and are found to be incompatible. To solve the discordance, people can alter either their behaviors or their beliefs to make them more consistent. This is not easily done, however, because awareness of contradictory beliefs often leads to "inner conflict," which can easily lead to shame, guilt, or avoidance. Avoidance occurs when one denies or compartmentalizes certain thoughts or beliefs. A simple example is that people continue to smoke cigarettes even though they know that smoking is extremely detrimental to their health, thus demonstrating human beings' creative ability to compartmentalize almost anything.[117]

After Jason decided that the counseling sessions were no longer helpful for him, I attended alone a few more times. At the beginning of one session, the therapist could tell that I was more restless than normal. "What's going on with you?" he asked. "Can you tell me how you are feeling?"

Instead of answering, I asked him to hand me a piece of paper and a pen. As he watched, I sketched a simple drawing: in the middle of the paper was a stick-figure woman. She was holding her arms straight out on either side of her body in order to stop two gigantic concrete walls from sliding in and crushing her. I labeled one of the walls "Church teachings on homosexuality" and other one "My son is gay." Both were edging inexorably toward the woman, whose mouth was opened wide in a silent scream and whose eyebrows were slanted downward in extreme sadness. She was going to be crushed—there was no doubt about it. There was no escape, no reconciliation, no truce to be reached here. The only possible outcome was the woman's death. "That's me," I said, tapping the point of the pen fiercely against the paper. "There's no way out."

The therapist leaned over and looked at the drawing. "They say a picture is worth a thousand words. I'd say this is an excellent depiction of cognitive dissonance. You're trapped between two immovable objects: your lifelong faith and the love you hold for your son."

"I want to keep them both. But I'm starting to believe it's not possible. If I have to choose, I already know which one I'm going to pick."

"Your son." It was a statement, not a question.

"Yes. Nothing could ever make me throw him out. But I still want to try and find a way to stay Mormon if I can. It's everything—my heritage, my family's foundation. I don't know how to survive without it."

"Well, you can continue to explore that space. Maybe you'll find a way to combine those two things, and maybe you won't. But whatever you decide to do is OK. And if you change your mind, that's OK, too."

I exhaled in relief and suddenly felt so physically weak that I slumped over on the couch in his office and rested my head on some overstuffed pillows. It were as if an iron string that had been holding me upright had been severed with a gigantic pair of scissors. The relief was overwhelming. *I can decide*, I thought. *I get to decide.*

As someone who had always considered herself an independent thinker, this was an embarrassing epiphany, to say the least. I had often questioned, pushed back a bit, wondered, and analyzed. Yet somehow, I had always stopped myself before venturing too far into dangerous, doubt-filled territory. Despite my occasional rebellious moods and dark questions, in the end, I always capitulated. As I walked out into the parking lot, I felt euphoric and hopeful. Maybe I can find a way to make this work, I thought. And if I can't, perhaps I won't be condemned by God.

Jason and I had known all along that our therapist would not be able to offer us any simple answers, but he did give us something very valuable. We realized that we were not alone, that other Mormons were coming out as gay, and that other families in addition to our own were falling down the rabbit hole.

During the same time that Jason and I were fumbling to construct a workable spiritual philosophy for our lives, Eric started dating. We were worried because he had met a couple of men online and then driven off to spend time with them without knowing much about them. We explained to him that our concerns had *nothing* to do with his being gay, but *everything* to do with his being inexperienced when it came to romantic relationships. We convinced him that before he went out with anyone, he would need to provide us with their name, cell phone number, and address at the very least.

His prior dating experiences had been limited to attending a few girls' choice dances at high school where one girl or another who had a crush on him would ask him out. Nothing ever came of these one-sided crushes, however, and we had chalked it up to Eric's shyness. At one point, he became close friends with Kelsie, a girl from his high school. They took a sign language class together and discovered that their personalities clicked. She was an outgoing, humorous, highly intelligent girl, and my daughter and I kept trying to persuade him to take her out.

"It's way too awkward," he would tell us whenever we mentioned Kelsie.

"How could it be awkward?" Leah, my daughter,

persisted. "Kelsie likes you, and it won't kill you to take her out on a date."

"Well, I just don't feel the same way about her as she does about me."

Leah rolled her eyes at him. "It's not like you have to *marry* her. Just take her on a simple date." Eric just stared back at her silently.

Meanwhile, I had mothers of teenage girls at church telling me that their daughters had crushes on Eric and hoped he would call them. I wasn't sure how to respond to their blunt hints. "I think he's just shy," I said. "We keep telling him to go on dates, but he won't."

Once we learned he was gay, the mystery was solved. But Jason and I were still worried about his new dating life. "If you were meeting a thirty-year-old woman, I would have the same concerns," I argued. "You're too young to be dating much older adults." He promised to be careful.

We were relieved to learn that Eric hadn't thrown out all of the morals that we had tried to instill in our children throughout their growing-up years. "Lots of these guys just want to have sex," he told me quite honestly after a few dates. "I'm not comfortable doing that with a stranger."

Thank goodness! I thought to myself. Aloud, I simply said, "I'm glad you're keeping yourself safe."

After a few months, Eric started dating a young man named Brian who was several years older than him. We met him after they had been on a few dates, and I instantly sensed he was a decent, caring person. He started hanging out with our family and coming over for dinners. Brian was in recovery and was completing his degree in counseling from a local university. He was Eric's physical opposite—short, dark-haired, and stoutly built. His eyes were a warm brown. He had one of the kindest hearts of anyone I had ever met and helped Eric calm down whenever he was becoming overly anxious about something. Within a short time, they decided to move in together. Although we thought they were rushing things a bit, we realized that we were no longer in a position to dictate the direction that our son's life would take. After he moved out, Jason and I hoped that his new partner could help him navigate the difficult road ahead as a gay, ex-Mormon man in Utah.

Our dilemma continued as we searched for ways to make sense of all the contradictions in our lives. We finally told both of our families that Eric was gay. Almost all of them were loving and accepting, but several verbalized their sadness to us; in addition, others worried aloud about how it would affect our religious beliefs. Since neither of us had figured that out yet, we simply told them we were still working on it. Meanwhile, the cognitive dissonance machine in my brain chugged along day and night, wheels spinning, but never making any discernible progress.

CHAPTER 16

Through a Glass, Darkly

I next turned to a chronological exploration of the Mormon Church's public responses to same-sex orientation. Although its teachings have softened in the last few years or so, at least on the surface, I found that the core doctrine remains unchanged: sexual relations between gay persons are an offense to God, and anyone who engages in such behavior will be unable to participate in full fellowship in the church, if at all. Even gay couples who are legally married are almost always excluded from participation.

Although the Mormon Church has taken a harsh stance against homosexuality since its founding, the church, along with most other European and American institutions, once accepted the "intense emotional and social relationships" that often occurred between two women or two men during the nineteenth century.[118] The so-called "cult of friendship" that thrived throughout most of this era portrayed such devoted friendships as platonic although they may very well have provided cover for erotic feelings as well, at least in some cases.[119] The citizens of the nineteenth century were much more scandalized by "inappropriate" opposite-sex intimacy than they were with open displays of physical affection between like-sexes and the sometimes passionate attachments that resulted.

But firm lines were eventually drawn between same-sex emotional/social intimacy and same-sex sexual intimacy. In 1851, Utah passed an anti-sodomy law, but it was quickly found to be unenforceable and was stricken from the books the next year. Then in 1876, the Utah State Legislature once again passed an anti-sodomy law, the penalty for which was a five- to ten-year prison term.[120] In 1879, when John Taylor was president of the Mormon Church, his oldest son, A. Bruce Taylor, admitted to engaging in homosexual acts. At that time information like this was generally kept quiet, but members accused of such behavior could be ostracized or have their lives threatened if the truth were discovered. A. Bruce Taylor left the state of Utah shortly after his "crimes" were discovered, and never married.[121] In 1882, first presidency member Joseph F. Smith excommunicated a group of teenage males who had been engaging in "obscene, filthy & horrible" same-sex activities. He explicitly claimed that such sins had caused the Biblical destruction of "Sodom and Gomorrah."[122] Other early church leaders such as George Q. Cannon, First Counselor in the First Presidency, prophesied in 1897 that the "Lord . . . [would] wipe them [homosexuals] out, that there will be none left to perpetuate the knowledge of these dreadful practices among the children of men."[123] This prophesy has obviously failed the test of time.

In the 1950s and beyond, the rapidly growing church moved to more fully correlate their doctrines, policies, and teaching materials as their membership expanded throughout United States and into several foreign nations. From this point on, the church ratcheted up their anti-gay rhetoric. Among other notable, official condemnations of the gay "lifestyle," first presidency member J. Reuben Clark addressed male members in the October 1954 priesthood conference session when he said that those who indulged in "that filthy crime of homosexuality" were not a part of the "Army of the Lord to fight evil".[124] In 1966, Elder Bruce R. McConkie, then an apostle, taught that "We hold that sexual sin [such as 'homosexuality'] is second only to the shedding of innocent blood in the category of personal crimes."[125] It is important to note that the "shedding of innocent blood" in a Mormon context does *not* mean murder; rather it refers to "blasphemy against the holy ghost," or assenting to the crucifixion of Jesus Christ after a person has received the "new and everlasting covenant" of the gospel that was restored by Joseph Smith.[126]

In 1962 Ernest L. Wilkinson, then president of Brigham Young University, along with Mormon apostles Spencer W. Kimball and Mark E. Petersen, decided that gay students were not welcome on the college campus. Rather than "dignify" the problem by making a public announcement, they decided instead that the church's *general authorities*[127] and campus leadership would exchange information behind the scenes about suspected gay students at BYU, the goal being to admit no one for whom they had "convincing evidence" of "homosexual" activities.[128] In 1965 Wilkinson decided to go public with the homosexual ban, announcing to the entire student body, "We do not want others on this campus to be contaminated by your presence,"[129] his speech thus invoking a common fear that mere physical proximity to a gay person might taint one's personal moral code. Gay students were invited to reveal themselves and depart posthaste.

In 1969, when I was ten years old, Elder Spencer W. Kimball's widely disseminated book *The Miracle of Forgiveness* was first published. The book went on to become deeply embedded within Mormon culture, especially throughout the 1970s and 80s when Kimball served as the church's twelfth prophet. In the book he took a hardline stance against any sort of sexual exploration or experiences outside of marriage, especially homosexuality. He solemnly intoned that homosexuality was a "grievous . . . sin against nature," and often came about as an outgrowth of "masturbation." Not only was it "repugnant" and "revolting," but it was also condemned by God.[130]

Perhaps even more dangerously, Kimball suggested that the "ugliness . . . of homosexuality . . . is curable and forgivable" to those who were willing to pay the price through sincere repentance. He warned that such transformation would not be easy and would involve "knuckles [that] are bloody" and a powerful mastery of self to "cauterize the wound." He continued that those who lacked the appropriate "self-will" would have to struggle with this destructive malady longer than those who had more faith. He then promised that "the cure is as permanent as the individual makes it and, like the cure for alcoholism, is subject to continued vigilance."[131]

This set up a dangerous cycle in the Mormon Church in which gay members desperately begged God to have their sexual orientation changed; failure meant that one was not righteous enough or sincere enough. When Kimball speculated that perhaps as an "extension of homosexual practices, men and women have sunk even to seeking sexual satisfactions with animals," the link between same-sex orientation and perversion was permanently established in church culture.[132] Same-sex intimacies were labeled as "unnatural" and "deviate," engendered by an "evil" impulse.[133] Furthermore, Kimball advised gay men to cure their "disease" by repenting, marrying a woman, and enjoying "the happiness of proper family life," which inevitably meant producing children.[134]

We were taught directly from this book throughout my years in seminary, a special religious instruction course for teens that was taught at high school campuses beginning in 1912 in Utah and which eventually spread across the United States. To this day, students in many western states are still released from their regular classes for one hour each day to walk to a church-funded building adjacent to their high school and receive daily religious instruction. When I was in high school, all students were expected to enroll, whether they wanted to or not. The only exception to this rule was made for the small handful of non-Mormon students who attended our school. On any given day, multiple students would find ways to skip the class (myself included once I became a senior), but the pressure from parents and peers to conform was exceptionally strong in Davis County, Utah. Thus, the Mormon-dominated environment of our youth taught us that the only thing worse than having the scarlet letter "A" emblazoned across our chest would be to have the scarlet letter "H" embedded in our heart.

Although the American Psychiatric Association removed the words "mental disorder" from its definition of homosexuality in the *Diagnostic and Statistical Manual of Mental Disorders* (DSM-II) in 1973,[135] Brigham Young University reportedly practiced electroshock conversion therapy for several years thereafter. The exact dates of the conversion therapy sessions are unknown, but at least one source has suggested a beginning date of 1959.[136] The sessions were held in the basement of the Smith Family Living Center, one of the buildings on the BYU campus, and remained active until at least 1983. In 1964 Spencer W. Kimball, who was then serving as an apostle, gave a speech to the religion faculty at BYU, partly because rumors had begun to swirl that such "conversion" sessions were being run in secret. He explained that "numerous people . . . [had] come through this special program," and that almost all of them had been transformed.[137] Mormon Church leaders were certainly not alone in their misguided, but at that time widely accepted, view that homosexuality could be cured using desensitization, electric shock, and exposure to pornographic images.

Controversy surrounds this topic because apostle Dallin H. Oaks has recently "categorically denied" that any electroshock treatments were administered to gay students from 1971 to 1980 during his presidential tenure at Brigham Young University. However, other researchers have denied Oaks's claims, insisting that his statement is less than credible. Prominent Mormon scientist and author Gregory Prince, for example, points to a thesis published by BYU graduate student Max McBride in 1976 that studied fourteen gay male students who were subjected to shock therapy. In 2016 the Mormon Church officially "denounce[d] any . . . reparative therapies," but that still doesn't answer the question about what Oaks did or didn't know during his BYU presidency. Readers will draw their own conclusions, but I believe that, at the very least, Oaks misspoke or perhaps forgot. At the worst, he seems to have purposely lied.[138]

In July 1973 as my peers and I were entering our teenage years, the church's official magazine for youth, the *New Era*, quoted BYU psychology professor Allen Bergin as saying that "homosexuals" are "psychologically disturbed persons" who are "compulsively driven to frequent and sometimes bizarre acts."[139] It is notable that Dr. Bergin apologized in 2022 to the creators of the "Latter Gay Stories" podcast, retracting his earlier statements:

> As a mental health professional and psychology professor from 1961 until my retirement in 1999, I was among the traditionalists who believed that homosexuality was a disorder and that it could be treated and changed to some degree. I was a professor of some renown at Columbia University and Brigham Young University, and my views have carried influence in some circles.
>
> I regret being part of a professional, religious, and public culture that marginalized, pathologized, and excluded LGBT persons. As a father of two gay sons and grandfather of a gay grandson, I've been given a personal education that has been painful and enlightening. To the general public, I say — Stop. Listen. Learn. Love. To myself, my posterity, my colleagues, my fellow church members, and my political leaders, I say — apologize and compensate those of God's children who have been afflicted by our treatment of them when they should have been embraced and loved. Give them their rightful place in society and in church so they may be nurtured and progress in their spiritual, social, and professional lives.
>
> We are all children of the same Heavenly Parents,

who I believe love and value all their children, regardless of sexual orientation, and who grant each of us the same opportunity to receive Jesus Christ's Grace. I will continue my efforts for the rest of my days to receive that Grace for myself and to point others toward His healing and redeeming power.[140]

In the October 1976 priesthood session of general conference, Elder Boyd K. Packer told the story of a young male missionary who confessed that he had knocked his missionary companion to the floor after the companion confessed his homosexuality to him. Packer commended the young man for protecting his virtue and advised the audience that in such cases, physical violence was allowable, even telling the listening audience that "somebody had to do it." Amidst the laughter of the audience, he explained that he had thanked the young man for doing the right thing. Interestingly, the church has since removed all written, audio, and digital versions of this talk, claiming that the talk has been "retired."[141]

Just a few years later in 1979, when I was one year into my undergraduate degree at Brigham Young University, Elder Vaughan J. Featherstone, a member of the *Seventy* (the third highest governing body in the church) gave a speech at the university in which he said that "to condone homosexuality is not an act of charity. Perversion is perversion. All the reasoning of the greatest minds in the world cannot change the seriousness of the transgression. Worlds without end, the homosexual cannot be exalted. That is it—as plainly, simply, and clearly as one can state."[142] Although his speech was entitled "Charity Never Faileth," he made it clear that no charity or forgiveness would be given to those who were gay, even by God himself. None of this stood out as unusual to my peers and me. It was part of the cultural milieu into which we had long ago been assimilated. Although I had questions for years, I still accepted the church's explanation that such proclivities were sinful, chosen because some people delighted in dangerous explorations.

It wasn't until 1987 that at least one leader announced that mixed-orientation marriages might not be a remedy for same-sex orientation, after all. Gordon B. Hinckley, who was then serving in the First Presidency, announced that "marriage should not be viewed as a therapeutic step to solve problems such as homosexual inclinations or practices, which first should clearly be overcome with a firm and fixed determination never to slip to such practices again"[143] Despite this announcement, there are many anecdotal stories of gay men who were still advised to marry a woman in order to reform themselves. And some church authorities continued to recommend marriage as a possible cure for same-sex orientation. In 1993, for example, Elder Spencer J. Condie of the Seventy claimed that homosexuality was a "habit" that could be successfully broken if men with these tendencies first sincerely repented and then married a woman. He shared the story of one formerly gay man who was able to successfully marry a woman and produce "several beautiful children."[144]

A few years later, in a 1995 General Relief Society meeting, President Gordon B. Hinckley introduced "The Family: A Proclamation to the World."[145] In a bold move, the First Presidency and the Council of the Twelve Apostles explained that this was the Lord's message not only to believing Mormons, but also to the entire planet. The proclamation starts out with two short paragraphs about the eternal nature of marriage and gender, in which the terms "biological sex" and "gender" are conflated. The church views gender as a set of inborn, essential characteristics, and argues that same-sex orientation is a temporary condition that will not exist in the hereafter:

"We, the First Presidency and the Council of the Twelve Apostles of The Church of Jesus Christ of Latter-day Saints, solemnly proclaim that marriage between a man and a woman is ordained of God and that the family is central to the Creator's plan for the eternal destiny of His children.

"All human beings—male and female—are created in the image of God. Each is a beloved spirit son or daughter of heavenly parents, and, as such, each has a divine nature and destiny. Gender is an essential characteristic of individual premortal, mortal, and eternal identity and purpose."[146]

The church had done more than draw a line in the sand —instead they built an impenetrable wall that would break gay members. Most members interpreted this document as the revealed word of God as to how husbands and wives needed to conduct their spiritual lives; it is still displayed prominently in framed images on the walls of many Mormon families. The pointed exclusion of gay members and gay marriage as acceptable before God was, once again, firmly ensconced at the heart of the church's official doctrine.

One year later in 1996, when Kelli Petersen, a seventeen-year-old lesbian high school student, tried to start a Gay/Straight Alliance Club at East High School, the Salt Lake City Board of Education decided to *ban all clubs* from their high schools rather than allow gay students to gather. Petersen had the support of her Mormon mother, who pointed out that "being gay . . . [isn't] a choice. You either are or you aren't." On the other hand, the president of the Utah Eagle Forum (which is an affiliate of Phyllis Schlafly's national organization) accused those with same-sex orientation of trying to recruit: "Homosexuals can't reproduce, so they *recruit* [emphasis added]. And they are not going to use Utah high school and junior high school campuses to recruit."[147]

The Mormon Church has significant political clout combined with almost limitless funds,[148] and it has exercised its power in fighting against many modern initiatives to legalize gay marriage. When California passed Proposition 22 in 2000, which defined marriage as strictly between one man and one woman, the church played an important, yet behind-the-scenes role in that passage. On January 16, 2000, church president Gordon B. Hinckley wrote an official statement that was read to every Latter-day Saint congregation in

California: "You are contributing your time and talents in a cause that in some quarters may not be politically correct, but which nevertheless lies at the heart of the Lord's eternal plan for His children."[149] Our son was eight years old and had recently been baptized into official church membership when that proclamation was read; little did we know that pronouncements like these would eventually have a profound effect on our family.

At that same time in California, a devout, young Mormon man named Stuart Matis was wrestling with his sexual orientation. As a returned missionary, he understood that same-sex orientation and Mormonism did not mix. He had spent years trying to sublimate his sexual urges through prayer, prolonged scripture reading, avoidance of social situations, and self-punishment; when nothing worked, his despair deepened, and he eventually decided that suicide was the only answer to his excruciating dilemma. "He would punish himself if he had a [homosexual] thought," said one of his childhood friends, Jenifer Mouritsen. "He wouldn't allow himself to go to a friend's birthday party or [wouldn't] watch his favorite TV program."[150]

Although his family had responded with empathy and love when he belatedly revealed the truth to them, they were unable to root out his deeply ingrained belief that he was broken in God's eyes. On the early morning of February 25, 2000, Matis shot himself in the head on the front steps of a California church *stake center*[151] building. He had pinned a "do not resuscitate" note to his chest. A few weeks later, his former Mormon mission companion, Clay Whitmer, who was also gay, committed suicide out of the same sense of despair that had tormented Matis.[152]

In 2010 when California passed Proposition 8, which amended the state constitution to make gay marriage illegal, the Mormon Church was also involved behind the scenes. Although the church at first downplayed its involvement, Fred Karger, who had worked for decades as a political consultant in California and had only recently come out as gay, followed the money trail in August 2008 when he discovered that the ProtectMarriage.com website was suddenly bringing in about "$500,000 a day." It didn't take him long to learn that the Mormon Church was behind this effort, leading to what Karger labeled a wildly successful "stealth campaign." Karger estimated that Mormon members had contributed "$30 million of the $42 million total raised in support of Prop 8, which passed easily in November 2008."[153] The backlash from these revelations grew heated, however, and the church found itself in the unprecedented position of being attacked for its political opposition to gay marriage, which can be traced back to at least 1995. After Mormons started resigning their membership in light of the church's newly disclosed funding activities, church headquarters sent church historian Marlin Jensen to California in an attempt to assuage angered members. Significantly, Jensen went on the record as apologizing for the "pain that Prop. 8 caused,"[154] although leaders since then have *not* apologized and have pointedly continued to claim there is no need to do so.

At the church's October general conference in 2010, which is considered by faithful members to be one of the means through which God reveals his will to the membership, Boyd K. Packer opined that "The Family: A Proclamation to the World" should be considered a "revelation." Immediately after referencing "Satan's many substitutes or counterfeits for marriage," he stated that "some suppose that they were pre-set and cannot overcome what they feel are inborn tendencies toward the impure and unnatural. Not so! Why would our Heavenly Father do that to anyone? Remember, he is our father."[155] His characterization of same-sex orientation as "impure and unnatural" proclivities that could be "overcome" if one showed enough faith led to thousands of people protesting his words at Salt Lake City's famous Temple Square a few days later.[156]

Coincidentally, I had decided to watch general

conference that weekend in 2010 after avoiding it for an entire year. I hoped I might hear something that would help me find answers to the unsolvable riddle that plagued me day and night. When I turned on the television part way through the program, Boyd K. Packer had just stood up and walked to the front of the church's new Conference Center, the "largest theatre-style auditorium ever built," to give his semiannual address.[157] As he stood at the magnificent black walnut pulpit, the wood of which had been harvested from a tree planted by former prophet Gordon B. Hinckley, the audience hushed.[158] The minute Packer started speaking, however, I knew that my hoped-for help would not arrive. As soon as I heard the words "impure and unnatural," I stood up, turned off the TV, and left the room. Another domino tipped over in the cascade of realizations that my lifelong spiritual home no longer felt safe. It was the last general conference I would ever watch.

CHAPTER 17

No More Goodbyes

I decided to continue my research with one of Mormonism's most well-known and beloved authors, Carol Lynn Pearson. I knew that she had married a gay man in 1966. Although she was aware of his sexual orientation, they naively believed that a righteous Mormon marriage could conquer all. But after eight years together and the birth of four children, the marriage fell apart. Although Pearson was emotionally devastated, she maintained a close friendship with her former husband and eventually cared for him when he came back to their home to die after contracting AIDS. Her 1986 book, *Goodbye, I Love You,* told the story of their marriage and was groundbreaking in its frank, empathetic look at a topic that had long been considered taboo in Mormon circles. As Berkeley professor Robert A. Rees noted in his foreword to one of Pearson's later books, for many church members, the 1986 book was "the first compassionate voice they had ever heard on the subject."[159] In making room for a frank discussion about the challenges that gay Mormons and their families face, Pearson's writings remain invaluable to this day.

I wondered how Pearson had managed to maintain her spiritual equilibrium. She was still a respected member of the church, yet she continued to openly advocate for change in the treatment of gay members. Her 2007 book, *No More Goodbyes: Circling the Wagons Around Our Gay Loved Ones,* seemed like the perfect starting point. As I read, I marveled that a practicing Mormon could be so outspoken about the deadly consequences of the church's teachings about same-sex orientation. Pearson tells one story about counseling a gay Mormon man who was in the midst of being divorced by his wife and who had been shunned by his children. He had emailed Pearson about his plans to commit suicide. Her counsel to him was completely unexpected, not only to him, but to me: she advised him to choose "healing" and to "come to terms with his homosexuality with self-respect." Somehow Pearson could see beyond the limitations of the culture she had been raised in and could fearlessly proclaim God's love for all: "God loves you just as you are, and 'abomination' is a word gone awry."[160] In boldly criticizing decades of public church teachings that to be gay was the most deplorable of sins, Pearson held up a lamp that shone on the path I needed to take.

After reading Pearson's book, I gave myself permission to search out other viewpoints, no matter their source. I found a podcast that I would have considered off-limits before my faith crisis called *Mormon Stories* and listened obsessively to episodes around the clock; the podcast focuses on Mormons around the world and their personal experiences growing up in the church along with the various challenges to their faith. Several of the episodes dealt with gay members, their families, and their heartache. At night I would lie awake trying to find some way to make all the pieces of this puzzle fit together. For me, accepting our son's sexual orientation as "real" only took a few weeks. The hard part was fitting this piece of information into my prior worldview. I hoped that if I tried hard enough, prayed enough, and read enough, I would understand how there could be a circle big enough to embrace me, my son, and my Mormon faith.

Of the hundreds of Mormon Story episodes that I listened to, some of the most crucial were a 2010 series of interviews that host John Dehlin held with Dr. William Bradshaw, a retired molecular biology professor who had taught at Brigham Young University for over three decades. After their son Brett came out to both Bradshaw and his wife, the couple experienced the same sort of vertigo that Jason and I had as they wondered how this unexpected twist would affect their family's eternal future. Much to Bradshaw's credit, he instantly and without any hesitation assured his son that he would always love him, no matter what. In addition, this brilliant and highly respected professor had the humility to admit that he was completely ignorant about what caused same-sex orientation before his son came out; to remedy this, he embarked upon an intensive period of study in which he read nearly all the existing academic literature about the subject.

To his surprise, he discovered that the most current research points to a biological basis for sexual orientation, which strongly suggests that it is not a choice. Bradshaw began lecturing about the probable biological foundation for same-sex orientation in 2004, and in 2010 he delivered a pivotal lecture on the Brigham Young University campus entitled "The Evidence for a Biological Origin for Homosexuality."

In his interview with Dehlin, Bradshaw enumerated his conclusions:

> The evidence is extraordinarily strong that orientation is the result of biochemical influences during the latter weeks of gestation in humans and the very early weeks postpartum. The conventional wisdom that homosexuality is caused by inept parenting finds no basis of fact. Men are not gay because their fathers were distant and uncaring or their mothers were stifling and overprotective. The evidence does not support the view that homosexuality is caused by sexual abuse in childhood or early sexual exploitation or experimentation.
>
> The brains of gay people and straight are not the same, and we know a lot about some of the hormonal affects, and the catalog of evidence is extensive.

It extends to studies of brain structure and brain function. It includes evidence from PET scans and from hormone measurements and from enzyme measurements and from demonstrated differences in the hearing function of gay and straight people. It comes from studies of things like finger length and a whole host of similar evidence. I've cataloged those and written about them.

In the Latter-day Saint community, there are strong sentiments that people can change. To cut to the core, there are probably some people, some homosexual people, who reside in the middle of the scale between totally homosexual on one hand and totally heterosexual on the other; in other words, there are bisexual people with some capacity for romantic interest in people of both genders who can function in a heterosexual marriage by finding ways to emphasize that one romantic attraction of the two that they're capable of. But although the evidence is hard to come by, the experience of most therapists and social scientists, psychologists [and] psychiatrists who have dealt with people across the country, the experience is that change at best is very, very, very, very rare and that, in fact, efforts for people to change unwanted sexual attraction often results in serious harm.

As I listened to his words, I felt a cool, soothing salve being applied to my spiritual wounds. Like Carol Lynn Pearson, Dr. Bradshaw had been willing to look outside the conventional wisdom of his Mormon community and had concluded that being gay was not a sin, a temptation, or a handicap—but was, instead, simply a biological fact.

Bradshaw added that he was convinced that levels of societal disapproval "that most of us can't even imagine" have led to higher rates of LGBT suicides when compared to heterosexual individuals. Thus, while being gay in and of itself does not raise the risk of suicide, rejection by family, friends, and society does. According to journalist Peggy Fletcher Stack, in 2013 out of the approximately 300 to 400 homeless youths in Utah, about "150 to 200 [were] believed to come from Mormon homes," either having been kicked out or having run away because of their sexual orientations.[161] In 2014 a group called "Mama Dragons" was started by eight Mormon women who found a lack of support and awareness at the highest levels of the church about how to help their gay teens. With nearly ten thousand members as of 2024, they've turned into a potent force whose main goal is to support, educate, and empower the mothers of LGBT children.[162] They've even opened their homes to gay teens "fleeing their families for fear of retribution or shunning."[163]

Jason and I already knew that we would never consider rejecting our son. After I read Bradshaw's comments about the connection between LGBT suicides and family or societal rejection, I was more convinced than ever that parental ignorance about the consequences of ostracizing their gay sons and daughters was deadly. I vowed to be one of the parents who loved and supported her child with a maternal ferocity, whether in public or in private.

Bradshaw's conclusions about the causes of same-sex orientation made much more sense to me than anything else I had heard during my decades of church membership; in addition, as I shared everything I had been learning with Jason, he, too, came to realize that sexual orientation was an inherent, unchangeable part of a person's identity. As we realized how destructive the church teachings about gay people had been, Jason decided that he no longer wanted to be an active member and told our bishop that he wanted to be released from his leadership calling in the Young Men's organization.[164] Although I fully supported his decision, I still could not bring myself to discard the church at that point.

It had been a lifetime anchor and was the heritage of all my beloved family. How could I leave it behind? How could I hurt the people I loved most by rejecting the way I had been raised?

I had grown up listening to faith-promoting stories about my pioneer ancestors. Both the paternal and maternal branches of my family came from Mormon pioneer stock; they had crossed the plains and endured unspeakable hardships to establish *Zion* (a dwelling place for the righteous) in the heart of the Rocky Mountains. My mother frequently recounted a story about one of our female pioneer progenitors who carried her sickly husband over a frozen river near Winter Quarters, Nebraska, to get to the next camping spot. To turn against that heritage would be an act of selfishness on my part. It would be seen by some as a betrayal of the family bloodline, an abdication of a sacred duty.

I could not think of any way to escape my predicament and still be a good daughter, sister, mother, wife, or friend. No matter what I did, someone would be hurt. I wondered at Jason's ability to cut himself off from the church relatively quickly and not to worry about anyone else's opinions about his actions. I decided that it was a combination of at least three things: First, Jason was the youngest in his family. He had never been tasked with being an "example" to his younger siblings. In addition, two of his older siblings had already left the church years ago. Second, Jason's family had been drifting apart for years; after his oldest brother's and his mother's death, the connections between siblings became even more tenuous because of geographical and spiritual differences. Third, Jason was a man. At the risk of oversimplifying, I believe that most men are not socialized to focus on keeping everyone around them happy, whereas most women are (or at least were for the decades before and during my own coming of age). The fact that my siblings and I were exceptionally close and that all of them at that point were still devoted to Mormonism added an extra burden that I carried but Jason didn't.

I was well and truly stuck. I thought back to my

experience of giving birth to our daughter. I had been in labor for hours, yet the baby was not making sufficient progress in the birth canal. My anxiety and pain were escalating (I had chosen not to have an epidural), and I found myself hyperventilating. Escape was the only solution. "I'm done with this!" I yelled out to the nurse. "I want to leave *now*." I tried to roll over and detach myself from the fetal monitors.

She patted my arm while clucking her tongue. "Oh, dear," she said. "I'm afraid this is one of those things you can't get out of until it's over."

After pushing even longer in a prolonged labor, I knew what the nurse meant. We don't get to opt out of certain experiences. Sometimes pain is unavoidable. And as for getting our hearts broken or breaking the hearts of those we love, that is just another thing we have to ride out—we don't get to quit because it hurts too much. It's a brutal guide, but it's an honest one. I hoped that whatever my decision, it wouldn't disappoint too many of the people who were part of my life.

CHAPTER 18

The Internet Bomb

During the presidency of Gordon B. Hinckley, who served as the church's fifteenth prophet from 1995 to 2008, the church embarked upon a more sophisticated style of interacting with the media; Hinckley's background in journalism and public relations suited him well for this undertaking. What neither Hinckley nor any of his successors could have imagined, however, was that an unprecedented technological revolution was on its way. Its arrival would not only transform the way the world created, stored, and consumed media, but would also have a profound impact on the church's ability to shape its own narrative.

Before the digital revolution, information had to be stored in a physical form, for example, on stone, paper, vinyl records, or film, among other formats. The Mormon Church has long stressed the importance of recordkeeping and eventually preserved its historical materials in the First Presidency's Granite Mountain Records Vault. Constructed during the 1960s in the northern side of Little Cottonwood Canyon near Salt Lake City, the vault was carved six hundred feet into solid granite and was designed to be impregnable. It contains a vast collection of microfilms—about thirty-five billion images in total—which are now being digitized. Marriage records, handwritten temple ceremonies, genealogy records, physical objects, and historical journals of both the faith-promoting and faith-destabilizing variety have been stored there in what has been called one of the "most secure locations in the world."[165] The public has never been granted access to the vault.

In addition, only a handful of academics and historians had been allowed to view records in other locations, such as in universities. Although the church claims that it has never hidden information, such claims are belied by statements of renowned Mormon historians, such as Richard Bushman, Jerald and Sandra Tanner, and D. Michael Quinn. Quinn was excommunicated in 1993 for his research about the continuation of polygamy in Utah even after its supposed "termination" in 1890. (The church now admits that polygamy did, in fact, continue.)[166]

However, the exponential growth of digital technology during the last twenty to thirty years has disturbed the equilibrium of Utah's largest, monolithic faith. The Internet has cracked open the previously impenetrable Pandora's box of historical information the Mormon Church would have preferred to keep locked away. Embarrassing realities are now accessible at the click of a mouse, and the long-buried ghosts of the past are rising up. For example, the church now acknowledges that Joseph Smith wrote at least four contradictory versions of his foundational first vision and that Smith's translation of the Book of Abraham has since been shown to be completely inaccurate by both Mormon and non-Mormon Egyptologists.[167] Since its founding, the church has been able to keep such things out of view, mainly through a practice of whitewashing its history and producing only sanitized, mainstream versions of its founding. The thinking has been that only top-level leaders and professional historians had the spiritual maturity to grapple with such difficult issues.

But according to author Charles Seife, digital technology's rapid growth has outpaced the ability of humankind (or its institutions) to adapt. Before the digital revolution, technological advances were slow and measured by comparison, and the people and societies exposed to them would have decades or centuries to slowly adapt to their interference until at last such innovations became part of the background. For example, experiments with steam power began in the early twelfth century and innovations and improvements upon the original concept have continued until the present day. But digital technology is different: it combines speed, flexibility, and interconnectedness like nothing that has come before it. The limitless nature of its reach illustrates its inherent danger: it is like a bomb that has been dropped into an unsuspecting village. Seife says it will be centuries before we fully understand what it has done to us.[168]

Church leaders have long warned their congregations to avoid anything that speaks negatively of the faith. Since the arrival of the Internet, the warnings have grown to include frequent predictions of the spiritual doom that will befall any who partake of the anti-Mormon information available online. This was the main reason that I avoided researching anything about Mormonism online for years: I dismissed the information as dangerous and of doubtful veracity. For someone who has not been raised inside an authoritarian faith, this may be difficult to understand. But once I committed to a temple marriage and became a parent, even the slightest doubt about my religious beliefs made me feel queasy. President Russell M. Nelson, the seventeenth and current prophet, asked all youth between the ages of twelve and eighteen to complete a seven-day fast from social media during a Worldwide Youth Devotional in 2018.[169] Later that same year, he called upon the women to complete a ten-day fast from social media and from any news that created "negative and impure thoughts."[170] Cynics asked why he didn't include the men, but most people understood that avoiding social media for a week would be the figurative equivalent of the little Dutch boy trying to plug up a leaking levee with his index finger. The Internet ocean is too vast and tumultuous to ever be controlled.

The Mormon Church at first reacted to the

unprecedented flood of information by becoming defensive. Belatedly, fumblingly, they tried to label everything that was negative toward the church or its founder, Joseph Smith, as heretical. Then they claimed that old, disturbing doctrines were either misunderstood or incorrectly explained by those who wished the church harm. More recently, they have been making at least some efforts to be more open about their history. But the genie was already out of the bottle, and the young twenty- and thirty-somethings who had been raised by orthodox parents began asking questions about the religion they had grown up in. The church's answers have been feeble at best and misleading at worst; hence, an ever-growing portion of millennials and Gen-Zers have abandoned the faith of their families. The leadership is acutely aware of this, and many alarming predictions and warnings have occurred in private meetings or communications (which have been leaked online) and during public church conferences and announcements since then.

In addition, the unparalleled access to information has had a profoundly negative impact on the number of convert baptisms and the retention of current members, especially young adults. It's far too early to predict the demise of Mormonism, and even many formerly devout members, myself included, don't necessarily want the church to disappear. But it is evident that the church now finds itself at a crossroads of dire import. Do they update their message to retain their youth? Or do they insist on holding the line to retain their older members? If they alienate the youth (as they are currently doing), they will lose their future tithe payers and families. If they alienate their adult group (those forty-five years old and up), they will lose their current tithe payers and families.

In Stockholm, Sweden, a concerned, top-level Mormon leader, Hans Mattsson, asked church headquarters for help in addressing the questions of members who had found disturbing material about the church online. Mattsson was a Swedish member who had been called to be an *Area Seventy*[171] in 2000, the first time a Swede had been called to such a high-ranking position. In large part due to Mattsson's efforts, an "emergency fireside" was held in November 2010 in Stockholm with approximately twenty-five bishops and stake presidents in the region; Church Historian Marlin Jensen and assistant Church Historian Richard Turley, along with Erich W. Kopischke of the First Quorum of the Seventy, were sent from church headquarters in Salt Lake City, Utah, to answer questions.[172]

The meeting began with the "assurances that these authorities knew all about the tough questions," but then quickly became contentious as Elder Jensen began to preach to those in attendance about choosing either God or Satan. As Mattsson scanned the faces of those in the audience, he saw them growing "impatient with the offensive tone of Jensen's words." They had come expecting answers to difficult questions; instead, they were admonished to protect themselves from the "spirit of the devil" and to repent. After three hours, the meeting ended with Jensen telling the members that he was "satisfied" with the meeting. Those in attendance, however, felt frustrated that their questions remained completely unanswered.[173]

In March 2012, with many troubled Swedish members still asking difficult questions, Ingvar Olsson, Area Seventy for Sweden, sent out a document to church leaders in Sweden. It contained a letter from Church Historian Marlin Jensen which he had titled "The Swedish Rescue." In the letter Jensen asserted that "the Church does not hide historical facts," a claim which belied everything that the Swedish Mormons had learned by searching the Internet. He insisted that the information simply wasn't "available," which is another dubious claim: "The Internet and digital records now make information about the Church available to many who because of language and other limitations have not previously known of this information. This does not mean that such information was hidden by the Church; it was simply not generally available."[174]

The letter contained no new information; neither had the questions previously raised in 2010 been answered. Then in the April 2013 general conference, Apostle Jeffrey R. Holland seemed to obliquely downplay the serious anguish that the Swedish church members had experienced, saying, "Please don't hyperventilate if from time to time issues arise that need to be examined, understood, and resolved. They do and they will. In this Church, what we know will always trump what we do not know."[175]

After some time, Hans Mattsson went public with his questions in a front-page interview with the *New York Times*. Despite Mattsson's open admission about his loss of faith, he and his wife Birgitta were never excommunicated by the Mormon Church;[176] instead, they resigned in 2016 after learning about the church's November 2015 Policy (leaked online), which barred children with gay parents from officially joining the church.[177] The couple eventually left Sweden because of long-term health problems that Hans had suffered; Birgitta described the move as "symbolic" as they left behind their old way of life and prepared for a new way.[178]

Several initiatives grew out of the Swedish events, including the eventual publication of the *"Gospel Topic Essays."*[179] Some of the topics covered are "Book of Mormon and DNA Studies," "First Vision Accounts," "Mother in Heaven," "Race and the Priesthood," and "Plural Marriage in The Church of Jesus Christ of Latter-day Saints," among others. While the essays have been an important attempt on the church's part to be more open about their historical and doctrinal dilemmas, their goal of being transparent has often collided with their goal of strengthening the faith. Published between 2013 and 2015 in electronic form, these essays (thirteen so far) have been available on the church's official website for years, yet most members still don't know of their existence. Some have speculated that the "soft rollout" of these essays, and the fact they were published without authorial attribution, means that church was hoping to tread the fine line between revealing enough to keep disaffected members in, but not enough to push stalwart members out. In effect, the church was attempting to "answer the hard gospel questions" of those who had already found disturbing theological issues online without troubling the "90% of members" who were not concerned about such issues.[180]

Good intentions notwithstanding, the "Gospel Topic Essays" have become a stumbling stone to many members who have admitted that the essays were the first source that pointed them to troubling doctrinal contradictions.[181] In 2014, Ganesh Cherian, a New Zealander who had served five years as a Mormon bishop, was disturbed enough by the new revelations contained in the essays to write a guest post on professor Gina Colvin's kiwimormon blog: "Is it possible that I have hurt people with doctrines and dogmas that in the light of these essays seem to sit on shaky ground? I understand how essential it is to 'sustain' the Brethren but these days I live with a caution that those ideals that I believe today could be dismissed by future First Presidencies."[182]

For example, in the "Race and the Priesthood" essay, the church says that "there has never been a Churchwide policy of segregated congregations," although there were some "instances of segregated congregations in areas such as . . . the U.S. South" due to "local customs and laws." Although a few black men were ordained to the priesthood during Joseph Smith's lifetime, Brigham Young later "publicly announced that men of black African descent could no longer be ordained to the priesthood."[183] One of the essay's footnotes refers to a letter written in 1907 by Apostle Joseph Fielding Smith (who later became church president). He stated that the belief was "quite general" among Mormons that the "Negro race has been cursed for taking a neutral position in that great contest [i.e., the premortal life]." Yet this belief, he admitted, "is not the official position of the Church, [and is] merely the opinion of men."[184]

However, an article written by Joseph Fielding Smith in 1924 says this: "It is true that the negro race is barred from holding the Priesthood, and this has always been the case. The Prophet Joseph Smith taught this doctrine."[185] Then in his 1931 book, which he wrote and published when he was an apostle, he says this: "That the negro race, for instance, have been placed under restrictions because of their attitude in the world of spirits, few will doubt. . . . It [was] a punishment for some act, or acts, performed before they were born."[186] Joseph Fielding Smith's views on excluding black men from receiving the priesthood seem to have been quite contradictory; this lack of alignment also encompassed the First Presidency and the Quorum of the Twelve, who, according to historian Matthew L. Harris, vehemently disagreed for decades about whether the "negro" priesthood exclusion was a doctrine or a man-made policy.[187]

If, according to the currently published Gospel Topics essay "Race and the Priesthood," the church's position on the "curse" upon the "Negro race" was not "the official position of the church" as early as 1907, one must ask why high-ranking church leader Bruce R. McConkie's 1958 version of Mormon Doctrine says the following: "The negroes are not equal with other races where the receipt of certain spiritual blessings are concerned, . . . but this inequality is not of man's origin. It is the Lord's doing, is based on his eternal laws of justice, and grows out of the lack of spiritual valiance of those concerned in their *first estate.*"[188]

The 1958 version accurately depicts the general beliefs of nearly all adult church members before the 1978 revelation that allowed black males to receive the priesthood. Although my own parents were personally non-judgmental in their interactions with Blacks, they never openly questioned the church's explanation as to why black men could not hold the priesthood. I remember my mother saying something about it being a confusing doctrine that would someday make sense or be righted in the heavens. Yet I also remember hearing McConkie's explanations about why Blacks couldn't hold the priesthood taught in church on Sundays and in my daily seminary classes throughout high school. After the 1978 revelation that allowed black males to receive the priesthood, an updated version of McConkie's book was published in 1979 that removed all previous references to black members being "cursed with a dark skin" because of ancient father Cain's "rebellion." However, the Book of Mormon itself still contains several troubling references to "dark" skins. Near the beginning of the book this scripture appears: "And he [the Lord] had caused the cursing to come upon them [the Lamanites], yea, even a sore cursing, because of their iniquity. . . . [In order] that they might not be enticing unto my people the Lord God did cause a skin of blackness to come upon them" (2 Nephi 5:21).

While some Mormon scholars have attempted to deny or contextualize any charges of racism in the church's foundational book of scripture, not all readers have been convinced by their arguments. And even as the church has, indeed, made great progress in its inclusion of black members, to the point of discounting some of the previous statements made by its highest leaders, one can see the logical dilemma this creates. If Brigham Young made a mistake—or was pressured due to political expediency or Utah's desire to join the Union—when he announced that "men of black African descent could no longer be ordained to the priesthood,"[189] have other prophets made mistakes, also? At what point does a prophet's divine utterance become suspect? After ten years, twenty years, fifty years? And if members decide that they can throw out something old, what's to stop them from throwing out something new and then, eventually, everything? Can I, as a member, decide to disagree with a current doctrinal policy because I believe that at some future point it will be discarded or cleansed as some other policies have been?

The problem is, of course, that a church that claims to

receive continuing revelation from God, that claims to possess more truth than any other religious or civic body on the planet, has set an exceptionally high standard for itself. Dallin H. Oaks, a member of the Quorum of the Twelve Apostles, told the Associated Press in a 1988 interview, "I don't know that it's possible to distinguish between policy and doctrine in a church that believes in continuing revelation and sustains its leader as a prophet."[190] Oaks knows that the church is on shaky ground if members can start protesting things that they view as mere "policies"; it is far safer if the church conflates the terms "policy" and "doctrine" so that members will view both as unimpeachable and irreproachable. If, however, there is even one instance where a previously embraced doctrine is shown to be erroneous, certainty disappears and pandemonium ensues; or at least such was the case when our son came out as gay. Once I discarded the church's doctrinal pronouncements about same-sex orientation as unsound, everything else in the church began to wobble. My carefully ordered life no longer had a center, and I watched in dismay as everything that had once been stable started to spin out of control; I finally understood what the poet Yeats meant when he said that if the "center cannot hold . . . things fall apart . . . [and] mere anarchy is loosed upon the world." *Mere anarchy*— what an artfully ironic way to describe the catastrophic loss of certainty.

CHAPTER 19

One-Armed Man

Life is precarious. What all parents learn too late is that after leaving the womb, their child wanders through a dangerous world, exposed to anything and everything. Decades ago, a man in my childhood neighborhood lost his adult daughter to a violent, senseless murder at a local university. Ten years later, at a church meeting, someone asked him how he had "gotten over" his daughter's death and moved forward. I still remember his response. He paused a moment, and then said, simply and without rancor, "It's like losing an arm. You eventually learn how to function as a one-armed man. But you never forget—not even for a moment—what it felt like to have two arms." Even before I had children, that statement burned its way into my brain, never to be forgotten. I could not imagine surviving a loss like that.

In almost every picture taken of our daughter and son together during their childhood, Leah has an anxious smile on her face as she tries to control her younger brother. She's trying to be the "good" big sister and help her brother not get into trouble. In one she stands in a pink and black polka-dot outfit, with her long, golden-red hair up in a side-ponytail, her arms cocooning her squirming brother in front of her. Eric is dressed in a onesie outfit with bright blue, yellow, and red stripes. He has an impish look on his face, his wide-open blue eyes looking around expectantly, the blond ringlets springing out in soft coils around his head.

In another picture our son sits on a small, white potty chair, turning his face to smile at the camera. His legs are helping him balance, but it looks like he might attempt to sprint away at any moment. Our daughter is kneeling next to him, trying to hold him in place while she grimly smiles at the camera. It wasn't until twenty years later that we saw the anxiety behind the smile. It was as if she knew, even at that young age, that her brother needed to be looked after. Perhaps she sensed that chaos was always lurking just outside the borders of the picture, and that if she stopped focusing on her younger brother, he might disappear.

As it turned out, she was right. Our son is brilliant, beautiful, creative, and caring. And because of his genetic heritage, he has dealt with some mental-health issues that have made every bit of progress he has carved out all the more impressive. The fact that he was raised inside an authoritarian church that has long condemned the "gay lifestyle" as something unnatural and perverse has surely contributed to his challenges.

The nature of authoritarian churches is that they demand total obedience and compliance from their members. Such churches spend a lot of their time, energy, and money on boundary protection. While boundary protection is an understandable response of any organization to an outside threat, it seems odd that a church that emphasizes Heavenly Father's love for all His children has gone to such vigilant extremes to protect itself from the "sinful nature" of its gay members.

The appeal of Mormonism lies in its claim to know the answers to some of life's most vexing questions: Where was I, if anywhere, before my birth? Why am I here on earth? What will happen to me after I die? When one is snuggly ensconced in the plush blanket of belief, the answers are comforting. However, when the blanket becomes threadbare, and one considers that perhaps this church has no special claim to divine knowledge, the resulting bleakness can be overwhelming.

Confirmation bias is the subconscious tendency that

all people have to search for and interpret information in a way that preserves their current beliefs and thus minimizes cognitive distress. It explains why individuals from a wide range of religious traditions are able to interpret information or events in ways that exclusively support whichever particular group they belong to. Anything that moves them in emotionally positive ways is interpreted as a sign from God that their church really *is* what it claims to be.

In truth, nearly all religious groups have reached those same conclusions: Mormons, Catholics, Moslems, and Protestants around the globe claim a special, oftentimes exclusive, connection with divinity. I was taught throughout my entire life that all earthly churches were privy to partial truths, but that Mormons were the only ones with the whole truth. It never occurred to me that perhaps we were all biased. Comedian Ricky Gervais sums it up succinctly: "How fortunate that we were all born into the correct religion!" How fortunate, indeed. The number one factor that determines people's faith convictions is their geographical location, or where they were raised. Deciding to throw out your gay child as an eternally lost cause based on the happenstance of your family history and the prevailing belief system of your current geographical location is surely madness, yet that is what many "religious" parents have done.

Of course, there are many people who never trouble themselves with such thoughts. "It will all work out in the end" is a common refrain and can be applied to almost any religious conundrum that might arise. For many people, hopeful platitudes like these are comforting enough to get them through a lifetime. But for devout Mormon parents of a gay child, there is no balm in Gilead. Instead, the parents now face a series of impossible choices: choose God or their child, choose official church doctrine or their child, choose their own salvation or their child. The Mormon Church claims this is a false dichotomy: parents don't need to choose, they say. Yet despite their somewhat softened rhetoric toward LGBT members, the church's doctrinal underpinnings are still firmly in place: even though Jesus loves everybody, members who live in an openly gay relationship or marriage will most likely be excommunicated. At the very least, they will be cut off from full activity and participation in the essential ordinances that Mormons believe are required to gain entrance into the eternal presence of God. In fact, gay members have become so dangerous to the body of Christ that they need to be cut off, both physically and symbolically: "If thy right eye offend thee, pluck it out, and cast it from thee. . . . If thy right hand offend thee, cut it off, and cast it from thee: for it is profitable for thee that one of thy members should perish, and not that thy whole body should be cast into hell" (Matt. 5: 29-30). And what if that eye or that hand is a gay child? Should *that* relationship be severed? Surely any parent whose heart still beats with human compassion will answer no to that question.

I know parents who have somehow found a way to continue to participate in the Mormon Church and love and support their gay children. I don't judge them for their decision; it was something I tried to do and couldn't. I know others who have kicked their gay children out of their lives in an attempt to purge their homes of the "evil influences" of the world. For those parents, I have no compassion. Unlike the Abrahamic test recorded in Genesis where Abraham was commanded to sacrifice his only son, Isaac, to prove his allegiance to God, there was no restraining angel to convince these parents of their fatal error; so they carried out their bloody sacrificial deeds under the guise of righteousness.

Back to the one-armed man. Once our children arrived, I knew that to lose either one of them would be a blow from which I would never recover fully. I finally understood the bereaved man's comment as I hadn't in my late teenage years. I saw that although life would continue in some way after the catastrophic loss of a child, it would be a much different life. I tried to imagine myself living forever in a heaven where my son was not at my side, where he was assigned to someplace less glorious because of his inborn sexual orientation. I saw myself transformed into a postmortal, female version of the one-armed man, forever existing in the hereafter, but forever bereaved. Such a fate struck me as bleakly unendurable, an endless twisting of my heart strings until they broke.

I decided to make one last-ditch effort to remain a member. Even though Jason had stopped attending church, and my own attendance had become sporadic, at our bishop's suggestion we set up an appointment with our *stake president*[191] to see if he could offer us the slightest hope that there might be some sort of reconciliation between our questions and the church's official teachings. As we entered his office inside the church building and sat down, my heart started racing, and my mouth felt dry. How many times had I sat in offices just like this over the years to receive official church callings? How many times had I been interviewed by men like our stake president so that I could qualify to attend the temple? I had received personal priesthood blessings in such rooms and had attended my father's funeral in a Mormon chapel. Our children had been confirmed to be church members in a building just like this. The memories that had once been so sweet had soured, leaving behind a taste of bitterness. I grieved the loss of the spiritual nourishment that my church membership had provided for decades.

I needed this leader to understand how completely we loved Eric and how deeply we had been wounded by the church's insistence that to be gay was to be sinful. I wanted him to acknowledge even a portion of our pain and show some compassion towards our child. At the last minute, I decided to bring along a picture of our curly-haired, beautiful baby boy, taken when he was about a year old. He was perched on a kitchen chair in his diaper, his plump, dimpled hands holding onto the back of the chair and his mouth opened in a happy grin to reveal several baby teeth. I wanted to emphasize a point: "I want you to know who we are talking about," I told the stake president while we looked at the picture together. "He's not a statistic or an abomination. He's our beloved son."

After we had conversed for a while about the church's stance on same-sex orientation, I asked the leader, "What should we do? Can you give us any hope?"

Our stake president leaned towards us, his eyes locked on ours. "I know what you need to do, but I don't think you're ready to hear it," he said in a somber tone.

My stomach dropped. Almost despite myself, I asked, "What is it?"

Then, while staring at the picture of our infant son, he solemnly proclaimed, "No unclean thing can dwell in the kingdom of God." This is a well-known scripture that occurs throughout both the Bible and the Book of Mormon (1 Nephi 10:21).

I felt like I was going to throw up. What? I thought. Was this really the advice that he was going to give us? To tell us that our son was unclean? To tell us that he was not worthy of divine love? How could this resolve anything? "So, how does this help us?" I asked.

"You must know that unless your son repents of his sins and returns to God with full purpose of heart, he does not qualify to live with God again in the hereafter," he said, his brows knit together into a straight line above his piercing, gray eyes. "As his parents, surely *you* can help him learn that better than anybody else can."

Something shifted inside me. Throughout our adjustment period of coming to terms with what it meant to have a gay son while also being active members of the Mormon Church, there had remained a tiny breathing space that I hoped I could hold onto, something that would help me reconcile the unreconcilable. As his words sank in, I realized that the space had disappeared and that nothing I could do would ever bring it back. Because of years of conditioning that I must always respect my church leaders, I carefully held my face in a neutral expression. But on the inside, I was screaming: Should we throw him out now since he is unclean, or should we wait for

God to do that in the hereafter?

    As Jason and I left and walked back to our car, he said, "I'm completely done with this church." I said nothing aloud, but the exquisite torture of considering what my religion had told me about my son's eternal future had been suffocating me for over two years. I knew that I had traveled as far as I could on this particular path if I wanted to remain psychologically healthy. I could find no way to reconcile the church's teachings with the reality of my son's life; I could find no compassion in its doctrine where I thought it was needed most. Instead, I had found only despair. After studying, praying, and searching endlessly, I finally had my answer. It was time to leave the faith of my fathers behind.

CHAPTER 20

Dear Bishop

I wanted to mail a letter of explanation to our bishop before I stopped attending our local ward. Bishops are the highest-ranking male leaders in each individual church unit; they are lay persons who have extraordinary responsibilities and burdens placed upon them. In addition to advising members whenever they have problems or questions, bishops keep the local ward functioning and running smoothly by delegating many callings, or unpaid church jobs, to other church members. They do all of this in their "spare time," since their church obligations are performed in addition to their regular career and family duties. Both Jason and I had worked in various capacities with our bishop and had come to know him well. We had found him to be an exemplary, honorable man, and we didn't desire to cause him any pain. I sat down at my computer and composed a letter, which I read to Jason before I sent it.

"October 29, 2011

"Dear Bishop:

"I will be taking a break from church indefinitely. You may see me on occasion, but most likely not very often. Therefore, I am asking to be released from my choir pianist, visiting teacher supervisor, and *visiting teacher* callings.[192]

"Jason and I both appreciate the time you have spent talking to us about Eric. However, after two years of trying to make sense of this situation, of twisting it every way that it could conceivably be twisted, we can find no answers in the

Mormon Church that give us any peace or comfort. We don't dislike the rank-and-file members—many are some of the finest people we've ever known. It's the doctrine that offends us—the supposition that *we alone* know what the next world holds. I find it impossible to neatly categorize people as either 'saints' or 'sinners.' I've always believed there were gray areas in the gospel—things that don't neatly fit into an oversimplified dichotomy. Despite my questions over the years, however, I have managed to go forward with faith based upon the things that have made me happy and that I believed would help my family.

"Jason and I have invested our entire life into our Mormon faith. We have served in callings that demanded many hours of time, taught church lessons, traveled to perform temple ceremonies in faraway locations, helped run the Boy Scouts program, organized compassionate service for sick neighbors and new mothers, packed and unpacked boxes for dozens of families moving into or out of various wards, and sung and played piano in the church choir. None of this makes us special or different; indeed, nearly all members give as much time as we did. We devoted ourselves to building a beautiful foundation for our family, a foundation that we believed nothing could shatter.

"Now, however, I face the terrible irony that the very hope I have relied upon for years has turned out to be treacherous. As a gay man, my son has no place in the church. He has been marginalized in the most extreme manner. While the church claims they love him, they have let him know beyond any doubt that his inherent orientation is perverse and will cause him to be damned. As my son has been marginalized —kicked off even the back row, so to speak—I have been marginalized, also. My life's work no longer amounts to anything according to the standard Mormon view. According to official church doctrine, my family has been shattered for eternity, left hanging on to the tenuously thin thread of hoping that Eric 'changes his ways.' I now understand that there are some things that faith can't change, things that are inborn and absolutely unchangeable. I *do* believe that a gay man might find it possible to suppress his natural desires, but I *don't* believe that he could ever find true happiness by doing so. It would be like living half a life—a lonely, dreary existence—without love, without emotional and sexual companionship, without family. What kind of parents would wish that upon their child?

"As I've watched Eric's progress on this journey, I have often thought how nice it would have been if he'd had a bench at church to sit on—with his gayness intact, and with his partner at his side. Instead, we've heard repetitive warnings of no exaltation, no eternal family, no hope. Losing my religious compass after fifty years has been excruciating. Losing my son would be unbearable. Eric is a good person, as you know. He has a good heart, a good soul. He doesn't try to hurt others, he feels their pain, he's smart, funny, caring—in short, an excellent son. But I can't keep attending a church that tells me that none of this matters—that he's somehow second class in God's eyes.

"I don't expect others to understand this, and I don't blame them for their ignorance. Nobody can fully understand this until it happens to them. The worst thing has been losing God in the process. At first I lost my trust in Him—I couldn't pray to a heavenly being whom I envisioned as a stern, heartless personage—one who pointed his finger in judgment at my son. Now I find myself deconstructing even further: Why would such a Being be necessary at all? For me, God has begun to morph into a cardboard character—a prop created to scare little children and later adults into behaving properly.

"I can't get through the next thirty years of my life hearing the unintentionally heartrending comments made at church. During one of the last relief society meetings that I attended, Sister Hunter[193] had created a paper chain made of multiple links. While holding the chain up in front of the class, she tore one of the links, and the chain broke in half. 'This is what will happen to our eternal families if even one link is broken,' she said. 'One broken link destroys everything.'

"I have respected Sister Hunter for years and know that her intention was not to hurt anyone. I also understand the fear that motivated her statements and that drives Mormons to make Herculean efforts to reclaim the 'lost sheep' in their families. But at that moment, I knew there was no way to ever reforge the broken link in our family. Specifically, there was no way to remake our son into something he wasn't and never would be—a straight man. *Nor did I want to remake him.* I thought he was perfect with all of his flaws and gifts, just like the rest of us. I got up that Sunday and quietly exited the meeting, realizing that once a seismic shift of belief occurs, you really can't go home again. I'm still not sure where my new spiritual home might be, but I know that it will not be inside a Mormon chapel.

"The exterior trappings of the church have never mattered much to me—now they mean nothing at all. I don't care about the fellowshipping events, training meetings, dinners, statistics, buildings, missionary farewells, conference talks, or any of it. Once you strip away all of the exterior structure, there's only *one thing left*—faith that God and Jesus Christ truly *did* speak to Joseph Smith and command him to organize a new church. Since I no longer believe that to be true, nothing that the church provides matters.

"Since my son has become a voiceless, disenfranchised person, cast off by the very church that once embraced him, I, too, have lost my voice. I can no longer be my authentic, true self in the congregation. Every question must be hidden, and every anguish must be silenced. It would be 'unseemly' to disturb the body of Christ by making my torment public; and quite truthfully, I can understand why most members would rather not hear about such things. They are struggling with their own difficult challenges and are hoping to find respite during their Sunday worship services; I am not self-centered enough to believe that my problems necessitate any more attention than theirs do. But the dissonance between my inner turmoil and my inability to honestly express it to the friends I have known for years at church is exhausting and terrible.

"My goal in distancing myself from the church is to try and find the peace that has completely eluded me for the last two years—two years during which I attended church, paid my tithing, attended the temple (for the first year), prayed nonstop, tormented myself, wept, paced the floor at night, talked to Mormon family counselors, talked to you, to the stake president, and to my husband. All to no avail. I cannot find the peace I seek within the Mormon Church. This is not a journey I ever anticipated taking, yet I find myself in the middle of it.

"Both Jason and I continue to wish you and your family the best in the future. In no way have you personally offended us, and we still consider you to be our neighbor.
"Sincerely,
Sister Taylor"

CHAPTER 21

Going to Hell in a Handbasket

And with that, Jason and I were both physically out of the church. However, cauterizing all the emotional wounds that were left would take me several more years and would require new ways of viewing the world. Jason was able to process the transition out more quickly, perhaps because he was an introvert who had never really enjoyed being part of an ecclesiastical community that promoted such rigorous religious and social obligations. I, on the other hand, missed the sense of community. The church had been a constant in my life, and despite the many questions I had always had, I felt an aching hole in the center of my chest.

Losing the religious foundation of my life in my fifties was akin to waking up on the edge of a precipice: vast darkness loomed ahead, and unplumbed depths gaped before me. I stood over that empty space on one leg—my arms waving as I tried to balance myself, and my other leg flailing in the air for the footpath that had disappeared before I could step onto it. Vertigo set in. The predictable path was gone, the one with the footprints of nearly all of my relatives and friends pointing in the same direction. The rail I had been holding onto for support vanished. I berated myself for imagining that it was ever there.

There was a nightmarish quality to the vertigo: a fun house-mirror derangement of everything. Foundational beliefs disintegrated and blew away like grains of sand. The landscape around me was transforming into something terrifying and new—or perhaps even nothingness. Into this blankness I stepped, not knowing if my feet would ever reach the ground again, or if I would tumble headlong into this newly opened rabbit hole, forever falling and forever dreading what might lie beneath.

This sort of free fall is so disorienting that it is almost impossible to explain it to anyone who has not experienced it. Imagine standing in front of a picture window looking out at a beautiful and familiar landscape with gently rounded hills undulating in waves of green beneath a clear blue sky. Leafy treetops wave in a cool, comfortable breeze. Now blink and look again. This time, around the edges of the landscape, there is an odd distortion, a pixilation of sorts. Instead of green hills, there are now individual dots that merely simulate the appearance of hills. The pixilation spreads until everything dissolves into random chaos. Life itself is unraveling, and that realization delivers a crushing blow. This is a personal hell that I wouldn't wish upon my worst enemy.

What happens when lifelong faith is lost? Old, familiar ways of thinking disappear. Parachutes don't open, wings are broken, and everything goes tumbling downward into pandemonium. I knew how Humpty Dumpty felt: "All the King's horses and all the King's men couldn't put Humpty together again." His perch of safety gone, he cracked into bits and pieces and never regained his equilibrium. The sense of loss is palpable, akin to a death: grief must be processed, and mourning must take place.

In Mormonism, once you're in, you're usually in to stay. Being a Mormon is much like stumbling into the "Hotel California" of the Eagles' fame: "You can check out any time you'd like, but you can never leave." I held on to the hope commonly expressed in post-Mormon circles that things would get better. Oftentimes, it was the only thing that got me through each day.

One day as I reflected on the unexpected changes in my life, I remembered some of my mom's pet expressions. Our mother was a very loving parent, but raising kids is never easy. When she said, "I've just about had it up to here with you kids!" while raising her flattened palm up to the top of her hairline, we knew we needed to make ourselves scarce. Other times she told us, "I'm at the end of my rope!" But sometimes, "You're going to hell in a handbasket!" came out of her mouth. "Hell" was a serious swear word back in Farmington, Utah, in the 1960s and '70s. Even though my siblings and I found it somewhat amusing when our mom swore, we knew things were grim if she did. I interpreted "going to hell in a handbasket" to mean that a person was happily and stupidly traipsing his or her way toward certain doom. I wondered what it would feel like to wake up with the flames of hell singeing my flesh after falling asleep in a nice, cozy handbasket, perhaps covered with a cheery, red-and-white-checkered dishcloth. Despite my adult cynicism about such dire imagery, this idea must have wormed its way into my subconscious because I sometimes worried that I might have done something serious enough to be thrust to hell. As soon as I tried to convince myself I hadn't, the thought came that maybe by doubting my sins, I was committing the biggest sin of all.

After writing the letter to my bishop, I had tossed and turned for months on end, trying to solve a divine riddle where even though the Mormon God was no longer trustworthy, I could still find someone or something to take his place. The various possibilities twirled in my mind until I was spiritually, emotionally, and physically exhausted. Jason knew I was depressed, but he did not know the dangerous extent to which it had progressed. Life had lost its savor. Days marked only the passage of time, nights were a torment. I couldn't sleep or find any escape from the drill bit that was boring into my heart.

I woke up in the middle of one particular night and experienced a moment of panic as I thought I saw the molecules of all of the solid objects in my bedroom dissolving into meaningless swirls. My sanity was restored when I realized that what I was seeing was simply a psychological manifestation of the fact that my worldview had crumbled, and I had nothing to take its place. I got up and started walking in circles in our kitchen, talking quietly to myself, trying to find some way out of the intractable mess I was in. "I need something bigger than myself," I said to no one in particular. I paced and considered. I had always thought the idea of a physical hell was an outdated remnant of mankind's superstitious heritage. The idea of burning in actual flames seemed the equivalent of the Greek mythological belief in Hades, in which a demonic boatman ferried his passengers along the River Styx to a place of literal torment in the underworld.

But hell as a mental condition seemed more likely and, ultimately, more terrifying. I could imagine what it would feel like to "burn" in remorse for eternity, twisting in tortured speculation about my failings. The acid of self-reflection would perhaps burn away the impurities that had clung to my earthly vessel, smoothing out the bumps and ridges of my imperfections. But what if one of those imperfections was my love for my son? Was I expected to remove him from my heart, to cast him off like an inconvenient bit of biological refuse? I knew that some Mormons believed that casting off unfaithful family members might be one of the sacrifices that God's purified people would be called upon to make. But I knew that I never could commit myself to such a brutal course of action.

Mormons believe in a detailed afterlife that is directly related to the degree of faithfulness they have maintained throughout their mortal lives. To believers, the *three degrees of glory*[194] are not symbolic but are instead distinct entities with specific entrance requirements. To enter the highest degree of Mormon heaven, or the "celestial kingdom," after being baptized and confirmed as official members, people must continue in faithful observance throughout their lives and show that dedication by achieving certain milestones: having their marriage sealed in one of the Mormon temples, paying a 10 percent tithe on their income, and serving others in whatever capacity the Mormon Church needs. Those who somehow don't qualify for the celestial kingdom will be consigned to a lesser kingdom, either the "terrestrial" or "telestial" kingdoms. The *terrestrial* kingdom is for those who were "honorable men of the earth, who were blinded by the craftiness of men" (D&C 76:75). Church members who have lost their testimony of Jesus will be assigned here. The lowest kingdom, the telestial kingdom, is reserved for those who never accepted Jesus or were liars, adulterers, and murderers. The lower kingdoms are places where people possess a certain degree of happiness but spend eternity living without their families (Doctrine and Covenants 76).

In addition, there is another, more awful place called "outer darkness," which is rarely spoken of, where the souls of those who have denied Jesus Christ after the Father has personally revealed Him to them will dwell eternally. According to Mormon scripture, the "torments" of this place are so horrible, so soul-wrenching, that only those who are consigned to these midnight regions for all eternity will understand what they have lost (D&C, 109, 133). There, even the light of Christ cannot shine, and the inhabitants will be psychologically tortured with no relief.

I knew that some would believe that since I had chosen my son over they church, I would, at the very least, be excluding myself from the celestial kingdom. And since I no longer believed in the Mormon truth claims, most members would conclude that I was likely condemning myself to an afterlife in which I would serve a period of time in hell before being redeemed to reside in one of the two lower kingdoms. Having experienced some severe bouts of anxiety at different times throughout my life, I imagined that this sort of punishment would be the equivalent of an eternal panic attack. Even the thought of it sent me spiraling into despair. In my mind at that time, the stakes were incredibly high, and the consequences were real.

Reflecting on all of this the night I had woken up, I

muttered to myself and walked back and forth for hours. I was hollowed out at the core; my eyes felt like I'd been rubbing sand into them. Then, shortly before dawn, I had an epiphany: using the unbending formulas of "Thou Shalts" and "Thou Shalt Nots," I had never believed myself to be righteous enough. Then came another, deeply disturbing insight. I realized that the religious mold that I had been poured into as a child had always been shaped by a large element of superstition and fear. A deeply buried anger bubbled to the surface. Had I really spent five decades of my life carefully following the detailed proscriptions of my church so that I could earn my way into heaven? In a nonreligious context, people who claim to be spokespersons for an unseen alien presence are placed in a straitjacket and prescribed a lifelong course of antipsychotics. But when the unseen alien becomes an unseen god, people are suddenly willing to listen, convert, and pay for the privilege. My lifelong religious heritage suddenly felt like a cage.

I knew that I must cease to fear. But how? I decided to openly challenge everything I had ever believed. In doing so, I knew that I was playing the highest-stakes game of my life. But I could see no other way to finally be completely honest with myself and whichever supreme being, if any, watched over my mortal journey. Tears pooled in my eyes, which were red-rimmed with exhaustion. I wondered if I had arrived at the pivotal point long since foretold by years of church indoctrination and if my next words might seal my doom. Since the only way forward was to risk everything, I stood in my kitchen and literally shook my fist at the heavens. "Damn you, God! Do you hear me? *Damn* you!" My rage chased away my fear. "What kind of parent throws her *child* away? No mother in her right mind would throw her child away! My boy —" I paused and gasped because the tears pouring down my face made it difficult to breathe "—my *boy*—comes before *you* and any fucking church on the entire fucking planet! I'm done living a life based upon fear, so this is your chance. Go ahead and smite me, but I will *never* change my mind!" I screamed several more F-words toward the ceiling just for good measure —I wanted to make sure my message was received loud and clear.

I waited, shaking with the intensity of my emotions. I was throwing out over fifty years of familial and social conditioning. A passage from Lewis Carroll's *Alice's Adventures in Wonderland* suddenly popped into my mind. I had read the Alice books repeatedly as a child, fascinated by the topsy-turvy adventures of a mildly disobedient girl; I was jealous of her fantastic journeys to a land where anything and everything could happen. However, there was always something a bit menacing about Alice's wanderings in Wonderland, an inescapable foreboding that something dangerous lurked at the periphery. The following passage occurs near the beginning of the book, shortly after Alice has found a bottle labeled "Drink Me" and gulps it down. As the potion in the bottle takes effect, she finds herself rapidly shrinking, and she begins to worry: "She felt a little nervous about this; 'for it might end, you know,' said Alice to herself, 'in my going out altogether, like a candle. I wonder what I should be like then?' And she tried to fancy what the flame of a candle looks like after the candle is blown out, for she could not remember ever having seen such a thing."[195] I, too, had wondered what it would feel like to disappear "altogether" and had resisted the terror that crept into my soul whenever I pondered the idea. I'll never do anything as stupid as Alice did, I had told myself during my childhood, so I'll be safe. Yet here I was a grown adult, risking more than my physical body: I was risking my soul.

I waited.

Then I waited a little bit longer.

Nothing happened. No answering thunderbolt from heaven—not that I really expected one. No choking fear seized me, no malevolent presence overpowered me; instead, there was only a sense of coming home to some long-buried, essential truth. I had finally declared where my ultimate loyalties lay. In that instant, I chose love over dogma and my son over religious expectations. The spiritual bedrock of my life was crumbling—the ground tilting at a dizzying angle—and I wondered how far I would fall as I slid down the ruins of my former worldview. But I was certain of one thing—I knew that unconditional love for my son had always been the *right choice*—the only choice I could ever have lived with.

CHAPTER 22

Leaving 101

It used to be almost unheard of for an older couple to leave the Mormon Church. Now, even lifelong members are leaving. When my husband and I stopped participating nearly thirteen years ago, we had been members for over fifty years. Jason had served a proselyting mission for two years overseas, after which we met at Brigham Young University (the church's official university that is supported, in part, by members' tithing donations). We were married in the Salt Lake Temple, attended weekly meetings with our children, and paid 10 percent of our income to the church for thirty years. We served in numerous unpaid church jobs, which didn't stand out as unusual—almost everyone we knew devoted the same, if not more, energy and fervor to building up the kingdom of God here on the earth.

The only thing that made us stand out was our exit. Many people find it nearly impossible to extricate themselves from something as deeply woven into their existence as Mormonism. It is a violent uprooting of something from the inner core of one's soul: it is devastating and destabilizing in every conceivable way. Hans Mattsson's description of his own trauma in leaving the church mirrored my own: "I felt like I had an earthquake under my feet. Everything I'd been taught, everything I'd been proud to preach about and witness about just crumbled under my feet. It was such a terrible psychological and nearly physical disturbance."[196] I understand why most members never even consider leaving. I had never imagined myself leaving, either. It was more than a rejection of my religion: it was a rejection of my heritage, my tribe, and my identity. But my husband and I had no choice. We had to save our boy.

Luckily, Jason and I ended up agreeing about our need to exit the church. I've heard multiple stories about couples divorcing after one of them began to doubt the church's truth claims. I've been very fortunate to have been married to somebody with whom I could openly and honestly discuss my questions.

That doesn't mean that it was easy to break the news to our families. Everybody knows how to join the church, either by being born into it or by converting. There are no manuals on how to leave, however. I've read accounts of disaffected members sending letters or group emails to their entire extended family telling them why they left the church and about all of the issues that led to their exit. Jason and I discarded that method as unworkable for us—it seemed too inflammatory. I read about others who held big family meetings and announced their decision in person. Again, that seemed like a surefire method for provoking a heated argument. Some delayed saying anything at all and just waited for their families to notice that something was different. Although our eventual goal was to be upfront with our families, we decided not to announce anything at first. We wanted more time to process on our own what it meant to be non-Mormon before we tried to explain it to anybody else.

I struggled intensely with this dilemma for another full year. It began to take a toll on my mental and physical health. I came down with a severe case of mononucleosis and was ill for six months. My family doctor told me to quit my teaching job and focus on getting better. I told him that we had a house payment to make and that I couldn't afford to quit. As a compromise, after taking two weeks of sick leave, I spoke to my principal about taking off one day in the middle of the week for three months so I could rest. She agreed and also allowed me to skip the numerous faculty meetings and trainings that were usually mandatory.

And still, I was living in dread of the moment when I would have to break the truth to my family. Finally, with the help of a counselor, I was able to see that my lack of authenticity would probably hurt them more than my honesty would. So, one at a time, on the phone, I told my sisters, my brother, and my mother. My father had passed away years ago, and I often wondered how he would have responded. I knew that he never would have stopped loving his gay grandson or my husband and me; both he and my mother were remarkably tolerant and easy going, especially considering the era they grew up in. But I wondered how he would have felt about our decision to leave the church ourselves.

My mother was understanding but completely heartbroken. She continued to attend the temple weekly and place all of our names on the *temple prayer rolls*,[197] hoping that we would somehow return to the believing fold. I worried about the toll that our exit was taking on her, but how do you explain to your aging mother that to climb back into the dismantled box of belief is impossible? That it would be, in fact, like climbing back into a coffin from which you have finally broken free? The only reason she stopped worrying about our salvation was that Alzheimer's eventually stole her memory, the one and only kindness ever to be granted from such a devastating disease.

The hardest person to tell was our daughter, Leah. She had been married in the Bountiful, Utah, temple only three months before her brother came out, and the last thing I ever wanted to do was to hurt her in any way. I felt like I was being squeezed between a vise grip: a temple-married daughter on the one side, and a gay son on the other. Now I found that trying to balance these incongruous realities was making me sick. As a mother I had always striven to be the one who kept the family happy and harmonious. How could I ever do that again?

I finally told Leah that we no longer believed in the

church's truth claims, and at first it was very difficult for her. Her husband told us that our news had greatly upset her and asked us not to speak to her about the church for the foreseeable future. After receiving his message, I threw myself on my couch and sobbed without restraint. I had hurt my daughter! She had never harmed anyone and was one of the most sincere, unpretentious people I had ever known. How could I live with that?

However, about a year later, both Leah and her husband left the church as well. I felt a great sense of relief at being united as a family in our newly evolving belief systems. One day I asked her what it had been like for her to leave. Had she felt sad? Lost? Angry? Her answer made me think that at least some of the turmoil I had gone through was worth it. "Actually, Mom, after the first shock wore off, it wasn't too bad for us," she said. "After watching you and Dad figure this thing out, we felt like you had already done most of the work for us." I was thrilled that our journey had made hers easier, but I feel echoes of sadness when I think of how disappointed some of our family members were and still are.

Jason, meanwhile, eventually told his elderly, widowed mother that he was no longer a believer. Despite being a lifelong member who had served in countless church callings, she had always held a grudge against the church's founder, Joseph Smith, because of his practice of polygamy. Both Jason and I had heard her express her disgust with polygamy on more than one occasion. But our leaving upset her because she feared that we were risking our salvation by not attending church each Sunday and taking the sacrament. Jason tried to explain to her why he didn't think that mattered, but she refused to listen.

After her death a few years later, one of Jason's older sisters pulled him aside the day after the funeral when the siblings had met to divide their mother's material possessions. They both climbed into the front seat of our car and shut the door so they could talk in private. I was close enough to see them animatedly discussing something. Although I couldn't hear anything, I could see by their facial expressions and hand gestures that they were both upset.

Jason told me afterwards that his sister had accused him of breaking their mother's heart. She told him that their mother had often cried about his disaffection from the church. Jason tried to explain to her that he had never wanted to hurt their mom, but his sister was not convinced.

"Well, I never thought that you, of all people, would do this to our family," his sister continued. "You went on a mission for the church! How could you do this?"

"I've done nothing to you. I've only done what I felt was necessary to protect my integrity and my son's mental health." The conversation ended when he got out of the car and slammed the door. They have never spoken again.

Eventually, of course, our family and closest friends found out about our exit from the church, not because we announced it, but because some of our behaviors changed. We no longer attended church or paid tithing. Getting our Sundays back essentially doubled our free time on the weekends, and we reveled in the freedom of sleeping in and not spending the day attending multiple meetings dressed in suitcoats and ties or dresses and nylons. We started drinking coffee. After a few years, I occasionally wore sleeveless tops and shorts in the summer, which were still very modest compared to the world's standards. I went out of my way not to be confrontational or to discuss religion unless somebody else asked me a pointed question. I knew how offensive it was when others tried to convince me that I was wrong, so I decided never to do the same thing to them.

Despite our taking care, however, we did lose some friends, mostly church friends with whom the church had been our only connection. One woman whom I had considered a good friend severed all contact with me shortly after learning about our son. She sent me a message on Facebook asking why I felt compelled to support Eric while he "played the victim card." I wrote her a long, angry letter in which I explained that being a gay Mormon had nearly destroyed our son's life and that by supporting him, we were not coddling him, but instead were fulfilling our parental duties. I read the letter to Jason. Then on his suggestion, I ripped it up and never sent it.

I'm sure there are some acquaintances who don't know that I've left the church because in most ways, I still look and act like a Mormon. I don't drink or smoke. I can fluently speak "Mormonese," and do so on occasion when the situation calls for it, not to be deceptive, but in order to join in the religious conversations that pop up constantly, especially in the state of Utah. If two or more Mormons are conversing, the church will inevitably come up: "How was church last week?" "Has your son received his mission call yet?" "I heard that you got a new calling!" "Can you help out with the young women's activity next week?" "Sister Davis needs a ride to the temple, and we were hoping you could help her." "Could you help take a meal to Sister Jones? Did you know she just had her baby?" Of course, there's nothing wrong with these types of conversions, but to a non-Mormon or post-Mormon, they can be awkward.

During the most turbulent transition period as I was leaving the church, I discovered Peter Berger's book, *The Heretical Imperative*. He argues that one must turn to "experience as the ground of all religious affirmations—one's own experiences, to whatever extent this is possible, and the experiences embodied in a particular range of traditions. This range may take the width and breadth that one chooses."[198] He continues:

> Implied in this option is a deliberately empirical attitude, a weighing and assessing frame of mind —not necessarily cool and dispassionate, but unwilling to impose closure on the quest for religious truth by invoking any authority whatever —not the authority of this or that traditional . . .

[belief], but also not the authority of modern thought or consciousness. The advantage of this option is its open-mindedness and the freshness that usually comes from a nonauthoritarian approach to questions of truth. The disadvantage, needless to say, is that open-mindedness tends to be linked to open-endedness, and this frustrates the deep religious hunger for certainty.[199]

Berger advocates, and I have since embraced, the turning away from outside authorities and the turning towards personal experience as the focus of religious thought. Ironically, members believe that Joseph Smith himself followed this same method when establishing a new church. What is lauded and celebrated in his case, however, is now condemned and feared in the modern church-member's case. I understand that the methods I choose to ascertain truth may not be to another's liking, and I allow them the freedom to choose their own methods. Likewise, I ask that they make no claims of superiority for their own methods over mine. For any traveler, there are no guarantees of arriving at the hoped-upon location with any sort of "certainty."[200]

After many long discussions about what the new philosophical foundation of our lives might be, Jason and I decided to seek goodness and truth by first focusing on the lessons we had gleaned from decades of living. This didn't mean we would arrogantly discard the wisdom of the ages from those who had gone before us and had passed down their own philosophies. Rather, we would seek wisdom wherever we found it, without being controlled or condemned by any exterior force. I, especially, would no longer listen to any outside authority who claimed to know more about my spiritual progress than I did myself. As a Mormon woman who had always been taught to "heed the counsel of the priesthood," I found a great sense of freedom in throwing off the bands that had restricted me and against which I had chafed throughout my entire life.

This *didn't* mean, however, that we needed to throw out everything from Mormonism. One of the Mormon teachings that we embraced in our youth has remained highly relevant, which is the critical importance of being "free to choose [and] act" (2 Nephi 2:27), which is often referred to as *"free agency"* by Mormons. Another concept that has always rung true to both of us is the inevitable "opposition in all things" that arises whenever people are attempting to accomplish something important or good in their life (2 Nephi 2:11).

In addition, we have found things of worth in the writings of the Greek and Roman Stoics with their emphasis on wisdom, courage, and temperance. Focusing on the "living in the moment" techniques of many modern meditative practices has also helped me, in particular, find a coherent life philosophy. Likewise, although neither Jason nor I desire to join any organized religion ever again, I have personally found many of Pope Francis's statements to be enlightening and consoling. Shortly after assuming the papacy in 2013, he made the following statement: "I prefer a church which is bruised, hurting and dirty because it has been out on the streets, rather than a church which is unhealthy from being confined and from clinging to its own security." His call to focus on mercy instead of authoritarian "obsessions and procedures" offers a healthy antidote to the practices of many orthodox religions, including his own.[201]

Eventually, we boiled our religious creed down to a single statement: "Do no harm." As we have discussed this through the years, we have decided that "Do no harm" is a better guide than "Do good." Doing "good" can imply a busybody mentality, or that the do-gooder has more knowledge or righteousness than the beneficiary. Thus, in doing "good," I might merely be trying to force my conclusions on another person under the guise of love and concern. "Do no harm" is cleaner and safer. It implies that a person can move forward with his or her own life's quest, helping others if needed, but without attempting to dominate or influence them.

For both of us, any religious traditions that invoke fear of punishment for questioning are no longer acceptable. I cannot believe that a benevolent creator, prime mover, or even the enigmatic universe itself would ever embrace such pettiness. Even if the final destination is ultimately unknowable, the contradiction inherent in a supposedly all-knowing, all-seeing supernatural (or natural) force that is simultaneously spiteful and ungenerous towards humankind's foibles stretches the limits of plausibility to the point of absurdity.

CHAPTER 23

Out of the Frying Pan

Jason and I had finally reached a place of balance: we knew what we believed and felt good about our decision to leave the church. Our families knew what we believed and had accepted it for the most part. Two years passed in relative peace. Then one day, I got a phone call from Eric's partner, Brian. They had been living together for about four years. "Eric and I need to come meet with you and Jason," he said. He sounded out of breath. "We need to discuss something important with you." I wondered why Brian was telling me this instead of Eric, but I didn't pry for details at that point. Jason and I agreed to meet with them the next day.

When they arrived at our house, it was evident something was wrong. Brian's eyes were red-rimmed as if he had been crying, and Eric slumped into our house with his head hanging down. Brian was pacing around the living room rapidly and waving his hands while explaining that Eric had something to tell us.

My husband and I sat there clueless as to what was going on. After a few false starts, Eric finally blurted out, "I've been taking pain pills."

At first I thought he was telling me that he had some sort of physical ailment that was requiring him to take the pills. "Are you sick?" I asked. "What's going on with your health?"

Eric let out a big sigh. "No, Mom. I'm taking them because they have opioids in them—you know, to get high." A complete silence blanketed the room as the four of us sat lost in our private thoughts.

"How—how did you get them?" Jason asked.

Eric had a hard time maintaining eye contact. "I started taking them from you, Dad. You know, those pills you got for your kidney stones." My husband had been to the emergency room over a dozen times in ten years for kidney stones, requiring surgery twice and an overnight stay at the hospital once. The doctors had given him a prescription for Percocet so that he could take a pill at home the minute another kidney stone started passing. Then Jason and I would climb into the car and I would race to the emergency room as he doubled over in agony in the passenger side of the car, yelling for me to go faster. More than once I watched him writhe on the floor in the emergency waiting room, crying and vomiting into a garbage can as he waited for somebody to take him back and hook him up to a morphine drip. I knew that the agony my very private husband experienced during these episodes must have been unbearable for him to come so completely undone in public.

I, myself, had taken some OxyContin several years earlier when I shattered my left leg into multiple pieces and broke my tibial plateau during a skiing accident. My pain levels had been unbearable for the first few days in the hospital, and I had thrashed back and forth on my bed while I incoherently sobbed and pleaded for help. Because of the severe nature of my injury, which necessitated a two-week hospital stay and two surgeries to implant metal rods and thirteen screws into my leg, I was given a prescription. The doctors feared that I might not be able to heal properly without some strong pain relief, so they sent me home with both OxyContin and morphine tablets. This was just before health care professionals were realizing how dangerously addictive OxyContin was. As a middle-aged Mormon mom, I was scrupulously careful to never take more medication than I had been prescribed. The pills helped me cope during the beginning of my lengthy and painful recovery, which began with three months in a wheelchair with no weight-bearing, and slowly progressed over eighteen months (and two additional surgeries) to walking with a walker, then crutches, then a cane, and then finally on my own.

Although I had followed all of my doctor's orders, including stopping both medications about eight weeks into my recovery, the moment I stopped taking the pills, everything crashed. All of the color seemed to have drained out of the world, and I felt like a five thousand pound chain was hanging around my neck. I dragged myself through my days listlessly, not caring whether I bathed or brushed my teeth or spoke to any of my family members. I couldn't sleep at night and noticed myself becoming agitated. After about two weeks of total bleakness, I noticed myself coming back to the world slowly but surely. It didn't take me long to realize that I had become dependent upon OxyContin and morphine despite following all medical instructions explicitly. I shared my insights with my family and flushed the thirty or so remaining pills that I had down the toilet with my teenage daughter supervising.

Both Jason and I knew how addictive these pills could be, and we were terrified for Eric. Brian started to cry in the middle of the conversation, and I found myself comforting both him and Eric. "It's so hard," Brian choked out. "I thought I knew everything about addiction because of my own recovery process, but it's different when you're watching somebody you love do it."

After discussing all of the options for a couple of hours, we decided that Eric would continue to live with Brian with the understanding that Brian would be monitoring Eric's behavior closely and would report to us if he suspected that Eric was abusing pills again. Eric was shamefaced and crestfallen. There was no doubt in our minds that he felt bad for what he had done; our only question was whether he would be able to maintain that attitude once the cravings started up.

Things that we had witnessed over the past two years now started to make more sense. Eric had started out excited to attend college classes after receiving a two-year academic scholarship to a state university. Then slowly, inexplicably, he started skipping classes and getting barely passing grades. His father and I encouraged him repeatedly not to give up on his education. We couldn't figure how a high school honor graduate who had always found school "easy" was now flunking out. We had wondered if he was depressed. We took him to counselors and discussed the situation endlessly. But now we knew—Eric's opioid use had derailed his life. We were hopeful that the worst was over.

For another few weeks things seemed to be going well, but then Brian phoned us. "Eric's using again," he said. He had caught Eric smoking heroin this time instead of using pain pills. We agreed that Eric would come home to live with us for a few weeks while we assessed the situation.

I called one of my lifelong friends who is the director of one of the county mental health centers in Utah. I told her everything and asked her what we should do. "I know this will sound weird," she said, "but be glad he's smoking it instead of injecting it. Injecting is *way* more dangerous and deadly." I thought it was strange that smoking heroin could be viewed as the "better" option, but I tucked her comment away and decided to watch for any signs of escalating use. After a few weeks, Eric was doing better, and he told us that he had stopped for good. Brian missed him terribly and wanted him to move back in with him. We agreed but told Brian to let us know the minute something went awry. Since Brian was in recovery and knew all of the secretive ways of hiding drug use, we figured he would be much better at catching Eric doing something than we would.

What followed was about a one-year period where Eric would slip up and get caught by Brian, move in with us for a while, then move back in with Brian. Every time he promised us this would be the last time. We kept believing him, partly because we were completely terrified about what it would mean if he kept using. Despite his promises, however, his appearance had become more disheveled, and the job that he had found working as a clinical lab assistant at a medical laboratory started to be impacted, also. We talked to Eric about his behavior and told him that he was going to get fired if he kept it up. Jason and I began discussing the possibility that he was using again.

Brian answered that question when he called us again. "He's been lying the whole time! I caught him with drugs in his car. I just need a break from this." I immediately went to the phone and called our medical insurance company to confirm our coverage for drug treatment options. We had suspected it might come to this, so I had done some legwork in advance of Brian's announcement.

Silently, Jason and I drove to Brian and Eric's apartment. We knocked on the door, told Eric to pack his things, and announced that he was going to attend a twenty-eight-day, inpatient rehab in Ogden, Utah. Eric was slack-jawed and pale. His eyes were glassy, and he had problems balancing. "You can't make me." He slurred his words and seemed to have trouble keeping his eyes open.

"Oh yes we can," I said. "You have no choice at this point. Brian won't let you live here anymore, and we can't have you live with us if you're putting your life in danger." Eric grabbed some of his things and threw them into the back seat of our car. While he was doing so, I had a chance to hug Brian and tell him that I loved him. "You know you're a part of our family," I whispered to him. "I love you like a son-in-law."

"I know," he said. "I'm so sorry, I'm so sorry." I thought he was apologizing for somehow letting us down, but when I told him that there was nothing to apologize for, he said something that I still remember and that sent chills up and down my spine that day in a wave of premonition: "No, I mean I'm sorry because I know what's coming, and it won't be easy."

With Eric's permission, I called his boss at the medical lab and explained that Eric would be attending inpatient rehab. His boss didn't sound shocked and told us that he had suspected something was up. Despite that, he said that Eric had been a hard worker and had done excellent work for them before the drug use started. He promised me that as soon as Eric was done with rehab, he could get his old job back if he wanted to. I counted this as a small grace in an extremely stressful time.

About two weeks later, we drove Eric down to his first rehab. He told us that it was a big mistake because he wasn't really a serious drug user. Some small part of me believed him. "Mom, you know I can quit anytime that I want to, right?"

"I guess so," I said slowly. "So why haven't you?"

"I haven't really wanted to before now, and besides, there are tons of people who have way more serious problems than I do." He paused. "But I guess I no longer get to decide that."

"Well, you're right about that," said Jason. We parked our car next to the rehab entry; then we walked Eric to the entrance, hugged him, and told him to follow every single rule. We promised to visit him and attend every parent and group meeting that we were allowed to participate in. As we drove away, we both sighed in relief.

"I think he's going to get the help he desperately needs," I said. "I feel like he's finally safe."

"I hope so," said Jason.

What neither of us said aloud was that we were already terrified about what would happen when the four weeks were up.

CHAPTER 24

Rehab, Relapse, Repeat

During Eric's four-week rehab, parents were invited to semiweekly educational meetings and group therapy sessions for families. The first time we attended a twelve-step Alcoholics Anonymous (AA) and combined Narcotics Anonymous (NA) meeting, we sat in a circle on some folding chairs. The circle was big—at least forty people, including patients and their families. As the meeting began, each person in the circle introduced him or herself to the others in the group. It was the standard intro: "Hi, my name is Sarah, and I'm a drug addict." The group nodded in understanding.

The woman to the right of Sarah spoke: "Hi, my name is Mindy. I'm the mother of an addict." The group murmured its support. I felt myself tensing up. We obviously did *not* belong in this group; in fact, I actually felt like an imposter for attending. Our son was not really a serious drug user; he was simply a depressed, gay kid who had taken a few pills and smoked heroin a few times to help him feel better about himself. He had told me himself that he wasn't actually addicted, and I had no reason at that stage to disbelieve him. Everybody else in the room is an addict, I thought. Oh, those poor parents. I'm so glad that *our* son is different. As we sat in the circle, I heard stories of overdoses, divorces, arrests, hospitalizations, suicide attempts, and death. I was thankful that our son's problem wasn't that severe. I had been completely persuaded by the lie that he could quit any time he wanted to.

When it came my turn to speak, I said, "Hi my name

is Laura. I'm here to support my son." (I purposely and conspicuously left off the "mother of an addict" phrase.)

The group leader looked at me. He raised his eyebrows a bit, and I imagined I saw a flash of understanding in his eyes. "Welcome, Laura," he said. I smiled nervously and congratulated myself on not giving in to the peer pressure in the room.

Our son was sullen and uncommunicative during the rehab meetings. Sometimes I noticed his cheeks flushing as we entered the room and gave him a hug. "Are we embarrassing him?" I whispered to my husband. He shrugged his shoulders.

Towards the end of the four weeks, I remember attending one of the parents' meetings where the group leader talked about the reality of relapse. "Remember," he said, "relapse is part of the recovery process."

I felt disoriented. How could relapse be part of recovery? Surely that wasn't true for everybody—surely only the seriously addicted patients relapsed. I raised my hand, "Does everybody relapse?" My voice trailed off as I realized that I must have sounded like an idiot. For the first time since the whole ordeal had begun, I considered that rehab might not be the *end* of the road, but the *beginning*.

"No," he said. "Not everybody does, but for the majority, relapse is going to be something that occurs more than once in the healing process." An exit door labeled "Total Recovery" slammed shut in my mind, and in its place I saw dark paths twisting out of sight towards destinations unknown. Now, looking back, I can almost laugh at my naivete. Weren't four weeks long enough to cure an addiction? It had been long enough for Sandra Bullock to overcome alcoholism in the movie *28 Days*. I didn't understand that persons with substance abuse issues have a red-eyed, crazed monkey clinging to their back—its arms and legs grasping them tightly, its sharp teeth nibbling on their ears and neck. Despite herculean attempts to shake it off, the monkey persists in hanging on and gnawing.

A parent in the group looked directly at me and said in a dismissive tone, "You realize that drug addiction is a *progressive* illness and that it *will* get worse, don't you?" I didn't respond because I thought her comment was abrasive and rude.

I suddenly thought back to the first time I had found out our son had purchased drugs off the street. He had come to me during one of the times Brian had kicked him out and told me that he owed a drug dealer some money. He was afraid that if he didn't pay up quickly, the guy would hunt him down and hurt him. "How much do you need?" I spoke calmly even as a sense of unreality settled about me like a shroud.

"Two hundred dollars."

I was relieved that it wasn't more than that. I went and withdrew the $200 and told him that I wanted to go with him so I could protect him.

He shook his head back and forth. "That's a really bad idea, Mom. You might be putting yourself in danger." Before he drove off alone to pay the dealer, he begged me, "Don't tell Dad." I waited for him at home, pacing back and forth, jumping every time my cell phone rang. I told myself and my son that this was a one-time deal and that there was no reason to upset my husband at this point. It was the first time in our thirty-year marriage that I had purposely been deceptive with Jason about my actions. I consoled myself that I was only protecting the long-term health of our family. Somehow, I hadn't thought about that incident again until this moment.

After Eric completed rehab, he returned to live with Brian. Brian had visited him several times during his treatment and had decided to give Eric one more chance. I spoke to Brian many times about how it wasn't *his* responsibility to keep Eric clean. I told him that if he even *suspected* something he should call us immediately. Brian promised that he would. He had been to one rehab himself over a decade earlier and had never relapsed since then. I thought he could be a good role model for Eric. Trying not to get my hopes up too high, I still found myself buoyed by the thought that perhaps the worst was over. I had always been an obsessive list maker—it gave me a sense of control over the vagaries of life. If I wrote something down and checked it off, it was done—right? I was soon to learn that checking off the rehab box for somebody else did *not* guarantee success. Instead, the person who was in rehab actually needed to want to change. And that required a special kind of motivation that was impossible to delegate.

One week after Eric's discharge, he confessed to Brian that he still had some drugs hidden in our home. We, of course, had no idea that he had squirreled away some heroin "in case of emergency." We had always told him that if he kept drugs in our home, we would be forced to kick him out for good. Brian and Eric arrived at our house, and together they did a thorough search of Eric's bedroom. Brian put all of the confiscated items into a brown paper bag, and together with Jason, they discussed what would be the best way to dispose of them. They quickly decided that our family's outdoor garbage can was not a good enough location since it would be too easy for Eric to retrieve them later.

Jason drove with Eric and Brian to a gas station about ten miles away from our home. Once there, Jason took the bag and stuffed it into one of the gas station's overflowing garbage cans. He made sure to push it far below the rotting layers of food leftovers and soiled baby diapers. He told me later that the entire time they were driving he was paranoid that they'd be pulled over by a cop and arrested for having a bag of illegal drugs in their car, so he had decided to go *under* the speed limit by at least five miles per hour and to drive as if his life depended on it. We were relieved that Eric had told Brian the truth, and we felt that it boded well for his ability to stay clean after rehab.

Two weeks later, right before I was to start a new job in a different school district, our son's addiction problem took another serious turn. My cell phone rang one hot August afternoon, startling me out of a reverie. I had been sitting on the wraparound porch of our log home, enjoying the scenery, and taking some deep breaths as I contemplated starting a new school year and leaving behind all of my colleagues and friends from my old school. I glanced at my cell phone and saw Brian's number. When I answered, Brian sounded out of breath and was speaking rapidly. "I can't keep doing this," he said. "I caught him *shooting up* in our bathroom! He was doing it inside our apartment! I can't believe how stupid I've been! He's been lying to me the whole time, and I told him that if he did it again, he'd have to move out for good."

My heart dropped and started doing somersaults in my stomach. "He's already relapsed?" I was in shock. Eric had barely completed his first stint in rehab, and although they had warned us that relapse was common, somehow I still hadn't understood the hypnotic lure of heroin's power. While we had been trying to convince ourselves that our son was getting better, he still had a demon shadowing him, whispering dark, destructive thoughts.

"Yes," Brian said. "He's out in the car right now, saying he doesn't care and that he won't talk to me anymore. I took his car keys away because it's not safe for him to drive."

"OK." My mind was playing out several possible scenarios. Was this the end for them as partners? I wasn't sure how much more Brian could put up with. Would Eric be able to get back into rehab this soon? Could we keep him safe at our home? "We'll be right there."

"OK, thanks." Brian's voice sounded rough, and I realized he had started crying.

I started crying also, the tears hot on my face. I loved Brian. He was a kind, patient man, and he and Eric had been together for over four years. I had a feeling this was the end of whatever relationship stability our son had managed to cobble together throughout his descent into a substance-abuse disorder. "It's not your job to be his parent," I told him. "That's our job. We'll be right there."

I told Jason the grim news. We drove in silence to pick up our son. Jaws clenched, my husband gripped the steering wheel of the car as if he were driving a tank into a battlefield. When we arrived at their small, downtown apartment, our son was sitting silently in his car, arms folded, face ashen, eyes closed.

We got him into our car, and then my husband drove him home while I got ready to drive our son's car home. I was left for a moment with Brian. "I love you," I said, throwing my arms around him. "You are family." We hugged each other for a moment. I felt the sun shining on my back and noticed that the sky was a bright, cheerful blue. White, puffy clouds drifted lazily overhead. The incongruity of the moment made me feel like I was losing my grip on reality—a sunny day, white puffy clouds, and a dangerously ill son. I wondered if and when the world would be made whole again.

Brian, who had finished his master's degree in counseling a year earlier and was working as a rehab therapist, choked back more tears. "You know, it's one thing to counsel others about substance abuse. When it's your own life, it's very different." I waved good-bye to him and drove home, strengthening my resolve to get things straightened out this time. Apparently, we had done something wrong the first time, but this time we *would* get it right. Comforting myself with this fiction, I drove home in a somber mood.

That night while I brushed my teeth, I caught a glimpse of myself in the bathroom mirror. I drew in a quick breath. The eyes that looked back at me belonged to someone I'd never met; as I continued to stare, I noticed that the outsider's mouth resembled mine, but it had fallen. It was me, but it wasn't me. This person was visibly aging as I watched. "I'm older," I said aloud to no one. The mirror answered that I was right. I felt my spinal cord compressing as if the gravity beneath me was pulling with one hundred times its normal force, as if my body had downshifted into a lower gear. As the weight of the world pulled me into a dark void, I collapsed onto my bed and wept at the lost hope that I now feared had been delusional.

After Brian kicked Eric out, I had two weeks until my new teaching job started. I wanted to focus on being totally prepared. Instead, I spent at least four hours a day making phone calls to doctors, rehab centers, insurance companies, and psychologists. I was consumed with worry and agitated to the point of not sleeping. My husband and I both lost weight. Eating didn't appeal to us anymore—it was simply too much effort to cook anything. Eating was something that the living indulged in, and we had fallen into an upside-down world where the usual rhythms of living had ceased. A curious dichotomy developed wherein my husband and I appeared fine on the surface but were becoming increasingly dysfunctional in private. Luckily, our marriage survived this phase. We knew that private breakdowns would occur; we also knew that every ounce of patience we possessed had been used up by our playing the role of successfully coping parents. Our tempers tended to flare more often; silly things that we would have laughed at in the past sent us into irritable, moody silences, and oftentimes we had to agree to simply walk away and let each other process whatever emotion we were experiencing at the moment.

My cousin, a local attorney, told me that she knew a couple who had both become heavy drinkers after their son's drug-addiction landed him in jail. Eventually, their marriage dissolved into an acrimonious divorce, with accusations being hurled like poison-tipped darts from both parties. We wanted to be sure that didn't happen to us; we wanted our son to have a home and a family to come back to. So, we continued our role-playing dutifully, always wondering when the performance would end, and reality would reassert itself.

I called my counselor friend again and somehow managed to choke out what had happened. "My son is acting crazy! I don't even know who he is anymore!"

"It's not him," she assured me. "It's the drugs. He's still in there somewhere."

"But how do you know that? How do you know he'll come back?"

"There's no guarantee that he'll come back. But for now, at least, he's still in there." I held onto that hope as tightly as I'd ever held onto anything and waited for the day when my beautiful boy would return to himself and look at me through loving, familiar eyes unclouded by the fog of addiction. In the meantime, I gazed into the alien eyes of a stranger.

CHAPTER 25

Opioid Monster

The opioid epidemic in the United States was created and fueled by big pharmaceutical companies pumping millions of pain pills into the health market. For years, doctors were routinely given incentives to prescribe opioid products, and they were given out for everything from minor surgery to childbirth recovery. Although opioid prescription rates reached their peak in 2012,[202] opioid deaths have continued to increase, most likely due to the easy access to heroin and more recently fentanyl, a synthetic opioid that is manufactured both legally and illegally in labs around the world. Although fentanyl has legitimate uses, such as treating patients with chronic or severe pain, it is fifty times more powerful than heroin, which means that a mere two milligrams of fentanyl, or the equivalent of a few grains of salt, can be deadly.[203] In fact, out of every ten pills seized by the Drug Enforcement Agency (DEA) and tested in laboratories, seven contained a "lethal dose of fentanyl."[204] What makes fentanyl even more insidious is that it's often mixed into counterfeit pills, such as Xanax, Adderall, Oxycodone, and Percocet. Pills purchased off the streets, on social media, or from a friend could easily be contaminated, and often teens and young adults have no idea that even a single pill can be lethal. Sadly, the overdose death train won't be slowing down anytime soon.

On a personal level, opioid addiction squats like a misshapen monster, its tentacles snaking their way into previously healthy families in an attempt to destroy them. The person with a substance abuse disorder has one claustrophobic goal—obtaining the next fix—and nothing is off limits in accomplishing that goal. People will lie, steal, betray, and manipulate. And even after they do it repeatedly, family members will still find it impossible to believe. Parents still see the child—the chubby toddler, the innocent grade schooler, the shy and awkward adolescent, or the beautiful young man or woman who their child was before becoming ill. They don't see the disease lurking behind their beloved's eyes; they don't know that the cerebrum has stopped functioning and that the reptilian brain has taken over. By the time they do become aware of their child's transformation, it's often too late.

We learned about all of these dangers too late, after the fact of Eric's addiction. We hadn't known that since reaching adolescence, he had been sneaking into our medicine cabinets and taking pain pills to minimize his spiraling anxiety and shame. Unbeknownst to us, the pills were only the beginning. Eventually, Eric started smoking heroin and then injecting himself nearly daily with heroin and cocaine.

I didn't know what a speedball was until our son explained it to me. It's a very potent, potentially lethal combination of heroin and cocaine. The cocaine hypes people up, and the heroin mellows them out; in this way, users are chasing an intense high where the negatives of both drugs supposedly cancel each other out. Speedballs are exceptionally dangerous and can lead to overdose, paranoia, stroke, heart attack, aneurysm, and respiratory failure. Treatment centers warn that a person who is "speedballing is essentially turning their body into an amateur chemistry experiment where marginal failure could lead to serious problems, and serious failure can lead to death."[205]

My son told me that speedballs were responsible for the deaths of Jason Belushi, Philip Seymour Hoffman, and Kurt Cobain, among others. I was horrified. How was it possible that my son had been doing something so deadly, so full of self-loathing? I had always believed that love was enough to save anybody, especially my own child. One of the cruelest ironies of being the parent of a child with an addiction problem is that no amount of love or desperation can fix anything. The child is left to his or her own devices, and the parent is left watching helplessly as a tragedy unfolds. Any family that experiences this is forever changed. If and when the trauma ends, the family will be either more healthy or less healthy. But they will never be the same. The beast that has blotted out the sun for years has devoured their innocence. Some things never return.

After we had learned more about the realities of drug addiction by sitting in group rehab sessions for family members, we realized that we were not failures. Like the other people in the room, we had tried our best. We had loved our son, and he had loved us. None of us were inherently defective —only human. Listening to the heart-rending stories of these families was eye-opening.

During one meeting, the director of the session, a lean, middle-aged man, stood and stared intensely at the group for a moment. His hair was iron gray and close-cropped to his head. I wondered what message lay coiled behind his laser-like gaze. "It wasn't until my son died of an overdose at age twenty-three that I realized that I was in over my head," he finally said. "We're all in over our heads, so don't kid yourselves. There's nothing to do but keep swimming, for your own sake and for your family's sake. And now, well—some days are better than others."

Another time, a woman stood up and announced that her husband of forty years had just left her because he couldn't cope with one more alcoholic relapse. She looked worn and aged beyond her years, with lines creasing her face and thin, gray hair hanging down in strands around her shoulders. "I couldn't stop, and I still can't," she sobbed. "I don't know what's going to happen to me and my family." Her two daughters sat across the aisle from us, their arms crossed in a defensive position, refusing to make eye contact with their mother. The daughter with dark black eyeliner and piercings through her nose, lip, and cheek got up and walked out halfway through her mom's confession.

Another older man who was sitting next to his adult son said, "It wasn't until my wife and I realized that we had no control over our son that we got our lives back. We finally stopped pushing, pulling, and punishing. We told him that we loved him and wanted him to live, but that we would no longer be his jailors. The choice was his. Luckily for us, he chose life." The son was sitting beside his parents with his wife and their young child.

Then his mother stood. "We opened our separate basement apartment to our son, but we told him that it was up to him to eat, pay for his own gas, go to work, or overcome his addiction. For a long time, we didn't even bother to go down and check on him. We were so burnt out that we couldn't bear it." She sat down and grabbed her son's hand.

Everything they said rang true. Despite our best efforts, our son had become addicted to drugs. Neither he nor we were evil. There was no quick fix for this, no silver bullet, no prayer that would ward off the devastation of the possible loss of a child. We were all fallible humans, slogging our way through mortality, hoping that we would eventually make it to firm ground.

As a mother, I had always hoped that the intensity of my love for both of my children would keep them safe, like a magical shield that would repel the most serious of life's challenges. I rocked them to sleep and held them, burying my nose deep into their wispy toddler ringlets and breathing in the clean, fresh smell of baby hair. I sang to them and read to them. I knew that they would face the run-of-the-mill growing pains, like insecurity and loneliness. I knew they would both have to pass through the crucible of puberty and hopefully come out on the other side with their selfhood intact. I knew that they would have to deal with issues of self-concept, self-doubt, and self-acceptance.

But drug addiction? Until I was standing nose to nose

with my son's illness and possible death, I would never have believed it. It made me question everything that I had once supposed to be true. If the child that I had carried for nine months could hide such things, what other monsters could be lurking in deeper, darker waters?

Our local library in my hometown of Farmington, Utah, possessed an old copy of Jules Verne's classic novel *Twenty Thousand Leagues Under the Sea.* As a kid, I had stared at the cover of the book repeatedly, mesmerized by the illustration that showed menacing tentacles rising up from the ocean floor, reaching toward the hapless sailors above. The large, yellow, protuberant eyes of the squid stared blankly ahead with dull indifference. In the impending disaster, the creature killed its victims simply because it could. Somehow, the indifference made it worse. Likewise, the addiction monster suffers no qualms, no morals, no remorse. Even as we create stories to explain its destructive power, there are no certainties as to why some victims are spared while others are not.

On February 25, 2022, the National Prescription Opiate Litigation Plaintiffs' Executive Committee reached settlements with the "Big Three" drug distributors and with opioid manufacturer Johnson & Johnson. The advantage of this strategy was that it combined the disparate lawsuits of over "90% of litigating local governments" nationwide, leading to a national victory, whereas some previous, localized lawsuits had failed. After years of work by plaintiffs and their attorneys, a groundbreaking settlement was reached in which state and local governments would be required to devote at least 85 percent of the allocated funds to creating "relief programs to help rebuild the devastation caused by the opioid epidemic."[206] As of August 2024, the settlement has expanded to include drug manufacturers Allergan and Teva, along with pharmacy retailers CVS, Walgreens, Walmart, and Kroger. As of this writing, a $45 billion dollar fund has been established with payments disbursed to nearly 5,000 beneficiaries in forty-three states.[207] But will it be enough?

Opioid addiction is a complex disease, and simply earmarking funds for treatment and prevention will not solve the problem. However, by holding the massive pharmaceutical manufacturers and distribution companies accountable for their contributions to an unparalleled wave of death and devastation, the settlement sends a clear message that business as usual is no longer good enough.

CHAPTER 26

Heart in a Blender

Life is messy. In fact, it's messier than any of us could have imagined when we were younger. Most of the families in our church looked perfect to me every Sunday when I was a kid—children's faces scrubbed, hair slicked back; mothers perfectly made up and immaculately groomed; fathers looking powerful in their white shirts and dark ties. Everything was well-ordered. We grew up thinking if we sat on that church bench and followed all the rules, we could hold life at bay —stop entropy from washing over us and destroying our stronghold. But stasis never lasts. Entropy is a pitiless foe, and the price for humanity's continuing existence is a lifelong battle against dissolution.

One of the most painful consequences of drug addiction is that trust is damaged in every significant relationship. The trust that has been given so naturally inside the family system for years must be rebuilt. We never, for a moment, stopped loving our son. But trusting him? Now that was an entirely different matter. It had taken five years of subterfuge to belatedly teach us that we couldn't trust our own child anymore. This shattering had caused a tectonic fault line in our relationship that we knew would be difficult to restore.

It's not a lack of love that holds families back—it's fear. Who would volunteer to have their heart shredded more than once? Who would open up their chest again for more slashing? The pop band Eve 6's 1998 hit "Inside Out" captured the daily turmoil I lived with:

"Swallow my doubt, turn it inside out,

Find nothin' but faith in nothin'
Wanna put my tender heart in a blender
Watch it spin around to a beautiful oblivion."

After Brandon kicked Eric out for good and Eric moved back in with us, I found myself trying to mask my anxiety. Ten times a day I casually asked, "How are you doing?"

Will today be the day he slips up? Heart in a blender. . .

He saw through my act, and his face closed like a fist. "Fine." He walked into his bedroom and shut the door behind him.

"Let me know if you want to talk."

Could he already be using again? Why is his face so pale? Heart in a blender. . .

Anytime his bedroom door was shut, I approached every hour or so and lightly knocked. "Do you need anything?"

Should I be watching him round the clock? Should we remove the door from his bedroom? Am I failing as a parent? Heart in a blender. . .

I told him that since I didn't trust him to value his own life, I was going to value it for him. If he didn't answer and was sleeping, I would enter and lie next to him on the bed for a few minutes to make sure that he was still breathing. I understood that he wanted his privacy. And I would have been more than happy to give it to him if I didn't think he was going to stick a needle full of heroin into a vein and end his life. There were so many things unspoken, bristling just below the surface. Every day was one in which my husband and I paddled like crazy underneath and tried to keep it all together above.

Even though everybody feels sorry for the person who's had a horrible surgical outcome, nobody wants to hear the gory details more than once. Despite their genuine sympathy, people become tired of hearing the same story over and over. Eventually, the wounded stop talking about what's eating their heart away. They know that patience has its limit, and they don't want to drive away the people who love them by repeatedly exposing their horrific scars.

A good friend of mine lost her husband in a terrible aviation accident when he was forty. "You know, whenever somebody asks you how you're doing, they really just want you to say 'Fine,'" she told me once. "So, you say you're 'fine' even though you know you never will be again."

I knew what she meant. "He's doing fine," I said when asked about our son's recovery. "And we're doing fine." It was all a lie. We were somehow still breathing, and our hearts were still beating. If that's what was meant by "doing fine," then I guess we were. It was unquestionably better than being buried six feet below the dirt, but it felt like a living death more than anything else.

Every day I asked myself a series of questions, aware that the answers could change without warning:

Is my son still alive? Yes.

Is he still using? Maybe. Please God, no.

Is he fighting as hard as he can? I hope so.

Is he lying to me? Maybe. Maybe not. I'm not sure.

Is my son happy? I don't think so.

Is he ever going to get better? I have no idea.

Is this ever going to end? Please, please, please!

Once again, *Alice's Adventures in Wonderland* perfectly captured the maniacal teeter-totter of emotions that I veered through every day. "I know who I *WAS* when I got up this morning," says Alice, "but I think I must have been changed several times since then." Later on she says, "It's no use going back to yesterday, because I was a different person then."[208] Every day, every hour, every minute, I swung from despair to hope and back again. There is no exit from this topsy-turvy world until the person who is addicted wills it; and even then, there is no guarantee of permanent peace. Still, we hung on, hoping, despairing, and dreaming of future happiness. Or at least of future calm.

After Eric had been living with us for a few weeks, our suspicions that he was using again became impossible to ignore. His behavior grew more secretive, and his expression became sullen. He communicated in nonverbal grunts or shrugged his shoulders when we asked him if he was OK. He would lie in bed for an entire day, neither eating, nor bathing, nor communicating with us. After intense discussions with Jason and many more hours of phone calls, I found a different hospital in Salt Lake City that accepted our military insurance and was willing to admit Eric for another inpatient rehab. I was elated that we had gained approval for a monthlong stay, with the possibility of requesting two extra weeks if the doctors felt he needed it.

Jason and I entered his bedroom together and stared at his pale face. "It's time," I told Jason. We both took a deep breath, and Jason started tapping Eric on the shoulder and telling him to wake up.

"Huh?" Eric asked when the tapping continued. His eyes were bleary, and his curly hair stuck out in odd angles around his face; in some places it was matted to his scalp.

"You're going back to rehab," I told him.

"Hmm?" He was confused and tried to roll away from us and go back to sleep. I noticed that there were spots of drool on his bed sheets.

"You're going back to rehab, or you're not living with us anymore," Jason said.

Eric shrugged.

I hurriedly packed a bag for him while he lay on his bed unmoving and untalkative. "You know we're doing this because we love you."

Nothing.

"You know that you're going to die if you keep doing this."

Still nothing.

Then suddenly he sat upright and said, "I'm *not* going to rehab, no matter what you say."

"Oh, yes, you are," I grimly replied as I finished my frenzied packing. My resolve was a steel trap that Eric would not be able to wriggle his way out of. "If Dad and I have to drag you to the car kicking and screaming, you're going." At this point, our son was much bigger than I was, and I knew if he put up a serious resistance, we were going to have problems.

Jason told him to get moving in his sternest, military-dad voice. Eric focused long enough to stumble into the car, and together we all drove downtown to the Salt Lake Behavioral Health Detox and Inpatient Rehab. There was no conversation at all in the car. When we walked him inside the clinic, a pleasant-looking woman in her forties greeted us and tried to help Eric feel welcome. He had gone into shutdown mode, a common behavior of those who don't want to accept responsibility for the turmoil in their lives. The woman explained that she was a counselor, chatted with me for a few moments, and then turned to Eric.

"It's time to come with me," she said kindly.

Eric looked at us with tears in his eyes. We approached him and hugged him tightly, both of us taking turns whispering into his ears, "We love you so much." "We know this is the best place for you to be." "Please, don't give up." Then Jason and I walked out of the hospital without looking back. I felt a slight loosening of the metal bands that had coiled around my chest for a full year, making breathing difficult. It's for the best, I thought. He's where he needs to be.

Four days later, we got a call from the hospital. Even though our Tricare military insurance had initially approved the rehab stay, one of the insurance adjusters who had reviewed the claim had decided that inpatient treatment "wasn't medically necessary." Phone calls and pleas fell on deaf ears. Our son was a statistic to them, and the statistical formula they used to determine eligibility for treatment said that our son didn't need inpatient rehab. We knew they were wrong, and as we drove to the hospital my husband and I discussed the possibility of our paying for his continuing treatment ourselves. We discussed the upper limit of what we could afford, but when we discussed the charge with the hospital's financial office, we found out that without insurance coverage, the out-of-pocket costs would have been $800 per day! For a six-week stay, that would have cost us $33,600. Our son's life was priceless, but we needed to keep up on our mortgage payments to have a house to live in. I was devastated. One of my best friends growing up had lost her teenage son to a heroin overdose after being told by her insurance that he didn't "qualify" for treatment. This nightmarish scenario spun in my mind like a hamster on a wheel.

Before we left the hospital, the same counselor who had welcomed us pulled me aside. "He's made some good progress here. I've seen him open up and start to take positive steps toward self-accountability." She put her arm around me. "I'm so sorry that your insurance won't pay for this—so very, very sorry."

I hugged her tightly. "We'll take good care of him."

Then Jason and I loaded him into the car and drove home. We were right back where we had started: Eric was living with us, and we didn't trust him. We told him that he needed to find at least part-time work if he wanted to stay with us. He half-heartedly applied for a few jobs, but nothing came of it. Four days after returning home with us, he told us he was driving down to Salt Lake to talk to an old friend from his previous job. We were worried, but we had decided that policing his every move was not only impossible, but unhelpful for all of us.

He told us that he would be back that night, but as the sky faded to purple and then darkened, there was no sign of Eric. He wouldn't pick up his phone or return messages. The nightmare was starting again. We didn't hear from him for almost twenty-four hours. The next morning, my cell phone rang.

"Hey, Mom, I'm in a downtown hospital right now. But don't worry. I'm doing OK."

"The hospital?" I was confused. "Did they admit you for more rehab?"

"No. I'm at a different hospital. I was driving around last

night and started feeling weird, like I couldn't breathe. Then I felt like I was burning up. So, I drove myself to the hospital parking lot. By the time I got inside and tried to talk, I passed out. I guess they took me to the emergency room and told me I'd have to spend a few days here."

He told us that he was in the ICU at St. Mark's Hospital in downtown Salt Lake City. Jason and I raced to the hospital. When we arrived, we found out how serious Eric's situation really was. He had both pneumonia and septicemia and would be kept in the ICU for a few days while they monitored his vital signs and pumped him full of intravenous antibiotics. The physician who came in stared down at our son with a sober expression and told him that he would very likely have died if he hadn't driven himself to the emergency room parking lot and then collapsed in the hospital's entryway. Then the doctor explained that Eric had developed pneumonia, most likely caused by years of heroin use, which had prevented him from breathing deeply. After that, a bacterial infection set in and started to spread from his lungs to all of his bodily organs. At that point, he developed septicemia, or severe sepsis, which, if untreated, has a high mortality rate and may result in lifelong side effects.

How did he get the bacterial infection? The doctor explained it was most likely from repeatedly injecting drugs with a dirty syringe or from having untreated, open wounds in the areas he was injecting. After six days in the ICU, Eric was transferred to another room where they monitored him for an additional eight days, all the while maintaining the intravenous antibiotic treatment.

Near the end of his hospital stay, during which friends and family members had rallied around him, another doctor came in and stared at Eric with a look of concern on his face. "You were very, very lucky this time," he said. "If you hadn't made it to the hospital in time, somebody would have found your dead body slumped behind your steering wheel, maybe even after just a few hours."

"I know," our son said, but he didn't seem to be taking this as seriously as I thought he needed to. He was smiling at the fact that he would soon be released from the hospital.

"You had the winning lottery ticket this time," the doctor continued. "Please promise me there will never be a 'next time.' You're young, and you have so many good things ahead of you if you can just hang on. You're lucky to have your family here with you, too."

"I know," Eric said again.

I sat by his bedside, holding his hand and taking slow breaths to calm myself.

"Go home with your parents," the physician told him. "Remember how many people care about you, and don't let me see you in here again."

We were terrified by our son's brush with death. As we drove him home, he promised to never inject himself with anything dangerous again. I fervently hoped he was telling the truth, but I had a gut instinct that more trauma was on its way. Unfortunately, I was right.

CHAPTER 27

Reality Check

Some people might wonder how two parents could be so naïve and unaware. But we weren't naïve, at least when it came to experiencing the realities of life. Jason had served for twenty years in the military and had seen what drug use could do to somebody's career. I had taught college and high school for over twenty years by 2015 and had seen students destroy their futures with drugs. I also had relatives and friends whose lives had been decimated by drugs and alcoholism.

We were both college-educated professionals: we talked to our two children every day, paid attention to them, supported them in all their activities, and tried to let them suffer the consequences of their own mistakes as best we could while they were growing up. I was fortunate enough not to have to work when our children were little, so they had an in-home parent who was as involved as possible in their lives. When they started grade school, I volunteered at their schools. I was a room mother, I attended parent-teacher conferences, and most of all, I listened to my children. So, what went wrong? How could this have happened to us?

According to the latest studies of the psychology of addiction, those with substance-abuse problems are *not* evil, and they are *not* weak. Instead, experts theorize that such persons have developed patterns of disastrously unhelpful responses and behaviors to deal with stress. As to why some people are more prone to addiction than others, there are theories about addictive personalities, genetic predispositions, mental health issues, and family and cultural environments.[209] For whatever combination of reasons, our son had gotten his foot stuck in the heroin bear trap; now he had to get himself out of it before it was too late. We stood by helplessly and watched as he gnawed at his mangled limb, hoping that he could escape before it killed him.

One day while Eric was napping, Jason went out and searched his car thoroughly. We had gifted the car to Eric a few years earlier, before we had known about his substance-abuse problem, and had transferred the title to him. Jason entered the house waving a piece of paper in his hand. "Look what I found!" His eyebrows were drawn downward into a scowl. "He sold the title to his car!"

"He what?"

"He took out a title loan on his car. They gave him $2,000 in cash for it. I guess that explains where he's been getting the money to buy more drugs."

I had heard of people getting mortgage loans, but I didn't know that such loans were also available for car titles. Jason quickly explained the basics to me: "You sell your car title to get access to fast cash. Then, if you don't pay it back in a timely manner, they get to keep your car."

"They can keep his car? Well, that's not fair."

Jason smiled grimly. "Any number of loan sharks would be more than happy to rip off their 'valuable customers.'"

"So what do we do?" I asked.

"We're going to have to drive down to Salt Lake right now and pay this damn thing off if we don't want to lose the car! Otherwise, they get to keep the car, and we can't replace it for less than the $2,000 we've already lost."

Jason called the loan company and told them that we were going to pay off our son's debt. The amount had to be paid in cash, so he wanted to confirm the total before we drove the sixty minutes to Salt Lake. "What do you mean it's $2,600?" I heard him say. He listened silently for a minute, sighed, and then said, "OK. We'll be there soon."

"What did they say?" I asked.

"Well, since no payments have been made, they just put out a notice for repossession, which means the car can be sold to recoup their losses and the accrued interest on the loan. So now we owe an additional $600 to take care of that mess."

We went upstairs and opened Eric's bedroom door. He was awake now and playing video games on a computer that he had purchased for himself a couple of years earlier. "We're going for a ride," Jason announced, "and you're coming with us."

"Huh?" Eric kept staring at the computer screen.

"Come on," Jason said. "We know about the title loan you took out on your car. We're going to drive down and pay it off, and you will be with us when we do it."

The three of us drove to the loan company in a stony silence. When we went inside the loan company, we forced Eric to walk in with us even though he said that he was embarrassed. "Too bad," I said. "If I have to be embarrassed, so do you."

We handed over the required amount of cash and started driving home. On the way, Jason said, "We don't trust you with your car title anymore. So we'll be keeping it with us. It was a gift, anyway, so we've decided to take it back."

"And," I added, "I'll be keeping your car keys. You've lost your driving privileges for the foreseeable future. When and if we believe that we can trust you again, we can negotiate an agreement at that point. For now, I don't see that happening anytime soon. And if you dare to lie to us or try to sneak away, you'll never drive anywhere by yourself ever again." Eric said nothing, but his scowl deepened.

Once we arrived home, Eric isolated himself in his bedroom, and Jason and I resumed our nonstop conversations about how to best help him.

"Do you think he's using again?" I asked Jason for the umpteenth time a few days after we had purchased the car back.

"No—and I'm tired of talking about it."

But ten minutes later he said, "I don't know—do you think he's using?"

"Let's talk about something else," I said.

We went round and round in conversational circles, dancing between hopeful delusions about our son's recovery and dire predictions about his demise. The last few months that Eric lived with us we started locking up credit cards, cash, valuables, and anything else we were afraid he might steal to buy drugs with. Jason bought two safes, and we hid the keys in places that we thought were unfindable. Yet our son somehow sniffed out the keys and got into things that we didn't want him to access. We changed all of our online banking passwords. We hid our car keys so that Eric wouldn't be able to drive away without us noticing. While every action we took was for our son's safety and for our own sanity, it did not lead to a peaceful coexistence.

Oftentimes the siblings in the family can see the truth before the parents can, and this, too, causes family trauma. Siblings resent the negative impact that their brother or sister's addiction is having on their parents' attention and health. They see it as a form of manipulation. As Eric's illness slowly took over our lives, his calm, loving sister refused to speak with him for a while. "I can't believe what he's doing to you and Dad! He's being so selfish! Why is he acting like an idiot?"

"Yes, his behavior is maddening, but he's your only sibling. If you cut ties with him, you won't have any siblings left."

"I don't care," she replied flatly. "For now, I don't want to have anything to do with him. If I change my mind, I'll let you know." She told us it was too painful to watch him destroy himself and us, too. She was angry at him for pulling us into the pit of despair where he had taken up permanent residence. I didn't lecture her. I knew why she was mad—I, myself, had spun from rage to sorrow to terror until dizziness became my new norm. But Eric wasn't my brother; he was *my son*. I loved him no matter what.

Once I became a parent, I loved my kids simply because they existed. They didn't have to do anything to earn my devotion: it was part of my parental obligation. With everybody else—my husband, siblings, relatives, or friends—it was a different story. I had expectations of them, and if they let me down, I had to work to forgive them. Our daughter was letting us know in no uncertain terms that her brother had broken her heart too many times.

Nobody talks about the siblings of the child with a substance-abuse problem. Parents are so busy wringing their hands over the self-destructive child that the child who is sailing along on smooth seas often gets overlooked. It's not that we didn't adore and appreciate our daughter—we did. She was and is an amazing individual. It's just that when one child seems to be catching an effortless breeze and the other one is in a sinking ship, parental instincts take over and all available energy goes into rescuing the floundering child. It's not fair. I can understand why ruptures occur and why they are sometimes never healed. But from a parents' perspective, it can't be helped. There is a terrible, inexorable logic to the parental math problem they face: they must save the drowning child before they can glance back at the safe child. Nobody has to tell them that—they can feel it in their bones.

CHAPTER 28

Bedlam in a Nutshell

Bethlem Hospital began its colorful history as a sanctuary for a Catholic religious order in thirteenth-century London. During the next four hundred years, it morphed into a sanctuary for any indigent persons needing help and then finally a place of seclusion (and isolation) for those deemed mentally ill by society. The nickname of the asylum became "Bedlam Hospital," and by the time the hospital was rebuilt in 1676 for the purpose of making London "a grander and better place for everybody," the linkage between "Bedlam" and "madness" had become permanent, and a new word slipped into common use in the English language.[210] The juxtaposition of the ornate, exterior façade and the atrocious conditions of treatment inside for the patients was a well-known irony. Patients were subjected to cruel and experimental treatments designed to "cure" them: bloodletting, beatings, submersion in icy water, forced consumption of laxatives, and "'rotational therapy,' which involved putting a patient in a chair suspended in the air and then spinning them around for hours." The fact that the public was allowed to pay a small amount of money and tour the facilities to gawk at the patients confined there made it even more notorious.[211]

Because of Eric's substance-abuse issues, our own lives had degenerated into a barely manageable state of bedlam. Insanity reigns supreme when a person who is using tries to maintain the appearance of normality. They mistakenly think that others can't see that they are disintegrating, can't see the telltale signs of hollowed-out eyes and blank stares. Our son's face took on the chalky white color of a cadaver, and he slept much of the time. I felt like a parole officer on twenty-four-hour duty as I constantly surveilled him, watching for any possible changes that might suggest another crisis was approaching.

There is no way to completely control any child, let alone one who is battling an addiction, and the most difficult life lesson I have ever learned was that I had to let go of my son. If my white-knuckled grip could have saved him, I would have held on forever. But it couldn't, and it was killing me in the process. I finally understood the cliché "There are things worse than death." I had heard people say such things but had always dismissed them. Certainly death, I thought, would be the most horrible thing of all: the final catch of mortal breath in the throat, the slow expiration of the final sigh, the headlong plunge into the unknown on the other side.

But now I knew the hard truth: living was a much more frightening proposition than dying. In dying I saw only two alternatives—either we continued on in some state, or we didn't. Either way I wouldn't have much choice in the matter, even if I desperately wanted to. But in living, the terror of the dead ends, one-way roads, and dangerous collisions were daunting. Each day there were a hundred ways to hurt someone I loved or to be hurt by them in kind. Each day threatened to ruin someone or something essential. Each day carried gifts and curses to be passed out willy-nilly to passersby who had no understanding of what they had received until it was too late. Life itself was the riskier thing —the bright, yet terrible, thing. Living was the brief moment between the unknown before and the unknowable after.

Eventually, I had to loosen my grip and watch my beautiful boy drift towards destruction. In my nightmares, I watched him leap into a murky, alligator-infested swamp. I threw out a life jacket, but he was too far away. I screamed, but nobody was near enough to hear. I was more than willing to jump in and swim to him, but I knew that I would be pulled under the churning, reptilian water before I could ever reach him. So I watched in stunned horror, anticipating the fatal flash of serrated jaws that would signal the end. I could barely breathe, let alone think. Something primitive in my brain had sprung to life, some ancient genetic imperative that whispered that my child's death would become my own unraveling.

As for living through each day, Jason and I had to find some way to stagger through our own lives, doing essential things like going to work, paying bills, and trying to stay somewhat healthy. I was thankful that we didn't have any younger children who would have placed additional demands on us. During the most intense part of Eric's drug use, I experienced almost intolerable levels of anxiety. I regularly laid next to him in bed while he was sleeping, checking for signs of breathing. I was afraid whenever his bedroom door was closed. I found it impossible to get enough sleep. I developed a nervous tic of constantly chewing on my fingernails and fingertips until they were painful stubs, and pieces of ragged skin had been torn far enough down my fingers to make them bleed. Ironically, the sight of the jagged skin edges made me want to tear some more. My goal was always the same—to create a perfectly smooth surface, a seamless transition from skin to cuticle to nail. But there was no way to create a perfect texture without constant picking. Any growth from the night before had to be removed, and in trying to fix it, I made it worse. I tried wearing bandages, gloves, and coating my nails in bitter tasting polish that promised to "stop the bite." But nothing worked. Tomorrow, I promised myself every day. Tomorrow I will not touch my fingers no matter what happens.

It occurred to me that I, too, was like an animal with its paw stuck in a steel trap—I was trying to chew off my own hand in order to escape the trap's serrated edges. If I couldn't control my son, his choices, his despair, his using, at least I could control this. I could chew on my fingers endlessly until they were seamless, clean, and perfect. Or, as my husband told me one night while watching me, "until there's nothing left but bone."

Then there were other moments when I was filled with a rage so fierce that I felt like my heart would explode. Those moments didn't last long, but when they struck, they were tornadoes that left me clutching my sanity as it flapped about me in the whirlwind. I would cover my face with one of my bedroom pillows and howl until I was breathless. Then I would collapse into intense crying jags that shook my body. The sadness was so intense that I wondered how I could continue to live with it. At first, Jason would try to comfort me during these bouts of crying. Later, he seemed overwhelmed by them.

When the burden became too great, I knew I needed help from someone with an outsider's perspective. I found a new therapist who was a little bit older than me. Her experiences as a mother and a Mormon made me feel like we had a common history. Her office had a comfortable couch with large, overstuffed throw pillows, and our discussions became an outlet for my turbulent emotions.

During one of our sessions she asked me, "What is the worst thing that could happen?" Although her question startled me, it came from a place of truth: "You *have to admit* the worst thing that could happen," she repeated. "Once you know what that is, everything else becomes a better outcome." She gazed at me expectantly through large, framed glasses that accentuated her eyes. She was waiting for me to rip my heart from my chest and verbalize the worst thing. We both knew what it was—every parent knows—but saying it aloud was brutal.

"The worst thing that could happen is—" I paused. I took a deep breath. I was terrified that I had to verbalize something so monstrous and angry at the woman who was forcing me to do it. My psychologist waited, her gaze insistent and yet somehow soft. "The worst thing that could happen is—" I broke off again. "He could die."

We both knew that this was the thing which must *not* be spoken, and yet somehow I had forced the words out. All the air seemed to have been sucked out of the room, and I felt dizzy.

"Yes," she said. "That is the worst thing." She said this matter-of-factly, without a shred of hysteria or sentimentality. We both fell silent, and I watched the second hand on the large, black and white clock in her office tick around the circle.

"He could die," I said again. "I know nothing is worse than that."

She paused for a few moments. "Now that you know the worst, go backwards from there and see if anything else other than his death looks as frightening." Of course, when viewed in the context of death, nothing else seems nearly so bad. I knew that was the point of the exercise, but it still didn't take away my fear.

"He could end up living on the streets."

She nodded.

"He could end up destroying his health."

"Yes."

"He could end up ruining relationships with his family."

Again, she nodded. I understood that all of these were better than his death, and even though none of these scenarios were positive, just admitting that a son living in any number of deplorable conditions was infinitely better than a dead son opened an inch of breathing room in my rib cage.

"Life is a fucking mess." I had already warned her to be prepared for a few f-bombs when we started our sessions together.

"Indeed, it is," she agreed.

As I drove away from the appointment, I thought of the closing lines of one of my favorite poems, "Ozymandias," written by Percy Bysshe Shelley in 1817. In the poem, a desert traveler stumbles upon the ruined statue of a formerly powerful leader, Pharaoh Ramesses II. Engraved on the statue is the pharaoh's haughty command, "Look on my Works, ye

Mighty, and despair!" The next three lines reveal the irony at the heart of the poem, as the command to "despair" is now revealed to be an impotent threat from a man whose power and glory long ago disintegrated under the relentless passage of time:

"Nothing beside remains. Round the decay
Of that colossal Wreck, boundless and bare
The lone and level sands stretch far away."

As a college student, I had read those lines with as much understanding as I could muster as a young woman. What would it be like, I had wondered, to stand alone, surrounded by nothing but a barren, empty wilderness, the ruins of a previous life destroyed beyond all rebuilding? After my son's addictions reached crisis levels, those lines needed no interpretation: they had been engraved upon my face, had wormed their way into my heart, and had finally taken up permanent residence deep in my bones. Decades after I first encountered it, I finally knew the answer to Jeremiah's rhetorical question in the Bible: "Is there no balm in Gilead?" No, I decided. There was no balm in Gilead. Unfortunately, there was no balm, no physician, and no hope of putting things right.

CHAPTER 29

Sober Living

After Eric was released from St. Mark's Hospital for septicemia, he spent a couple of weeks living with us. During the worst period of his drug use, we basically had two full-time jobs: teaching school during the day and trying to find help for Eric each evening and weekend. I spent hours making phone calls to our insurance company, doctors, psychiatrists, and rehab programs across the county. Neither Jason nor I had any delusions left about our ability to keep our boy safe. Despite these ongoing efforts, however, we had discovered that the existing resources for addiction and mental health issues are shamefully inadequate. This is a costly lesson that society has yet to learn, and one that has fatal consequences. Jason and I were college-educated, competent adults, and we were barely able to keep our heads above water while trying to work our way through a labyrinth of insurance rules and procedures. I can't imagine how a family without a bit of extra money or insurance could survive this process.

After calling nearly two dozen rehab programs, I was dismayed by the exorbitant costs. One location in Provo, Utah, told me that it would cost $33,750 for our son to spend ninety days there. If for any reason he left the facility early, we would be charged $14,000. A rehab center in Draper, Utah, would have cost $39,000 for three months. Another place in Midway, Utah, told us it would be $18,500 per month for the first two months, and then drop to $8,000 for the third month, for a total of $45,000 for three months. I called the Alcohol and Chemical Treatment Program (ACT) in Ogden, Utah, where our son had completed his first four-week rehab stint in September and October of 2014. Because our insurance would not pay for another treatment with them so soon, we learned that for twenty-eight days it would cost us $28,000.

Finally, after a suggestion from a counselor, I learned about a program called Next Level Recovery. One of their treatment options was a Sober Living Adult Intensive Outpatient Home in downtown Salt Lake. The Sober Living Home was an accredited and surprisingly affordable option for persons needing transitional support. Since it combined daily drug checks with in-home counseling, we thought it would be a good fit for us. We moved Eric in near the end of April 2015 and drove back home. But from the beginning, he didn't like living there. He called several times a day, asking us to let him come back home because he was anxious and lonely. I told him that he had to stay because we could no longer monitor his behavior closely enough on our own. I spoke to the home supervisor several times on the phone, and he assured us that he was keeping a close eye on our son. He said that Eric was attending the required meetings and that he was being cooperative if not congenial. Once again, for a brief moment, we hoped that he would be safe.

After living there for only two months, however, Eric tested positive for heroin use and was kicked out of the facility, which had a zero-tolerance policy for drug use. He blamed it on another resident, claiming that he had dropped a tinfoil packet of heroin near the showers and that once Eric had seen it, he couldn't resist smoking it. He called us and told us that he was stranded on the streets of Salt Lake City with no way to get home or to pay for a place to stay.

We drove down to pick him up, discussing different options all the way there. I told Jason about a long-term rehabilitation place I had recently discovered called Odyssey House of Utah, an adult treatment center with both inpatient and outpatient programs. Located in downtown Salt Lake City, Odyssey House is considered one of the best drug treatment centers in Utah. When we picked Eric up after his expulsion from the sober living facility, we told him that we had found a better place for him. I explained that his new living arrangements in Odyssey would include constant in-house supervision, group and individual therapy, and work training programs. I told him that they were holding a spot for him that would open up soon, and that he would be going there. He didn't protest at that point, but he didn't agree, either.

Two weeks later, when we all drove down to Odyssey House together, Eric had started to twist and turn in the seat, wringing his hands and chewing on his ragged fingernails.

"I don't want to go. I can't do this. I'm so anxious, I can't stand it."

I exhaled in frustration. "You have to go. We've been over this before. If you don't go you will die, and we refuse to let you die."

At this point Jason and I were beyond exhausted. Odyssey was going to cost us $3,600 a month, which was less expensive than any place else I'd been able to find. We figured it was like a second mortgage payment, a mere trifle compared to the value of our son's life.

"I can't go in there," he said again.

"Yes, you can."

"No."

"Yes."

We pulled onto the pleasant, shady road that led to Odyssey House. The street was lined with luxuriant shade trees, and I felt a sense of peace wash over me. This could be the right place, I thought. It had formerly been a family residence, but since 1971 it had served those in the community who were battling substance-abuse issues. It was a dark gray brick building with bright white pillars and windowpanes. A sky-blue shade awning over the front porch gave the building a cheery, inviting look.

Jason and I parked the car across the road and spent another thirty minutes trying to convince Eric to get out of the car. Finally, with a sigh of resignation, he got out and slammed the car door behind him. He stood by the side of the car and inhaled a cigarette. He had taken up smoking during the last few years to calm his nerves, and he knew that tobacco was not allowed at Odyssey.

After he stubbed out his cigarette, all three of us climbed the steps that led to the front door of the center and knocked. We were greeted by a young, friendly counselor who told us that Eric would need to complete a lengthy intake interview and that we should say our goodbyes. We hugged him tightly; he stood stiff and unresponsive. The staff promised to take good care of him, and I somehow willed myself to walk out the door. I knew that we would be unable to see him in person until he was acclimated to the program. We drove home with the smallest flicker of hope that this time things would work out.

Five days later, feeling like our son was finally in a safe place, Jason and I drove for ten hours straight to Coeur d'Alene, Idaho, for our first out-of-town break in over fifteen months. We had never dared leave Utah while Eric was unsupervised, knowing that at any minute a phone call might bring us bad news. We had just checked into a local hotel and ordered a pizza. I had collapsed onto the bed, exhausted from our long drive. "This is going to be a well-deserved break," I told Jason. Before he could even kick his shoes off, his cell phone rang. It was ten o'clock in the evening, and I was nervous about who might be calling us at this late hour.

My husband answered his cell phone and muttered a few terse replies. "Yes. . . I see. . . I understand. . . When did this happen? Thank you for letting us know."

"What's going on?"

"Eric's disappeared," he said. "They have no idea where he is." The ten hours of driving we had just completed still thrummed through my bones like a persistent toothache.

We knew that Eric had been having a hard time acclimating to the program because his counselor had allowed him to call and speak to us after forty-eight hours even though it was against the rules. During that call home he told us, "I want to come home. I'm too anxious."

"You have to stay," I said.

"I want to come home."

"You can't," Jason said.

The counselor put the conversation on speaker phone and explained that she had allowed him to call us to help ease his mind somewhat. "We're going to do our best to help him," she explained. But we knew that Odyssey was unable to hold residents against their will. Although patients were closely supervised and had detailed, daily work requirements and mandatory counseling schedules, if a patient decided to walk away, the center was legally unable to restrain him.

"So, you'll just let him walk away?" I had asked a few weeks earlier when I first talked to them about their program.

"Oh, we'll do everything in our power to get him to come back," they had reassured me. "The counselors and residents will follow him if we see him leaving and beg him to return." I was hoping that Eric didn't know about this potential escape clause.

"Eric," I said while we were still on speaker phone with the therapist.

"What?"

"You absolutely cannot leave; do you understand me?"

Pause. "Yes."

"You have to stay there," my husband added. "We know this is really hard, but this is the only way we know how to help you now."

"Ok."

"Eric, do you want to say anything else to your parents?" the counselor prompted.

When there was no reply, I said again, "Whatever you do, do *not* under *any* circumstances try to leave."

And now, just three days after that phone call, Eric had disappeared during an outside work detail, and nobody had seen him leave.

"What are we going to do?" I asked Jason. I knew what the answer was, but my body and mind were screaming for rest.

"We've got to go back—*now*," my husband said. Silently, we rolled our suitcases back into the hall we had just left. We walked to the front desk and explained that our reservation that we had booked for four nights needed to be canceled due to a family emergency.

"We're still gonna have to charge you for tonight, on account of the late notice," the hotel clerk stated flatly while staring at his computer screen and avoiding eye contact with us. The blue light of the screen illuminated his face.

"That's fine," I said. I was too tired to protest. We paid for a single night, climbed back into our Suburban, and hit the road. The ride back to Utah was heavy with repressed emotions and physical exhaustion. We hardly conversed at all; we had no energy left for anything extraneous. And any time we did start to talk, the conversation drifted inexorably to our son, which always led one or both of us to call for a "time out" when we couldn't stand to talk about it anymore.

We had no idea where our son was. Near the end of the return trip, with over seventeen hours of continuous driving, Jason's head started to dip forward and spring back up quickly. "Are you falling asleep? You know we can't afford to get in a car wreck right now."

"No, I'm fine. But keep talking to me until we get home to help me stay awake." For Jason, that was as much as admitting that he was about to pass out. I sat up watching him drive for the last three hours, tapping his arm and face about every two minutes to make sure he was awake, plying him with Diet Cokes, and talking to him nonstop.

When we finally got home, we found our son asleep on the basement floor in a sleeping bag. Popcorn was strewn around him on the carpet and a couple of empty Mountain Dew cans were tipped over next to him. He was sleeping on his stomach, with his face squished into the carpet. There was a small, discolored spot on the carpet that looked like drool.

We woke him up, and he told us that he had walked to the downtown light railway system, Trax, and gotten as close to home as he could. Then he had hitchhiked the rest of the way. He was clearly exhausted, but also, in our best estimation, not high. Just to make sure, I laid down on the couch for an hour or so and listened to his breathing.

When I was sure he was safe, I stumbled upstairs and collapsed into bed after nearly thirty-two hours with no sleep. I twisted and turned all night, with nightmares of being stuck in a waist-high swamp, trying to wade my way to higher land. The muddy water pulled at my legs like quicksand, making a hollow sucking sound. I was only able to advance a few inches at a time and feared that I was going to sink under and suffocate.

The next morning we told Eric he was under house arrest. He would not be allowed to drive anywhere or leave the house for any reason. We took away his cell phone. I called Odyssey House and told them that we had found our son; they told me that if we could get him to return the next Monday, they could hold the spot for him. Jason and I took turns watching Eric like a hawk, telling him that he couldn't shut the door to his bedroom and that he needed to tell us before he showered or used the bathroom so we could wait outside the door. He clearly wasn't happy about the situation, but at this point his happiness was no longer our concern. At this point, only one thing mattered—saving his life.

CHAPTER 30

Rock Bottom

After spending the weekend under house arrest, Eric was scheduled to go back into Odyssey House on Monday, August 3, 2015. Jason and I knew that he didn't want to return, but we told him he had no other options. I had carefully hidden his car keys in a secret location in my walk-in closet. That morning, as we were preparing to drag our son back to rehab, I heard a car engine turning over and tires peeling out on our gravel driveway.

I ran to the kitchen window and saw Eric's car speeding away from our home. "No! No, no, no!"

Jason came rushing into the kitchen. "What happened?" His face looked haggard; his nerves were as frayed as mine.

"Eric just drove off in his car! This can't be happening!"

"I thought you hid the key!"

"I did! I did! There's no way he could have found it in the last fifteen minutes!"

I ran to my closet and looked; sure enough, the key was missing. I had no idea how our son had found the key so quickly. I collapsed onto my bed. "He's going to die! There's nothing we can do!"

My husband sank onto a nearby chair and lowered his head into his hands. I blamed myself for not hiding the key better; perhaps my husband did, too. Later, we realized that our son's decision to run away again was his own and that we were not to blame for that disastrous choice.

For the next two days, I repeatedly called and texted Eric. We had no idea where he was, and my fevered brain created numerous disastrous outcomes. During that same time, Jason checked one of our safes and discovered that Eric had stolen twenty silver coins, which were valued at about four hundred dollars. Jason had no idea how Eric had found the hidden key to the safe, but it did explain how he had financed his latest getaway.

Finally, Eric called me back. He told me that he had been living out of his car for two days and agreed to meet me in the parking lot of a downtown grocery store. I drove down to meet him under a gray, ominous sky that mirrored my mood. Jason and I agreed that we had to get him to go back to rehab. At this point, no other viable options remained. It was rehab or nothing. We had decided that I would go alone to reduce the chance of Eric feeling overwhelmed. I spotted his car in the far corner of one of the downtown Smith's Food and Drug parking lots. As he opened his car door and climbed out, I noticed that his car was filled with garbage. His cheek bones stood out, emphasized by both his gauntness and his paleness.

We walked into the store together and bought him a few new t-shirts, deodorant, underwear, caffeinated drinks, and some food. Then we returned to my car where after about an hour of pleading, I got him to agree to follow me to the parking lot that was behind Odyssey House's head office.

We drove to Odyssey separately, and then an intense, four-hour debate started in the parking lot. The staff knew that I was trying to convince him to return to their program, but they were unable to physically drag him in. Our conversation was circular, never progressing, never resolving itself. As we talked, Eric paced and chain-smoked. A drizzle started and soon turned into a downpour, forcing us both to move inside my car.

"You need to go *back* into rehab," I said for the thousandth time.

"I won't, I can't."

"Why? It can't be worse than dying, and dying is about all you've got left at this point. You *do* want to live, don't you?"

He paused awhile before answering. His eyes were ringed with dark circles, and the light behind them was snuffed out. "I'd rather die than go back to rehab," he finally said. "And you can't change my mind."

I stayed longer anyway, hoping I could persuade him. We sat in my car as the rain poured down. A few stubborn weeds grew between cracks in the asphalt, and hundreds of cigarette butts littered the ground. I guessed a lot of people about to go into rehab came out here to inhale their final cigarette, like a condemned man. I hoped that by silently sitting I could outwait him, but he was too stubborn to give in. I begged him one final time to reconsider. He refused.

I had driven down to Salt Lake with an ultimatum, but I dreaded the thought of delivering it. My husband and I could no longer endure the torment of watching our son destroy himself. We had lived through four rehab stints: one completed, one terminated by our insurance company, one terminated by Eric's continued usage, and one ended by Eric's disappearance and now refusal to reenter the program.

If I could have given my life for him at that point and saved him, I would have done it without a second thought. Jason would have done the same thing. We had discussed it many times, always arriving at the same dead end. We couldn't save him—he would have to save himself. However, early on we had decided that if we both agreed that we could no longer let him live at home, we would know that the time had come. Up until this final conversation with Eric, either Jason or I had always held out hope that things might change. We no longer believed that, so the time had come to kick him out.

So after four hours of pleading, I drove away. I left my son behind in a dirty car in a littered parking lot. I drove away pounding the steering wheel with my fists, screaming curses into a sullen sky. A blinding rainstorm now battered my car and mirrored the tears streaming down my face. I had delivered the ultimatum that if he was unwilling to reenter Odyssey House, he would be joining the ever-growing throngs of people without permanent shelter who roamed the streets of downtown Salt Lake City. We were no longer willing to enable his drug use.

I called my husband while I was driving home to get some reassurance that I had done the right thing. I was angry that I had been the one tasked with announcing our decision to our son. "No mother should ever have to do this alone! I feel like you abandoned me."

"We've already discussed this," Jason said. "Eric has always listened better to you than to me, and you did the right thing." His reassurances fell on deaf ears.

"It's easy for *you* to say I did the right thing because *you weren't here*! I feel like I've just signed his death warrant."

"You didn't sign it, I didn't sign it—he did."

He was right, of course, but his words brought me no peace. I had seen the look in Eric's eyes when I told him he couldn't come home. I had seen the desperation and the utter emptiness there, and I couldn't bear to think that my words had contributed. I felt like I was driving to my own funeral as I headed home in a hard rain that fell in solid sheets.

I was angry at my husband for not being there. I was terrified that my son was throwing his life away. But most of all, I felt a growing fury at the idea of god that I had been raised with—the Mormon God who would never give us more than we could handle, who would somehow work all the tangled skeins of our mortal lives into a beautiful, meaningful tapestry on the other side. There was no way to untangle this. Our son was burdened by the double shame of supposedly failing his family and his God. He couldn't "pray away the gay," as many gay Mormons have been admonished to do by well-meaning, but dangerously uninformed, ecclesiastical leaders. He couldn't pray it away because it was simply who he was.

During the years of Eric's drug addiction, I had tottered through my days like a high-wire aerialist—one slip, and it would all be over. Yet somehow I had continued to perform my professional teaching duties. Every day I would get up, put on a brave face, and go teach the high school students I cared about. I truly wanted the best for them, and I put every ounce of my remaining energy into being the best teacher I possibly could. To the outside world, most of whom knew nothing about our family's challenges, I probably seemed fine; inside, I had been erased. I started to wish that I could somehow be blinked out of existence—an empty spot in a room; a watery, fading footprint on a hot concrete step; a final exhalation camouflaged by the wind. I wanted to disappear forever. My sacred obligations to my family stopped me from doing anything rash, but over the next few months, the wish for oblivion kept tapping at my chamber door.

CHAPTER 31

Hiroshima Day

Three days had passed since I had left Eric in the parking lot behind Odyssey House's main office on August 3, 2015. I had been calling and texting him ever since, hoping that he would pick up my calls. Jason and I were frantic with worry and were second-guessing our decision to give Eric the ultimatum of either reentering rehab or living out of his car. On that hot morning of August 6, when Eric finally replied, I had called 911 shortly before noon to report a suicide threat. Since that call, Jason and I had remained frozen, unwilling to move from our deck's bench.

Suddenly, my phone rang, and I nearly dropped it in my haste to answer. "Is this Mrs. Taylor?" an unfamiliar voice asked.

"It is." My pulse was pounding in my ears.

"This is Detective Ferrell with the Salt Lake County Police Department," he said. "Did you call in the suicide report on your son?"

"Yes, yes! Do you have him? Is he OK? Are you with him now?"

"We have canvassed the entire hospital parking lot and don't see any cars matching the description you gave."

The borders of my world were unravelling one thread at a time; I wondered when the tattered strands would reach the center. I wanted to stop the day and hit the rewind button.

"Do you think he could have gone someplace else?" the detective asked.

"I have no idea."

"Does he have a cell phone? Can you give us his number?"

I rattled off the cell phone number and asked if they could track him through it. The detective explained that if the phone was turned on and the SIM card hadn't been removed, they could. I wondered what the odds were that our son hadn't thrown his phone out the window and driven away.

Jason and I waited as the minutes crept by, then nearly an hour, an hour and a half. Suddenly the phone rang again. I flinched as my heart galloped in my chest. "Ma'am, we have found your son," Detective Farrell said. "He is parked outside a Motel 6 in Provo. We are going to approach the car, and we need to know if he has a weapon."

A weapon? I thought. Why would that be the first thing they asked? But then I remembered the stories about policemen who sometimes mistakenly shot unarmed suspects. In asking them to help my son, had I inadvertently put him in danger? "No!" I cried. "He does not have a weapon!"

"Are you sure?" the officer asked.

"Absolutely! He has never been violent!" I could hear the edge of hysteria in my voice; no doubt the police officer could, too.

"Ma'am, I will have to call you back once we have apprehended your son."

My mind was whirling. Why had our son driven to a Provo motel? What was he doing? Was he safe? Had the detective believed me when I told him that Eric would never be violent? I imagined a cadre of officers approaching him with their bulletproof vests and their guns ready. I hoped that our son would be sober enough to turn himself in without any attempt to resist or escape. Jason and I sat mute, waiting for the phone call that would decide the future course of our son's life and our own.

About an hour later, Detective Farrell sent me a text message with a grainy photo attached. It looked to be an image captured from a video surveillance tape. The text read, "Can you confirm that this is your son?"

I looked at the photo. Yes, it was definitely Eric. He was standing in the middle of a short line of people, looking up towards a ceiling-mounted video camera. There was no hoodie pulled down low over his forehead, no sunglasses, no attempt at all to disguise himself. Instead, he stared directly into the camera. His expression revealed a person with no hope, no future, and no more exits. It was the face of somebody who had given up on life. I had never imagined that a person whom I had spent years loving could be so utterly, completely empty.

I showed the photo to my husband, and he quickly called the detective back on speakerphone. "Yes, that's Eric. Did you arrest him inside the motel?" Jason asked. We were both confused about the line he was standing in.

"No," Farrell answered. "We found him at the Provo motel and have taken him into custody, but we also received a phone call this morning from the bank just across the street from the Salt Lake Behavioral Health parking lot where we originally looked for Eric."

"OK—"

"You're sure this is him?" Farrell asked again.

"Yes," I said. "But I don't understand what this has to do with the bank."

"The bank was robbed a few hours ago," Farrell said. "They called us shortly after it happened, and when we got the 911 call about your son being in the parking lot across the street, we thought there might be a connection."

"You're telling me Eric robbed a bank." I spoke as if I were a bad actor rehearsing a line for an upcoming play.

"Eric did *what*?" Jason gasped. "No—this isn't possible. He's *never* been an aggressive kid, never done anything like this."

"Mr. and Mrs. Taylor, I am going to have to call you back later," Detective Farrell said. "We're double-checking something else right now. Good-bye."

Jason and I stared at each other. Then we stared back at

the photo. "Look!" Jason said.

"What?"

"The man standing behind Eric has a gun concealed in his hand." He pointed to a somewhat disheveled man standing close to Eric in the photo. His right hand was close to Eric's lower back.

I tapped on the photo and zoomed in. "I think you're right," I said. It looked like the tip of a gun barrel was poking out of the man's jacket and possibly touching Eric's back. "Do you think it could be his drug dealer? I'll bet Eric was forced to rob the bank!"

"That's it!" Jason said. In our delusional state of mind, it was the only way to make sense of the photo in front of us. "We've got to call the detective back immediately. We've got to tell him that Eric was being threatened."

Jason dialed the detective's number using my phone and the call was picked up quickly. "Hello," Jason said. "This is Eric's father. My wife and I just noticed something crucial in this photo you sent us." We put the phone on loudspeaker while Jason explained our drug-dealer theory. When he was done talking, there was a prolonged pause.

"Mr. and Mrs. Taylor, I understand that this is shocking news for you to have received," he said patiently. "But I can assure you that the man behind Eric did *not* have a gun in his hand. We have already analyzed the video images and talked to the bank employees and the other customers who were there at the time. Nobody is threatening your son in this photo."

"But—" I blurted, "are you absolutely sure? There is *no way*—"

"I'm positive," the detective answered. "Eric has already admitted that he acted alone, and he told us that he asked the bank teller for $600 in cash."

"Only $600? Well, that doesn't sound like very much money," I said in a hopeful tone of voice.

"Ah, yes. It doesn't. But he took it from a bank, which potentially makes it a very serious crime."

I didn't understand at that point that any robbery committed inside a federal bank is considered a federal crime and that the penalties are usually harsh.

"But—did he hurt anybody? Did he threaten anybody?"

"No," he didn't. Both Jason and I expelled a loud breath. "We have confirmed that Eric did *not* threaten anybody and did *not* have a weapon on him. In this case, Eric is very lucky that he didn't have a weapon. We've also spoken to bank teller, and she confirmed that he seemed embarrassed and soft-spoken when he passed her the note asking for $600 in cash."

This was the tiniest bit of good news, but it saved me from collapsing. "He's never hurt anyone," I said. "He's just depressed."

"Well, he sure didn't seem depressed when we picked him up in the motel parking lot," the detective said, his voice hardening. "He was joking and laughing with us; in fact, he seemed to be enjoying himself."

"That's not who he *really* is," Jason said. "He was probably high and out of his mind. Or maybe he was relieved to finally be caught."

"Um-hmm."

"Look," I said, "I want him placed under a suicide watch the second he gets to jail. I'm afraid he might find a way to finish this somehow."

"Understood," Farrell said. "We'll communicate that to the jail. I'm sorry, but I've got another call coming in." Then he hung up.

"Do you know what today is?" Jason asked in a leaden tone.

"What?"

"It's Hiroshima Day. Exactly seventy years ago today, the U.S. dropped the atomic bomb on Japan, instantly killing thousands of people and ending World War II."

"And?" I could not have cared less about a history lesson.

"Today is our family's personal Hiroshima Day, don't you think?"

Even now, several years later, we still refer to the day we got the phone call from the police as Hiroshima Day. It was a private tragedy, played out on an infinitely smaller scale, unnoticed, unknown, and unimportant to the rest of the world. Yet a devastating bomb had just been dropped that would scatter and perhaps destroy our lives.

I called my immediate family members to warn them that they might see something upsetting on the news or in the newspaper. Jason and I somehow stumbled through the rest of the day on autopilot. Every so often one of us looked at the other, took a deep breath as if we were about to say something, then lapsed into silence.

And indeed, that night on the local evening news, there was a brief report about a young man being taken into police custody for robbing a bank. The reporter mentioned Eric's name, and a picture of his face flashed on the screen momentarily. I was bothered by the report because it didn't mention that the suspect did *not* have a weapon and that he had only taken a few hundred dollars. I thought it was making him out to seem dangerous when, in reality, he was just dangerously depressed.

The next day, Friday, August 7, we received our first phone call from the Salt Lake County Jail. It was Eric. He had been allowed to make one call, and he called us. Jason put the call on speakerphone. "Mom and Dad, I did something really, really stupid." His voice was barely audible.

"We know," Jason said. "We've been talking to the police." We didn't tell him that they had caught him because I had called in a possible suicide attempt. "We know about *everything* that happened."

After a moment's silence, Eric said, "I only wanted enough money to buy one last dose of heroin. I never planned to leave that motel alive."

A horrible question arose, but I had to ask it despite myself. "How come you didn't go through with it?"

"The hotel clerk told me I couldn't check in until they

changed the sheets and cleaned up the room," he said softly. "She told me it would be another hour or so."

For the want of clean sheets in a cheap, run-down motel room, our son had been delayed just long enough so that the police were able to apprehend him in the parking lot. His car was filled with empty syringes and other drug paraphernalia. If the room had been ready, if the sheets had been clean, if I hadn't called in the suicide report, if Eric had turned off his phone. . . . I realized how close we had come to having our lives obliterated.

I'll never know why or how it all worked out the way it did, but the universe paused for just a moment in our favor. I didn't believe then, nor do I believe now, that a supreme being somehow protected our son. That doesn't lessen my gratitude one iota, but it doesn't explain what happened, either. There are too many tragic stories of babies and children and young mothers and fathers who are struck down too early, who don't get protected, and who die in the middle of an uncompleted life. Nor am I misguided enough to count it as a sign of righteousness on our part, for we, like most people, were simply doing our best to muck through the messiness of each day. For whatever reason, at that precise instant all the individual events and seconds of the morning had lined up exactly in the way they needed to for our son to be arrested and kept alive. The magnitude of this unearned gift from the universe will forever be engraved on my heart.

CHAPTER 32

No Guarantees

After Eric was arrested, he declared himself indigent since he was no longer living with us and had no means of income. We heard that a pro bono attorney had been assigned to his case. We also heard that while some counties had highly competent pro bono attorneys, others did not. We decided that we couldn't take the chance of risking our son's future with the possibility of incompetent legal representation.

One of my cousins who had been practicing law for years in the state of Utah did some research and provided us with the name of a lawyer who she thought would be the best fit for Eric, a man named Daniel Stewart.[212] This defense attorney had decades of experience and had worked with many of the judges in the state. He charged a substantial retainer fee up front in order to secure his services. His fee was higher than we had anticipated, and although we were by no means wealthy, with a bit of financial stretching it was possible.

We didn't want our son to get out of jail immediately; we were afraid he would overdose. But neither did we want him spending years behind bars for taking $600 from a bank. We believed the potential penalty to be far too harsh for the crime committed, especially since no threat of violence or weapon had been involved. If the goal of imprisonment was truly correction, we felt that a shorter sentence could provide that. We were convinced that a longer sentence would be counterproductive, not only for our son, but also for the state that had locked him up. It seemed far more sensible to let him do some time, pay restitution to the bank, and get the mental health services he desperately needed. The lawyer we found agreed.

When we first hired Mr. Stewart, I sent him a lengthy email detailing our son's life history and drug issues. Part of that statement included the fact that our son had come out as gay and that, as a result, our family were no longer participating members in the Mormon Church.

Mr. Stewart's telephone response to my email was compassionate and heartfelt: "I think we can clearly see that this is not a dangerous young man—this is a young man with a drug addiction who is crying out for help."

A sense of relief rushed over me. This stranger, even if we had paid him, really seemed to care about our son. As we talked further, he told me that his own son had also become addicted to heroin a few years earlier. Like Eric, his son had been raised in the Mormon Church, and after coming out as gay, had left his family's religious heritage behind. Then his son had joined the military but was eventually discharged after his drug addiction developed.

"The thing that finally saved our son was a full year in rehab," Mr. Stewart told me.

"A full year! Where did he go?" I knew how much a single month cost.

"He qualified for treatment at the VA Hospital in Salt Lake because of his prior military service. Without that help. . . ." His voice trailed off.

"Whatever it takes to get our son clean is OK with me," I said. "But I can't see anything good to his being in jail for more than a year."

He agreed with me. "Oh, there won't be anything good that comes from a sentence longer than that. At first, the jail environment can teach new prisoners a thing or two, but if they stay in too long, whatever benefit they gain is lost. Rather than helping nonviolent offenders, we are hurting them."

What was the perfect balance between helping and hurting? I kept turning over the possibilities: Helping or hurting? Too short? Too long? Finally, I realized that I had no say in the matter and would have to sit back and watch and wait. This lawyer soon became a lifeline for us and our son. He was the only person who stopped us from veering off into total despair. We spent several hours on the phone with him and exchanged multiple emails. He visited with Eric a few times in jail. Soon, almost every phone conversation with our son started with, "Mr. Stewart says . . . ."

Shortly after Eric was arrested, Jason started searching the Internet to see what the penalties might be for such a crime. What he found was worse than grim—it was completely terrifying. We learned that in 1934 it had become a "federal crime to rob any national bank or state member bank of the Federal Reserve System" and that penalties attached to these sorts of crimes are far heavier than those attached to most other types of robberies.[213] Jason read that federal bank robberies could have sentences ranging from one to twenty years. While there was a wide range of punishments that accounted for all sorts of circumstances, the fact that federal charges might be involved was a devastating possibility. We didn't share this information with Eric because we thought it would distress him even more.

Our son's lawyer told us that Eric's crime, although nonviolent, still might involve a federal prosecution since it occurred inside a bank. He warned us that if the feds became involved, we could be looking at a much more serious penalty, both in terms of time and placement. He said that the best outcome would be to have the state of Utah prosecute our son on a drug possession charge, but he couldn't promise that that would happen. "There are no guarantees" became the most repeated phrase in many of our conversations.

Early on, Mr. Stewart told us that Eric was one of the few clients he had represented who still had any sense of clarity about him, whose eyes hadn't been permanently dulled by repeated drug use. How our son survived all of this without losing his life or his cognitive abilities is a mystery to me. I don't believe it was a miracle—I don't believe in any god stingy enough to parcel out miracles to the favored few. There are too many good people who never get the miracles they pray for—who was I to assume that any fortunate twist of fate meant that my family was somehow special?

It occurred to me more than once that our son was locked up with a dangerous group of men. There were violent offenders in the jail, and although they were kept in a separate wing, the mere fact of their presence spooked me. And even in the low-security wing that Eric was housed in, serious fights broke out multiple times, leading to lockdowns for all prisoners in their cells for twenty-four hours at a minimum, and sometimes longer.

Eric's bank robbery had been his final cry for help; he had reached the end of his ability to cope. He had passed the bank teller a note asking for cash in smaller bills. She had given him $600; he had thanked her and left the bank. Throughout his imprisonment, a single question kept running through my mind: How could a child who was so deeply loved lose all hope?

CHAPTER 33

Lifeline

Two years prior to our son's arrest, I had gone to see my family doctor because I knew something was wrong with me. I was dragging myself through my days with what felt like a two-ton weight hanging around my neck, and the utter exhaustion reminded me of how I had felt in high school when I had contracted mononucleosis. When I went to work each morning, it was all I could do to leadenly place one foot in front of the other and climb the two sets of stairs to my classroom. At the top of the staircase, I would be out of breath and have to pause for several moments. I had been physically active for my entire life, so this crushing fatigue was troubling.

"I've never been this tired," I told Dr. Henley as I settled onto the blue exam table in his office.

He knew about Eric's drug use because Eric had been a previous patient of his. As always, he opened the visit with, "How's your son doing?"

"He's not OK. He keeps relapsing. We've tried everything." I pulled in a heavy breath.

The doctor checked my lungs and my heart and then poked and prodded around my abdomen. I winced when he touched a couple of spots near the upper right side just under my ribs. He peered at me intently. "Just lie here and rest while we wait for the bloodwork."

After he left, I lay there staring at the ceiling. I can't do this anymore, I thought. I have nothing left to give.

A few minutes later, the door swung open, and Dr. Henley walked in. He pulled his chair up to the exam table and looked at me silently for a moment. "The test for mono was positive, and your liver and spleen are slightly enlarged. And I don't even need to ask if you're stressed because I can tell by looking at you that you can't keep carrying this burden. It's going to break you."

I felt a rush of hot tears pooling in my eyes. "I know, but there's nothing I can do."

His gray-blue eyes were kind, but his tone was direct: "You need to quit your job. You can't keep this up."

"I can't quit," I said. "We have a house payment to make, and I don't have the luxury of lying around for a couple of years waiting for our son's drug problems to go away."

He brought his hands together near his face and tapped his index fingers together. "Let me tell you something about heroin. I've treated patients who were wonderful people until they got hooked on pain pills. Once they progressed to heroin, they abandoned their children and families and became shadows of their former selves." I knew that he was a father himself. "I know how strong the mother-child bond is," he continued. "I think it's probably the strongest force on the planet, and if heroin can make a mother neglect her own child —" He blew out a breath. "Anything that can make a mother do *that* is the most destructive thing in the world."

I listened silently, dabbing at my eyes with the tissues that had materialized in his hand. "In your case, the mother-child bond is killing you. You can't throw out your son, but you can't live with the stress, either."

"Well, I can take two weeks off work," I said. "Then maybe I could start taking one to two days off each week so that I can keep up with my students but have some time in the middle of the week to recuperate."

"That's better than nothing." He paused for a moment as if considering what to say next. "I'll tell you what I know about rehab success. If you want your son to have the best possible chance at recovery, you should pray that he is arrested."

That caught my attention, and I sat up on the exam

table. "Arrested?" Never before had I considered that being arrested might be a good thing.

"I know it sounds shocking, but studies show that jail time can be a more effective deterrent to repeated drug use than many rehab programs are."

His words made sense, but I couldn't quite accept them. Jason and I had tried so hard to help our son stay clean that an arrest sounded like a huge step backwards. "It's a *good* thing?" I asked.

"Not always," he said. "And there are dangers that come with being locked up. But in Eric's case, I think it would help."

I left the exam room with his words echoing in my mind. Later that day I told Jason what the doctor had said; after discussing it, we still were terrified by the prospect of Eric being arrested. I have often been grateful that this kind, wise man suggested the possibility that a stint in jail might actually be a helpful thing, and I tucked those words away in a safe place in case I ever needed them again. Two years later, that conversation with Dr. Henley would ring true with the force of prophecy. His advice proved to be the tiniest toehold on the sheer vertical cliff that Jason and I now found ourselves hanging from.

After our son was locked up in the county jail, we knew that he was, at least temporarily, locked away from his demons. But I continued to wrestle with mine round the clock. Was he safe? Was anybody threatening him? Our son, despite his drug use, was a handsome young man. He had expressive blue eyes and a striking facial structure. I could imagine that he would be appealing to any number of prisoners who were in there.

No parent wants their child to be locked up in a cage. It's true that our son broke the law and did something incredibly stupid. It's also true that he was suffering from deadly substance abuse problems. Jason and I had wanted Eric to be locked away somewhere that would keep him safe, such as a long-term, inpatient hospital program—something that could save his life and snap him out of the haze of addiction. Although our family doctor had warned me that jail time might be the only way to save our son's life, when it did occur, it was one of the most frightening experiences of our lives.

Our son was like a fish out of water. He was introverted and intensely private. He instinctively knew to lie low, avoid confrontation, and bide his time. The mental agonies he experienced while being locked in jail must have been horrible; to this day, he refuses to speak about it.

Once we figured out how to deposit money to his phone account, Eric called us repeatedly, up to five, six, or more times per day. A privately owned, outside entity collected money from the families, and the prices for these calls were much more expensive than regular phone rates, costing us about $300 per month. We could afford it, but we suspected that most of the other people who were incarcerated could not pay for such luxuries. One of the first times he called, he begged us to bail him out, but Jason and I had already discussed that possibility and decided that bailing him out would be a catastrophic mistake. We had put the phone on loudspeaker so all three of us could be in on the conversation.

"You *have* to bail me out!" he pleaded. "I cannot stand to be here! Please! Please! Please!" He sounded frantic and out of breath.

"We can't bail you out because we are trying to protect you," I told him.

"If you really wanted to help me, you'd get me out of here!"

"We're not going to do it," Jason said. "We don't trust you right now to take care of yourself, so we're leaving you in."

"How much is the bail?" Eric asked. Our lawyer had told us that bail had been set at $25,000.

"It's too much for us to even consider right now," Jason said. "And Mr. Stewart told us it's a bad idea."

"I will lose my mind if I have to stay in here! If you won't bail me out, I'm going to find some other way to get the money on my own!"

We knew that was an impossibility because we were his only reliable connection to the outside world. I knew that the air inside his cell was stuffy and hot. Our son no doubt looked out of his transparent cage door and wondered why we wouldn't bring him home, why we didn't love him enough to do that. Telling him "no" every time he called asking us to get him out was an exquisite form of torture. It left no external marks, but it tore off pieces of my heart each time he asked.

"No, no, no, no, no, no, no, no."

"No—we can't bail you out." *Because we want you to live.*

"No—we can't bail you out." *Because we value your life more than you do.*

"No—we can't bail you out." *Because we love you enough to make you hate us.*

Before his arrest, Jason and I had dragged him out of bed and forcibly driven him to more than one emergency room. We had heard his tearful apologies, his heaving his heart into his mouth to cry out that he didn't know how to stop using. I dreaded getting a text or a voice message on my phone; every message I had received in the previous two years had only brought bad news: your son has run away from rehab, your son is in jail, your son is in the emergency room, your son has been kicked out of sober living for a drug violation, we don't know where your son is. For several years, I flinched whenever my phone rang or a text message appeared.

I experienced a case of sympathetic claustrophobia. Knowing that *he* was locked up locked *me* up, too. I was trapped inside an invisible cage that followed me wherever I went—to work, to the store, to bed. I was trapped with him. His father and I had both cried more tears than we ever had before. Would there ever be an end? Surely there was a reservoir that was nearly empty—surely our eyes would soon be dry.

During a phone call about one month after he was arrested, Eric complained bitterly that everybody else was getting bailed out except him. "They go out high-fiving each other and laughing, and I know they've done way worse stuff than I did."

Jason repeated our stock response: "Eric, we know this is hard. You also know we won't bail you out. You're just going to have to come to terms with that. It doesn't mean that we don't love you. In fact, it means that our top priority is keeping you alive."

"That's it!" Eric yelled. "I *never* want to speak to you *again!*" He slammed the phone down only a few minutes into our phone call.

Jason and I stared at each other, shocked into silence. How was this our child? The years of loving him seemed to vanish in an instant, leaving behind nothing but ashes. Jason reached over and grabbed my hand. But before we could fully process our son's rage or our own heartbreak, the phone rang again. It was Eric. "Mom, Dad, I'm sorry," he said crying. "I'm sorry! I love you, and I don't have anybody else left." We understood his grief; in fact, we shared it. This emotional seesawing was brutal to the extreme, and we never knew what would happen next.

Eventually, Eric stopped asking about getting out. But we knew that he clung tightly to our emotional and physical support. We never stopped calling him, visiting him, writing to him, depositing money into his commissary account, or thinking about him. He knew that we were his only remaining lifeline; what he didn't know is that we needed him as desperately as he needed us.

CHAPTER 34

A Visit to the Zoo

It took us a couple of days to learn how and when we could visit Eric at the Salt Lake County Jail. No drop-in visits were allowed, and since there were only certain days and times available, appointments had to be made up to seven days in advance. Prisoners were allowed two thirty-minute visits from groups of up to three people every week. For Eric's first visit, I had told Jason that he would have to go alone since I couldn't bear to see Eric locked up; however, the morning of the visit, I relented. I decided that my son's need for emotional support outweighed my fear.

When we arrived, we had to show government-issued ID cards and then lock our cell phones, sunglasses, watches, and hats into keyed lockers that were provided. We were required to be there at least thirty minutes before our scheduled visit, but not earlier than forty-five minutes in advance. We were not allowed to carry anything in with us for our son. Next, after passing single file through a metal detector, we were herded into another stark waiting room. One guard stood at the head of the room while we waited for our thirty-minute visitation to begin. A small, ceiling-mounted TV screen showed grainy images of mindless sitcoms and local news stories. We sat on wide, backless, concrete benches, along with all the other mismatched humans who had somehow washed into this waiting room along with us. Most families kept to themselves; I rarely saw people conversing with anybody outside of the small group they entered with. They all seemed lost in their own private thoughts, trying to disappear or to become anonymous or to make sense of whatever particular chain of circumstances had brought them here.

I have no complaints about the jailers and guards themselves. Some were kinder than others. Some tried to be courteous to visiting family members; others looked bored or irritated. Most of them were doing their best in a difficult, dirty job that nobody else wanted, no doubt trying to pay the bills and care for their own families. It would have been easy to become jaded by the flotsam of disheveled humanity that washed in and out of the backwaters of the Salt Lake County Jail. I saw prune-faced, twitchy meth addicts visiting their loved ones who were in jail while they themselves could hardly stop picking on their scabs or writhing on the concrete visiting benches. I saw heavily pregnant women who had aged prematurely, dragging their toddlers behind them to visit with the biological fathers of their children.

Being a prison guard must be one of the most stressful jobs in the world. They endure hours of boredom punctuated by moments of bottled-up, impotent rage that explode at even the slightest provocation. When a fight broke out, prisoners were locked in their cells for twenty-four hours or even longer. Whenever they declared a lockdown, we waited in suspense to hear from our son. Was he safe? Had anyone been seriously harmed? There was no way of knowing until the lockdown was lifted and the men were allowed to line up at the pay phones that lined the halls. I heard the desperation in our son's voice whenever he called and wondered how much more he could take.

For our first visit, after we had waited for about twenty minutes, guards pointed us in the direction of the visiting rooms, and we walked down a long, concrete hallway in silence with other groups of visitors. Jason and I had mistakenly assumed that we would be able to sit in the same room with Eric and embrace him, which we thought was essential to his mental health, but unfortunately, no physical contact was ever allowed.

Once we arrived at our assigned location, we were all funneled into a narrow room that held up to five groups of visitors on one side of a thick, plexiglass window. Five small, circular, metal stools—seemingly designed to cause extreme discomfort to whoever sat on them—were bolted to the floor. After we waited for another five to twenty minutes, the prisoners appeared on the opposite side of the windows, escorted by guards. There would be anywhere from one to five men who had small partitions separating them from each other, ostensibly for security purposes. I worried that it would be easy for a prisoner who was angry to cause serious damage by moving or reaching into the next partition before a guard could intervene.

We were surprised to see that there were no phones or visible openings or slits through which we could communicate. Instead, visitors were expected to press their ears up against the acrylic windows and listen intently while their loved ones on the other side tried to yell through the impenetrable barrier. Reportedly, there were lines of 1/16-inch holes that had been drilled into the window frames to allow voices to pass through but nothing else, such as wires or drugs.[214] Whether or not the holes actually existed, I just know that conversing in such a way was nearly impossible.

Jason and I were able to make out about 75 percent of what our son was trying to communicate, and this was only after repeatedly yelling and using copious hand gestures. When it was our turn to "talk" back to him, we yelled as loudly as we could against the transparent partition while he tried to discern at least a semblance of what we were communicating. Unlike those who were locked up, the visitors had no dividing walls between them, so while we were yelling at our son, families who were a short distance away from us were yelling at their incarcerated family member. It often became a shouting match to see who could scream the loudest. If one of the other prisoners became especially infuriated, which happened on more than one occasion, the entire room of visiting family members and friends were a captive audience to flaming explosions of vulgar language and obscenities communicated with wildly gesticulating hands. We always felt lucky during our visits if there were no or only a few other visitors in the room with us, but it didn't happen often.

As we visited with Eric, I noticed that the metal counter on our side of the room was smudged with fingerprints and most likely harboring the germs from a thousand unwashed palms—each handprint a testament to those who came to cry with or yell at their loved ones being held captive in the zoo.

Jason and I always drove to the jail on Wednesday afternoons and Saturday mornings and only missed a single visit during Eric's incarceration unless the prison was in lockdown mode. From the time we left from work, waited our usual thirty to forty-five-minutes for the visit, completed the actual thirty-minute visit, and finally drove back home, it was about a three- to four-hour round trip, depending on traffic and road conditions. We were making this trip twice a week on top of our fifty to sixty hours of work as full-time schoolteachers. Visiting our son soon became the only thing that we did outside of work. There was no time, energy, or desire to socialize with anybody, including friends and family. Energy was a precious commodity, to be hoarded at all costs, and only to be spent in maintaining our sanity, our marriage, our jobs, and our son's life. We were experiencing the psychological version of tunnel vision. We could see nothing and deal with nothing outside of getting through every twenty-four-hour period that our son was locked up. Nothing else mattered.

Part of the exhaustion that came from interacting with our son during his jail stay was that we needed to keep our spirits somewhat lifted and at least pretend to feel hopeful. As we drove down to visit him, we often rehearsed aloud what we would say, and gave each other feedback on whether or not our comments were too negative or too idealistic. We didn't want to cause him to despair or to develop false hope.

"I'm going to tell him he has to just think positive and endure this situation," Jason said one afternoon as we drove to the county jail. "I had so many times in the Navy that I wanted to give up, but I stuck it out and I survived it."

"Yes," I said. "But you are also very different from Eric in temperament. I don't want him to think that you're telling him he has to handle this like you would in order to do it 'right'."

"I'm not telling him that, I'm just telling him that everybody goes through hard times."

"Yes." I stared out the window silently and thought about how many times we had had this exact conversation, only in different words. I blew out an exasperated sigh through pursed lips.

"What? You don't seem to agree. Whenever you sigh like that, I know you're not done talking." His voice sounded on edge, but I could tell that he was trying to be accommodating.

"I want to tell him that I understand how difficult this is and that I completely understand it if he's depressed."

Even though we disagreed about the exact tone our conversations should take, between the two of us we tried to provide him with a balance of toughness and tenderness. After each visit, we left emotionally drained. Seeing other families sitting in there, stonelike, with the same weary expressions of frustration and hopelessness stamped onto their faces made it worse. I tried not to stare at them, and they tried not to stare at me. But I could imagine what they were thinking. "Did you ever think you'd end up in here?" Or "Oops! He did it again." Or "What the hell do we do now?"

We worried that our son would soon pass the point of instruction and harvest the bitter crop of a hardened heart and a twisted soul. We watched and waited as we hoped that he would escape his confinement before it devoured him. Each time we saw him, his eyes looked like they had sunken deeper into their sockets. The bones of his face became more pronounced, and the haunted, hooded look never left his face. He slumped over heavily as if he were wearing a sack of boulders around his neck. I knew that he was suffering from the twin burdens of despair and shame. I also knew that prisoners sometimes committed suicide while locked up; I fervently begged whatever powers might be that my son would *not* become the next suicide statistic.

CHAPTER 35

The Cube

In 1997, audiences were terrorized by a Canadian sci-fi horror film called *The Cube*, in which a group of individuals wake up inside a massive building with a Rubik's cube structure that rotates and changes its configuration at seemingly random intervals. Each time the cube transforms and its thousands of rooms are shuffled, new dangers are unleashed. Wire-thin razors slice hapless characters in half; doors that seem to open to escape routes actually open into black pits of nothingness; and with each rotation of the giant matrix, new horrors are thrust upon the characters, who eventually succumb to claustrophobic madness.

It wasn't until our son was imprisoned in the Salt Lake County Jail that I got a partial glimpse into what life inside a claustrophobic cage would be like. Each time we entered the building to visit our son, I felt like a prisoner myself. The jail's exterior, with its gray, cheerless, concrete walls, sends a somber message: "Abandon hope, all ye who enter here." Opened in 2000 at a cost of $135 million, the jail is classified as a maximum-security building, yet holds minimum-, medium-, and maximum-security prisoners. Those assigned to the minimum-security areas are housed in seven-by-ten-foot boxed enclosures with floor-to-ceiling, two-inch thick plexiglass walls. Inside the cells, there is no privacy, for one cell wall abuts the next. Prisoners can watch each other sleep, urinate, and dress. The only exercise areas are tiny spaces enclosed within "tall, sheer walls." The jail, which has a capacity for about 2,000 prisoners, was constructed with a podular design, with cells built around open, common areas. A single guard can easily see any one of the thirty-two housing units that he supervises, which has led to increased safety because every cell is within "direct sightline" of at least one guard.[215] Cells have locking doors, but no bars, which also increases visibility.

Nearby Oxbow Jail, completed in 1992, is a minimum-security facility that has been through multiple closures and reopenings, depending upon the number of prisoners in the county jail. Oxbow Jail was fully reopened in 2018 as a facility for nonviolent offenders;[216] unfortunately, during our son's incarceration, Oxbow was mostly closed and could therefore only accept prisoners who met certain narrow criteria. Because of this, Eric was assigned to the much larger, and potentially more dangerous, county jail.[217]

In the county jail, prisoners had no access to any extra supplies for their first two weeks until somebody on the outside deposited money to their commissary accounts. Once we figured out the procedure to provide funds, Eric could afford what were considered "luxuries" to the men who were locked up: foam earplugs, tiny packets of tasteless instant coffee, hard candies, small pieces of soap, deodorant, and three-inch golf pencils for writing letters. Prisoners were not provided with pillows but were given a thin mattress to lie on. Those lucky enough to have funds contributed by their families or friends could purchase their own pillows, which were limp, nearly flat pads that prisoners usually placed over their own faces to block the lights that were left on twenty-four hours per day inside the cells for security reasons.

Each cell contains two small, combination-lock safes; nonetheless, petty theft ran rampant. One day Eric didn't lock up his meager commissary purchases for only a few minutes because he was sitting just yards away at a table in the commons area where prisoners took their meals. Just before he returned to his cell, he saw another prisoner dart in and out of it in a fraction of a second: if he had blinked, he would have missed it. Several other prisoners had also seen this man slip into our son's cell and told him who had done it. This prisoner had apparently made quite a few enemies by his habit of pursuing five-finger discounts at any opportunity.

Eric was incensed when he saw that some of his things had been stolen, yet he faced a dilemma: if he reported the theft, there was the risk of everybody being put on "lockdown," a twelve to forty-eight-hour period where all cell doors were locked shut and nobody could leave their cells for any reason. But if he didn't report it, he might be viewed as a soft target. After he decided to report the theft, the man was moved to a new location, and our son never saw him again. It struck me as bleakly ironic that our son would expect any level of honesty from the people he was incarcerated with.

He had a few different cellmates during his time in the jail. His favorite was an older man who played guitar and often sang to assembled groups. This was one of the few forms of entertainment available to prisoners, in addition to watching old movies on small, wall-mounted televisions with blurry resolution at best. There were hours of boredom interspersed with three meager, substandard meals per day, occasional showers, and chances to wait at the pay phones that lined the hall and were always in use. Prisoners often attended whatever few group activities there were, usually run by local volunteers. Our son attended a group session run by an elderly Mormon couple who sweetly and sincerely told him that Jesus could help him overcome his drug addiction if he had enough faith. Even though he didn't find their sessions to be helpful, he went anyway just to have something to do.

His least favorite cellmate was one he had about four months into his incarceration. This man held drug chats in their cell, inviting in a few prisoners at a time and instructing them on how to get drugs as quickly as possible after they got out and whom they should contact to accomplish this. These tutoring sessions made our son understandably nervous. When he communicated this to me during a phone call, I emailed our attorney and asked him if we should consider bailing Eric out under the circumstances. Mr. Stewart answered almost immediately and told us that bailing our son out would send the wrong message to the judge. He said that it would be important for Eric to still be locked up when the judge sentenced him; otherwise, it might send the message that he hadn't fully paid the penalty for his robbery. We followed his advice, and Eric remained in jail.

Gossip abounded as prisoners told stories about their comrades who had caused problems. One story circulating concerned a former prisoner who had taken a running leap and plunged over the guardrail from the upper floor in his section, landing headfirst on the concrete floor below before he could be stopped. Another story recounted the tale of a convict who showed his displeasure at the tasteless prison meals by squatting atop a table during supper, emptying his bowels, and throwing the resulting substance at the guards who tried to stop him. Based on our son's reports, there was good reason for this convict's admittedly unusual method of getting his point across.

The food he was served was subpar at best: gristly meat that he often was unable to choke down; watery, instant potatoes; and canned, mushy, unidentifiable vegetables. More than once, our son became ill after eating. He told us there were wild rumors that the canned meat was being produced in a dog-food factory. The portions were small, which regularly resulted in prisoners being hungry unless they were fortunate enough to have funds donated that allowed them to purchase snacks at the jail commissary.[218] Eric told me that he spent hours reminiscing about all of the times we had cooked together during his growing-up years; he wondered if he'd ever be able to eat real food any time soon. While he was dreaming about more edible meals, he craved cigarettes, coffee, and candy. He told us that after about three weeks, his craving for opioids had ceased, but that his raging hunger for sugar had grown exponentially.

Eric read around the clock to stave off boredom. He would send us book requests, and several Saturdays on our way home from visiting him, we would stop at bookstores and purchase the requested items. Jail rules stipulated that no books could be mailed in from family or friends. Instead, once books were purchased, they had to remain at the bookstore; then the bookstore was required to follow a strict series of procedures to get the books into the jail. In addition, prisoners could have only a certain number of books with them in their cells. Once the maximum number was reached, they had to turn their books in to the jail library before they could check out anything else. We spent several hundred dollars on books, which we were happy to do for our son, but once they were turned in to the library, they became the permanent property of the jail.

Prisoners had zero access to the Internet or any websites. Even receiving letters from the outside was a lengthy, complicated process. We were given a photocopy of the mailing rules, which we took home and memorized. Most of them were designed to limit the many creative ways that prisoners had devised to receive drugs from the outside world.

"Mailing Rules:

- Incoming mail will be <u>opened and inspected</u> for contraband before being delivered to the prisoner.
- All materials, except paper products and photographs up to 4x6 are considered contraband.
- Incoming mail containing the following [prohibited items] will be returned to sender. In some cases items will be removed and discarded. If this cannot be done without destroying text or pictures, they will be returned.
- **Prohibited Items**
  - Stamps - Soiled or Stained Paper - Tape - Stickers
  - Glue - Lipstick - Staples - Correction tape or liquid
  - Paper clips - Nude photographs - Watermarks
  - Prisoner to prisoner correspondence (unless pre-

approved)

- Crayon - Instant Photographs - Photo Stickers
- Glitter or Confetti - Paint marks - Marker or highlighter
- Mail containing more than four (4) Photographs
- Blank greeting or post cards - Laminated items
- Enclosed blank paper, envelopes, or other writing materials will be discarded.
- Stamps and stamped envelopes are contraband and will be returned."

There were more rules than this, but soon we knew them all. However, my eighty-year-old mother had a letter returned to her because she had drawn a red heart using a colored marker on the outer envelope. Apparently, prisoners in the past had found ways to smuggle in drugs using such markings. For security reasons, every letter that we sent in was ripped open and scrutinized.

A few of Eric's friends wrote occasional letters to him. Some family members wrote him, too. His father and I wrote him multiple letters per week. We knew that these missives from the outside world were one of the things helping him to stay sane. Jason was a level-four math teacher, which allowed him to teach all high school math courses, including calculus and statistics. Eric had always been good at math, so at his request, Jason sent in sheets of complicated math problems. Once Eric had tried to solve them, he and Jason would discuss the answers and any questions that Eric had during our phone calls with him.

I had to dig deep to find interesting, uplifting things to say. Sometimes Eric and I wrote silly limericks back and forth to each other, seeing who could come up with the most ridiculous rhymes. One of our favorites was one that I composed:

> The cannibal chief was a sinner
> Who cooked his own brother for dinner,
> But the guilt that he felt

Has made him quite svelte:
He eats vegetables now, so he's thinner.
Another favorite was one that I found online:
An amoeba named Max, and his brother
were sharing a drink with each other;
In the midst of their quaffing,
They split themselves laughing,
And each of them now is a mother.

When I ran out of anything of substance, I resorted to repeating gossip stories about the movie stars, actors, and politicians whose escapades were reported round the clock on various websites. My son and I both knew that I was scraping the bottom of the barrel whenever I reported a celebrity's failed marriage or unsuccessful cosmetic surgery procedure, but we both played along, pretending like these trivial topics were worth repeating. In truth, they were simply a smokescreen to mask the despair that Eric, Jason, and I were drowning in as the minutes, hours, days, and weeks ticked past. Eric's life in the cube was suffocating us all.

CHAPTER 36

Dubious Distinction

For years, Utah was one of nearly twenty states that did not require jail inspections or outside oversight.[219] Gary DeLand, a former Salt Lake County jail administrator, worked as a private contractor with the state, providing training guidelines which were used throughout the state but kept hidden from the public. Public outcry called for more transparency inside the jails when Utah achieved the dubious distinction of having the highest rate of deaths for incarcerated persons in the United States in 2014.[220] In 2017, Senator Todd Weiler announced his decision to sponsor a 2018 bill that would mandate that jails "submit certain policies to the Legislature." He stressed that the jails needed to open those policies up to scrutiny and that the "legislators [needed] to have that data."[221] In 2018, after pressure from several sources, DeLand held a news conference in which he claimed that his rules were "some of the nation's best but they needed to be kept confidential." Senator Weiler replied that he was "very uncomfortable that we have taxpayer-supported facilities with taxpayer-paid-for standards that are secret."[222] The Utah Sheriffs' Association then announced that it would make at least some of those 600 standards public, but some confusion remained about whether existing standards or new standards would be released on the Association's website. Finally, in 2021, after a successful lawsuit against the Davis County jail by the American Civil Liberties Union and the Disability Law Center, jail officials were required to release the complete jail standards to the court, which reviewed them and "redact[ed] sensitive information" before making them available to the public for the first time.[223]

The *Salt Lake Tribune* reported that the agreement to provide public transparency would help explain why suicide was the "most common cause of death in [Utah's] county jails," especially in the first few hours following a person's arrest.[224] The fear that our son would become one of those suicide statistics never left my mind. Because I had insisted that he be put on a suicide watch after he was arrested, he was housed in a single-occupancy cell which supposedly had closer monitoring than the regular cells did. After a few days of observation, it was decided that Eric was not a suicide risk, and he was moved into the regular jail population and assigned a cellmate.

I was still very concerned about Eric's state of mind, which I communicated to his lawyer and, through him, to the jail. Eric had been prescribed Zoloft and Wellbutrin for anxiety and depression some years earlier. Although he had stopped taking both of them during the height of his drug addiction, I was convinced that he needed to start taking them again. After two months of my repeatedly asking about his access to medication, he was finally given these two drugs. He reported to me that he felt "a little bit better," but was still having problems sleeping. When I passed that information on to the jail's nurse, I was told that it was a "common side-effect of detoxing from opioids" and would eventually get better.

Since Eric's incarceration, I have paid more attention to the goings-on in jails and prisons throughout the state. One particularly disturbing story involved the death of a twenty-one-year-old woman named Madison Jensen, who turned herself in to the Duchesne County jail in order to receive help for her heroin addiction in 2016.[225] According to The Office of the Medical Examiner, Jensen had died "of a probable cardiac arrhythmia caused by dehydration in the setting of opiate withdrawal." Although Jensen was vomiting continuously and suffering from diarrhea, the Duchesne County nurse who was tasked with monitoring Jensen's health neglected to treat Jensen or to respond to her medical crisis. Deputies and Jensen's cellmate Maria Hardinger reported Jensen's worsening condition to nurse Jana Clyde, who still "made no assessment" and refused to "check on the welfare of the victim."[226]

Nine months after Jensen's death, Clyde was charged with negligent homicide in a lawsuit brought by Jensen's father, Jared Jensen. Medical records showed that Jensen lost at least seventeen pounds in the four days she was incarcerated. "When she says she didn't eat or drink for four days and you still didn't put an IV in her arm, you dropped the ball on her," he said.[227] Although the lawsuit was first dismissed by District Judge Lyle Anderson in 2018, in 2020 the Utah Supreme Court and Court of Appeals overturned the decision and ordered a new criminal trial. Federal judge Dale Kimball, the new judge assigned to the case, wrote: "There are questions . . . as to nurse Clyde's training and a reasonable jury could find Clyde . . . disregarded the risk to her [Jensen] by not obtaining adequate treatment."[228] Then in December 2022, Clyde was found not guilty; however, the presiding judge, Judge Torgerson, condemned the "obvious institutional failures" at the Duchesne County Jail. Based on that ruling, the court granted Jared Jensen's request to have the previously dismissed county defendants added back to the lawsuit, which means the civil trial will continue. Jensen has vowed to never stop fighting for justice for his daughter.[229]

While Eric was in jail, he was losing weight, not sleeping much, and detoxing from a heroin and cocaine addiction. I wondered how carefully they would monitor him and if they would believe him if he told them that he needed help. The arresting deputy had earlier made light of my warning that my son was seriously depressed, telling me that he seemed "just fine" after he got arrested; his flippant attitude still nagged at me.

The fact is that the prison system is perfectly designed for one thing—locking people up in cages and limiting their exposure to the outside world. I don't fault the policemen, the guards, or the staff in this system. I think most of them are doing the best they can with the resources they have. However, when it comes to *helping* prisoners, especially nonviolent, drug-addicted, or mentally ill prisoners, most prisons in the United States are failing dismally. According to Alisa Roth, author of *Insane: America's Criminal Treatment of Mental Illness,* when one tries to "turn an institution designed to punish into one that is meant to cure," problems abound. The central conflict stems from a clash of philosophies between the "mental health care" and "criminal justice" systems and is nowhere near being resolved to anyone's satisfaction. Add to that persistent underfunding, "extreme overcrowding," and a chronic and critical shortage of qualified doctors and staff, and one sees why the essential needs of prisoners continue to be unmet.[230]

For a long time, the system has been unintentionally set up to guarantee failure in most cases. Prisoners have long been given very limited access to counseling, treatment options, or adequate medical or psychiatric care. Our son had to wait nearly two months to be allowed to access his medically prescribed antidepressants. While he was waiting, his spirits sank, his weight plummeted to an all-time low, and his once snugly fitting prison uniform flapped around him like a tent on a flagpole. Dark circles surrounded his eyes, and he had trouble maintaining eye contact with us when we visited. Convicts are given a one-size-fits-all mental health treatment, which often means limited or no treatment, largely due to the same issues that Roth points out in her book: overcrowding, underfunding, and understaffing. I often wondered how safe Eric really was inside his cage.

In June 2022, Governor Cox of Utah attended a ribbon-cutting ceremony in Salt Lake City for Utah's newest state prison, the Utah State Correctional Facility. With a capacity of nearly 3,700 prisoners,[231] the new prison will offer nonviolent offenders a lifeline: a chance to learn new job skills and to receive counseling about their maladaptive behaviors. Steve Turley, the director of the Clinical Services Bureau at the Utah Department of Corrections, says this rehabilitation approach is a good fit for nonviolent prisoners, who will have the chance to earn rewards for good behavior, such as more visits from friends and family and more commissary trips. One of the most notable improvements in the new prison is that nonviolent offenders can have "visits from family members or significant others that are not separated by walls and glass, during which they can hug their loved ones and are allowed one kiss at the end of the visit." This kind of physical contact could have made a world of difference to our jail visits with Eric. Unfortunately, we were never permitted to touch him or even be in the same room with him.

Some have criticized the new building as "too nice" for prisoners, who will have access to therapy rooms, multiple nondenominational chapels, libraries, barber shops, and computer labs, among other advantages. But Turley points out that almost 95 percent of those locked up in Utah state prisons will eventually be released and make their way into "your neighborhood, my neighborhood." He argues that it's only in our best interest to help these people reengage with life successfully after their debts to society are paid.[232] Despite diligent efforts at providing top-notch mental health care, however, the new prison at first found itself short-staffed and trying to process a "backlog of thousands" of prescriptions.[233] As of April 2024, however, the Utah Prisoner Advocate Network director, Molly Prince, has announced that services at the jail are "absolutely improving" since Brian Redd took over as the new executive director in 2023.[234] I can only say that as a member of the public who witnessed the old level of care in the Salt Lake County Jail, the new prison seems to be light-years ahead in at least attempting to offer adequate treatment options.

Unlike the nearly windowless Salt Lake County Jail where our son was housed, the new facility provides access to "natural daylight," which should improve the mental health of "both officers and inmates alike."[235] About five weeks after Eric was arrested, he was transported to the Salt Lake County court system inside a prison van to enter his guilty plea to a reduced charge of attempted robbery on the advice of his attorney. He and several other prisoners were moved together, all of them in their bright orange prison garb with their ankles and wrists shackled. Eric told us it was his first glimpse of the sky since his arrest. He admitted that the smell of the rain and the sight of the gray, overcast sky with its clouds gave him goosebumps and brought him to tears.

There will always be a tug-of-war between those who believe their family members are being mistreated during incarceration and those who believe that the public has already spent more than enough money on helping convicts. My own experience has taught me that if the critical mental health needs of prisoners are not met, there will be a much higher cost, not only in terms of dollars spent, but also in the price paid by the various communities that will eventually welcome these offenders back to society.

CHAPTER 37

Getting Out

When Eric pled guilty to attempted robbery on September 19, 2015, the original sentence imposed was up to five years in the county jail. Our biggest fear was that if he were forced to serve out the full length of that sentence, his life would be destroyed. Our attorney, Mr. Stewart, requested a new hearing and planned to argue that our son was a nonviolent offender, a young man in the grip of a substance-abuse illness who had been suicidal and had got himself arrested on purpose as a cry for help. We hoped that the judge would agree and find that the original sentence was overly harsh. After having his hearing delayed twice, Eric learned that he was finally headed to court on Monday, December 14, 2015, to hear the judge's decision. The weeks leading up to the hearing had been a time of high anxiety for all of us. Each day crawled by in slow motion, the minutes dragged out in what seemed to be an eternity. We tried to keep Eric's spirits up, but secretly Jason and I were terrified that the outcome might not be what we had all hoped for.

I was at school teaching one of my English classes that Monday afternoon when my phone started buzzing. I had been on a nervous watch all day, pacing and looking at my phone every few minutes. As a teacher, I forbade the use of cell phones during class, and I had always held myself to the same standard. On this day, however, I told my students that I was expecting an emergency message and explained that I might have to answer and leave the room.

When I glanced at the buzzing phone and saw the

phone number for our son's attorney, I instantly felt like I had breathed in too much nitrous oxide. Dizziness and nausea overtook me, and I could take only shallow, superficial breaths. I told my students to keep working on their assignment and quickly went to the hall and closed my classroom door behind me. I somehow managed to force out a few words: "Hello. What's happened?" I gripped my phone tightly so that it wouldn't fall out of my trembling hand.

"The judge agreed with our argument and has decided to release your son today." I swayed and leaned against the wall for support. Thankfully, and perhaps partly because then-Utah Governor Gary Herbert had signed House Bill 348 into law on March 31, 2015, the judge had agreed with our attorney's plea for a lesser sentence. H.B. 348 was an attempt by the state to substantially reduce the nonviolent prison population, thus saving the state millions of dollars and leaving more room in the burgeoning prison population for the truly dangerous criminals.[236]

"Today?" I was beyond thrilled but had expected that we'd have more time to prepare for Eric's homecoming. Exhilaration flooded me, warming me from the tips of my toes to the top of my head, and I realized that it had been years since I'd last felt any hope: feeling it well up inside of me now was like the embrace of an old friend whom I'd expected never to see again.

"Yes. Today. You will need to be at the jail from four o'clock on since Eric could be released anytime from then until midnight."

"Midnight? That late? On a winter night?"

Our attorney said that for some reason, prisoners often seemed to be released very late in the evenings, which was not only inconvenient for them and their families but also dangerous. He said he had seen prisoners released and standing outside the Salt Lake County Jail in the middle of the night, with nowhere to go and no money to get on the city bus.

As soon as we were done teaching for the day, Jason and

I left school and rushed to the jail. We were in the middle of a nasty winter snowstorm. On the way down, I fretted with each passing minute. "We're going to miss him! He'll be standing out there all alone! Drive faster!"

"I'm going as fast as I can," Jason said. He gripped the steering wheel tightly, trying to see his way through the gray, gloomy sky that was filled with large, wet snowflakes. The snowflakes turned into a thick, icy slush as soon as they hit the road. The last thing we wanted was to get in a car wreck before we could get there.

Once we arrived, the waiting game started. We checked in with the correctional officer, told her who we were, and provided the name of our son. She directed us to sit down on one of the hard chairs that were pushed up against the walls in the waiting area. We soon learned that the "waiting area" was aptly named as the minutes stretched into hours and my nerves grew taut with anticipation and dread. I wondered if something had gone wrong, if the judge had changed his mind, or if there had been a mix-up on the release date. There was a large, heavy metal door that prisoners walked through when they were released. We stared at the clock that hung on the wall above the door. Every so often, somebody would emerge from behind the door with a victorious look on his or her face and be greeted by one, two, or three people who surrounded the person with hugs and high-fives.

Most of the people who exited looked like they had led a hard life: missing teeth; fading tattoos; greasy, unkempt hair; and lined, prematurely aged faces. Five o'clock came and went. We watched the secondhand crawl around the circular clock in a maddeningly slow arc: six o'clock, seven o'clock, eight o'clock, nine o'clock. We talked to the correctional officer twice to make sure that we hadn't somehow gotten the time or the date mixed up. But we were fearful of angering the guards and somehow prolonging our son's release. I wondered how the other groups of waiting people felt. Were they scared? Or was this commonplace for them? I never had the guts to ask.

Ten o'clock came. The door swung open to reveal a disheveled young woman who was walking hesitantly. She came and sat on one of the seats not too far away from us. From where I was sitting, I could smell a strong body odor. She sat quietly and stared at the floor.

Female prisoners are an especially vulnerable part of the prison population. Because most of them have children on the outside, they are forced to rely on the support of their families, friends, or sometimes even strangers. And oftentimes, their families are so dysfunctional that caring for a child is the last thing they can do. I wondered what sort of cycle was being set up with jailed mothers and neglected children. It seemed like a recipe for disaster.

Nobody was there to meet her, so I watched to see when somebody would show up. After about twenty minutes had passed, I walked over to her. When she looked up at me, I could see that she was quite young, probably in her early twenties. I asked her who was coming to get her. She looked up at me with washed-out, vacant eyes. "I don't know."

"You don't know? Did you tell anybody you were getting out? Like your family?"

She looked down at her hands and twisted them in her lap. "I don't know anybody's phone numbers." She stared at me like a lost child. "I don't know where my mom lives anyway."

"You don't know where your mom lives?" It was freezing outside, and the snow was falling in a thick blanket. The young woman didn't have a coat or a jacket. I feared that eventually they might kick her out into the night. Anybody left outside in that weather would freeze to death, assuming they weren't assaulted first.

"But don't you know anybody?" I persisted. "A friend? A relative?"

"I have a baby boy." As she smiled up at me shyly, I noticed that she was missing a couple of upper teeth. "He's staying with my friend."

"Well, call your friend, then. I'm sure your boy wants to

see you."

The smile wavered on her face, and she dropped her head. "I can't remember her name," she said softly. "It's kind of hard for me to remember things." She started chewing on her lower lip.

"You don't know the name of the friend who has your baby?" As I was idiotically repeating everything she said, it dawned on me that this young woman was dealing with severe cognitive deficits. "You can't remember who she is?"

"Nope," she said, her mouth turning down at the edges.

"I have my cell phone," I said. "See if you can remember her last name and we'll try to call her."

We spent about thirty minutes trying different names, different phone numbers, and different addresses. Each time we'd call, the person on the other end would say, "I don't know who you're looking for. We definitely don't have a baby here."

The young woman slumped down in defeat. "Well, I guess I'm spending the night here."

I was shocked. This woman, who clearly had some sort of a learning disability, had no money, no coat, no friends, and no family that she could remember. What was she going to do? I had always heard that recidivism was particularly high among those prisoners who lacked supportive family connections on the outside. I couldn't see this girl lasting a night, let alone a week on the outside with no reliable support system.

At that moment, the door swung open to reveal our son. He was dressed in a one-piece, white paper jumpsuit with a long zipper up the front. On his feet he had a pair of bright orange, jail-issued Crocs. That was it. He had no idea where his clothes, shoes, cash, or cell phone had ended up after his arrest. His car had been impounded shortly after he was taken into custody, and after paying a hefty fee to get it back, we had driven it home and parked it in our driveway. We knew there were no personal belongings left inside.

The sorrow I felt for the young woman's plight was

momentarily forgotten as my husband and I hurried toward our son and threw our arms around him in a group hug. "We love you! We love you!" we whispered over and over. The joy at that moment was overwhelming, but a tiny part of my brain was aware of the young woman staring at us, her mouth hanging open. I knew that she wouldn't have any kind of homecoming.

It had taken us nearly sixty minutes to drive from work to the jail in the snow and the traffic. With the snowstorm still raging outside, it would take us at least ninety minutes, if not longer, to get home. Our son told us that a kindhearted guard had offered him a coat since all he had on was a thin paper suit. It was nice to know that someone on the inside had treated him with basic, human compassion. "It's all right," our son had told him. "My parents will be here."

And what about the prisoners who had nobody waiting for them? What would happen to them? For a second I considered asking the young woman to come with us, but I quickly rejected the idea as insane. She didn't know her family's phone number or the name of the person who had her small child. What if somebody showed up and she was gone? Would we be accused of kidnapping her? I had no idea what kind of messy situation we might be getting ourselves into.

I approached the officer on duty one last time and said, "There is a woman in the waiting room who just got released who has *no* idea where her family is. She doesn't have anybody's phone number. I can tell she has some sort of mental impairment, but I'm not sure what it is. It's freezing outside— can you let her spend the night here or try to help her contact her family?"

The officer nodded crisply but didn't make eye contact, and I wasn't entirely convinced that she would do anything. Meanwhile, I just wanted to get out of there and get our son safely home. It was now 11:30 p.m., and we were all exhausted.

Just then, a guard came out of the same door through which our son had exited.

"Here's your commissary money," he said. "You've got about fifty dollars left." He held out an envelope with a wad of paper bills and some coins inside along with a receipt.

I took the envelope, turned toward the young woman, and handed it to her. "Here. This is the rest of our son's commissary money. Take it—maybe you can get a hotel room for the night."

She looked up at me in surprise. "You're giving me money?"

"Yes," I said. "Now go talk to that guard and have her look up the information in your file. Maybe you can find the phone number of the person who has your son. Be careful—don't spend the night outside. It's too cold."

She nodded, and my husband and son, who were waiting impatiently for me, opened the waiting room glass doors into the freezing night. A blast of frigid air took my breath away after my prolonged stay in the small, stuffy waiting room. As we walked out, I turned back to look at the young woman one last time. She sat clutching the paper envelope I had given her, staring ahead blankly at the concrete wall.

We drove off into the storm, taking our son back to safety and what we hoped would be a new start. Yet I found myself thinking of this young woman for months. Had she found her son? Was she back in jail? Was there any hope of a happy ending for her? What kind of world was it if fifty dollars was the best hope of redemption for a lost soul?

CHAPTER 38

Blackbird

Our son was one of the fortunate people who had a home and family to return to. Many are not so lucky. According to the National Association of Housing and Redevelopment Officials (NAHRO), there are multiple causes of homelessness: a shortage of shelter beds, lack of affordable housing, insufficient wages, and racial discrimination, among others. Some groups of people more likely to experience homelessness are survivors of domestic violence, people on the LGBT spectrum, people exiting the criminal system, veterans, and unaccompanied youth under the age of eighteen. If one adds untreated mental health or substance abuse issues to the mix, the situation becomes more dire. And the problem isn't even close to being solved: NAHRO reports that after years of steadily dropping, homelessness among families and children rose 15.5 percent between 2022 and 2023.[237] Before our family's ordeal, I had looked at the dirty, unkempt men and women who shambled around the streets of our nation's largest cities with a sense of unease and distaste. I viewed them as pitiable creatures who nonetheless must have made serious mistakes to end up at the bottom of the social ladder.

Now, I look at them through a different lens: I see them as somebody's child, somebody's parent, somebody's spouse, somebody's sibling. I see that the safety net meant to address their issues is hopelessly inadequate, underfunded, and stretched to the breaking point. I no longer see them as strangers, but as the lost souls whose swelling ranks our son had once inhabited. Instead of averting my eyes to the ugliness of their existence, as I did before, I gaze at them now with a new understanding. On the rare occasions that they look back at me, I see the haunted eyes of my son.

The process of rebuilding a life that has been scorched by the flames of addiction is difficult at best. New relationships must be built, and oftentimes prior, dangerous relationships must be cast aside. New ways of coping must be learned to replace the old, maladaptive behaviors that have been relied on for years to dull the pain in a person's life. Educational opportunities have been delayed; professional connections have been severed; and the albatross of remorse hangs heavily around the neck of the recovering individual. Perhaps the most difficult part of this journey is self-forgiveness. In some cases, that forgiveness is never granted by the immediate family.

One of the conditions of Eric's being released to live with us was that we could have no firearms inside the house since he still had a felony listed on his record. My husband moved every single gun he owned to an undisclosed storage location. We were never afraid that Eric would hurt us or anybody else —his loathing was fully focused on himself. However, once we notified our insurance company that our son was once again living with us and that he now had a criminal record, they canceled our homeowner's policy. It didn't matter that we had been customers of theirs for over thirty years, that we had never missed a payment, and that my husband was a military vet. My husband appealed their decision, but they denied our request.

A few weeks after Eric was released from jail, he admitted to us that he had stolen some money from us back when he'd been using. He wasn't quite sure of how much he'd taken, but the amount didn't really matter. Jason and I both felt that his confession was enough—it was knowing that he was making efforts to restore our faith in him that mattered most.

Eric spent eighteen months enrolled in one of the Adult Probation and Parole (AP&P) programs that the state of Utah offers. Our attorney suggested the program, and we were ecstatic when Eric was accepted. During the period of Eric's supervision, he had to check in every day to find out whether or not he had been chosen for random drug testing. Several weeks he had to test more than once, and he never had a week where testing was skipped. The first time Eric met his parole officer in downtown Ogden, I had driven him down and attended the appointment with him. The officer looked at me with obvious surprise. When I asked him if there was a problem with a parent attending, his answer was telling. "No, there's no problem at all. In fact, I'm glad you're here. It's just that I've never had a parent attend with their child before." He looked directly at Eric. "You're lucky that you have somebody who cares enough to come down with you." The officer, a robust, dark-haired man in his mid-thirties, told us that he had asked to join the AP&P program because he wanted to make a difference in the lives of ex-convicts. He was young enough that he hadn't burned out yet; I hoped the stresses and strains of the job would not jade him too quickly.

After that first appointment, Jason and I decided that it would be better for Eric to follow through on his own; we didn't want to be responsible for his compliance. On occasion, his parole officer would drive up to our house unannounced, knock on the door in his bulletproof vest, and drop in to see how our son was doing. On his black vest the words PAROLE AGENT were emblazoned in huge, bright yellow letters. He always had another officer with him, and they both carried guns. I'm sure some of the neighbors in our conservative, Mormon town wondered why we had police officers pulling up to our front door; at this point in Eric's recovery, however, the neighbors' thoughts were the least of our concerns. Our son's participation in the AP&P program was absolutely essential in providing Jason and me the peace of mind that we needed to allow Eric to live with us again.

After successfully completing the AP&P program and having his charge dropped to a misdemeanor, Eric continued the arduous task of refashioning his life. His long-term partner, worn out by Eric's many failed rehab attempts, had ended their relationship while our son was in prison. In addition, many of his former friends disappeared. The heat of his incarceration had burned through past alliances like the hot sun burns through the ephemeral morning mist. Two friends notably stayed in touch with him, but one particularly devastating blow came from a very close work friend whom he had spent many hours confiding in before his arrest. Eric had gone to spend one of his first evenings of freedom visiting this friend and her husband. Although she knew that it was against the rules for him to be around any drugs or alcohol, she and her husband spent the night drinking heavily and smoking pot in front of our son while he watched in growing discomfort. Finally, hesitantly, he told her he was uncomfortable being there while they drank and got high.

She exploded in anger. "You fucking hypocrite! I never want to see you again! Get out of my house now!" Her drunken husband stood and lurched toward my son.

Eric was shocked. "I am only saying this because I care about you—"

"What a self-righteous prick! Who do you think you are to be telling me *anything* about how I should live my life?" Her face was red, and she was slurring her words. Ironically, this friend had suffered the death of a previous boyfriend who had crashed his motorcycle while intoxicated, and she and Eric had originally bonded while helping each other cope with the tragedy.

Awkwardly, our son stood to go. "I hope we can talk about this later," he said, while inching his way toward the door. "I still care about you—"

Her husband glared at our son. "Get the hell out!"

The next day Eric sent her an apology text and assured her that he hadn't meant to hurt her feelings. She responded by rubbing salt in the wound. She texted back that she and his former coworkers used to sit around laughing about his arrest. "We used to talk about you all the time. We all thought it would have been better if you had died while shooting up in the bathroom at work. What a fucking loser!" Whether her statement was true or was instead a wild exaggeration fed by her own deep sense of inadequacy, the brutality of it completely devastated our son and struck a deep wound into my own psyche. With friends like these, our son had no need of enemies.

And these are just some of the obstacles to be surmounted. Dealing with the grief of lost time and of the infliction of pain on others takes a long time to process. Self-loathing is common. Forgiveness is hard to come by. Employers often don't want to take a chance on hiring someone with a prior conviction, despite lip service to the contrary about helping the citizens in their communities. I can understand this reluctance to some point; however, as one of my son's friends who was in recovery said, "Former convicts are the best workers out there. They have everything to lose if they mess up and are willing to work harder than anybody else to prove themselves to their bosses."

After months of searching for jobs and being repeatedly rejected, Eric's elation at getting released from jail was slowly seeping away like helium from an old balloon. He became more depressed each day and began to isolate himself in his room away from us. We were terrified when we saw some of the same signs that we had seen before when he was using, but thankfully this time he did not relapse. He did go through a period where he drank heavily to cope with his depression, but unlike before, he confessed the truth to us and enlisted our help. Although we were relieved that only alcohol was involved, our son told us that he thought alcohol was almost as dangerous as heroin because it was so much more readily available and socially acceptable.

Finally, through the help of our school principal, who knew our son's personal story, Eric was granted the lifeline he needed and offered a full-time job at a metal manufacturing company in Clearfield, Utah. The hours were arduous: twelve-hour shifts that necessitated his getting up at 4:45 a.m. to make the sixty-minute commute to work. The work was grueling and repetitive, but our son was grateful to have a job. At first, my husband would set his own alarm for 4:30 a.m. to make sure Eric was up; eventually, we realized this was not helping our son become self-sufficient and Jason stopped doing it. Despite a few more setbacks with anxiety and depression, he was able to stick out the job for almost eighteen months. This toehold in the employment cliff was enough to set him back on his feet, and he was eventually able to move to a different company with higher pay and better benefits. Still, this first job was critical, and I believe more employers need to reconsider their hiring policies when it comes to helping nonviolent offenders find work.

I have told this story to the best of my recollection although I have had to look backwards at events that occurred over a fifteen-year period. For the sake of brevity, I didn't include descriptions of every single phone call, text message, or setback during the years of our son's active drug use; however, every incident described in this book is accurate and is based upon extensive journal entries, letters, emails, jail records, and medical records. I now have the opportunity of hindsight and the gift of the passage of time; things that were once unbearable to consider have been softened to some extent because of the outcome of our son's experience. But I am not the same person I was before this story began; neither is my husband or my son or my daughter. Certain experiences that pass through us leave behind markings—new stories are created to explain the previous chaos, and sometimes events lose the intensity that they had in the moment. It is good that time dulls things, an unexpected kindness, perhaps, from an often indifferent universe. I won't ever forget what happened, but I never want to experience anything like it again.

I no longer have recurring nightmares about Eric relapsing or dying, as I did during the first two years of his drug use. In my dreams, I would watch him repeatedly plummet off sheer cliffs or drown in quicksand as I stood helplessly nearby, my mouth frozen open in a silent scream. There were also the nightmares in which I gazed down in horror at our son's colorless face and blue lips as a sheet was slowly pulled back from his lifeless features by some unknown hand. These nightmares almost always woke me up, my heart thumping as if it were trying to claw its way out of my chest. The nightmares have finally passed, but the concern still lingers. I know that Eric is still haunted by his former actions. Some paths were closed off to him during his years of active drug use. His addictions put his life on hold, and while his peers were moving forward and achieving the important milestones of adult life, he was literally fighting for his own. Yet he has moved bravely forward, committed to fighting for a better future.

So what does the future hold for our son? It looks brighter than it has for years. Eric continued counseling sessions for almost two years following his release; he also attended mandatory workshops on recovery techniques. After three years, he was able to meet a new partner and move out of our home to start over. He found a permanent, full-time job, and he and his partner eventually bought an old, fixer-upper home in a city near us. Slowly, painfully, like old, infected wounds, our son's lacerations from the past began to heal. The healed skin would never look the same: the scars would always be there, slightly raised and reddish, to remind all of us how close he came to losing his life. They now serve as permanent reminders, not of a life wasted, but of a life recovered.

When our son was first living with us after his release, he bought an old guitar, found a local teacher, and learned how to play very quickly. He had played the cello during junior high and high school and eventually had auditioned for and been selected to play in the orchestra at Weber State University in Ogden, Utah. His drug use had derailed this, but I knew that he still loved music and found solace in it. We listened to him practice and enjoyed hearing him sing along at times in his clear, baritone voice. The first song he performed at a public recital was The Beatles' "Blackbird." As I listened to the lyrics, I knew at once why he was drawn to this song:

> Blackbird singing in the dead of night
> Take these broken wings and learn to fly.
> All your life
> You were only waiting for this moment to arise.
> Blackbird singing in the dead of night
> Take these sunken eyes and learn to see.
> All your life
> You were only waiting for this moment to be free.

I know that recovery is ongoing, that it is a daily battle that must be continually fought. Although I can only imagine what that constant battle feels like, I trust my son; I trust in the goodness of his heart and in his solemn promise to never give in to such disastrous habits again. But I am not naive. I know that addiction is a chronic illness that can never be cured, but only managed. According to the National Institute on Drug Abuse (NIDA), approximately forty to sixty percent of all heroin users relapse at some point.[238] Since Eric went through more than one relapse before his arrest, both my husband and I now believe that those experiences were essential steps on his path to recovery.

I have also come to understand that a delayed or altered voyage is not always a disaster. Sometimes missing an exit or taking a wrong turn can lead a traveler to an unexpected, or even better, location. Perhaps this was the *only* voyage that our son could have taken, the one that he needed to take all along to exorcise the demons that had perched on his shoulder due to a happenstance combination of his genetic inheritance, our family's religious heritage, and the vagaries of chance. His life—messy, painful, brilliant, and glorious—is just one version of all the broken, beautiful lives that surround us, including our own. This book is a love letter to my boy, for whom his father and I would have gladly carried every piece of pain . But love—ripping, sharp, terrible love—restrained us and forced us to watch as his broken wings healed. Now he soars into a limitless sky, finally free from the infernal, red-eyed, chattering monkey that clung to his back for years.

CHAPTER 39

No Way Out

It wasn't until several years after our son's release from the Salt Lake County Jail that I was able to bring myself to open his jail and medical records and the numerous letters we had written to each other during his incarceration. Even then, as I started combing through the documents, I felt an old, familiar sense of disorientation set in. How was it possible for us as his parents to have been so wrong? How were we unable to see the depth of our son's turmoil? We had devoted the better part of twenty years to the hands-on parenting of our children. We were by no means perfect, but we read together, played together, laughed together, and loved each other.

Once Eric reached his teenage years, Jason and I attributed some of his moodiness to teenage angst and some to a genetic predisposition that he had inherited from both sides of the family. Never once did it occur to us that he might be struggling with something deeper, a realization that he would never be the perfect Mormon son. I've searched for the intersection between his religious upbringing and his drug addiction, and I believe it took root when he was taught that being gay was a sin, an abomination before God. Little did we know that this constant refrain was working its way through his system like a slow-acting poison. He had a terrible secret to keep: he liked boys instead of girls, so God must hate him. If God hated him, he hated himself. At a very young age, he learned that he was broken.

Since our son came out in 2009, I have continued to track the Mormon Church's official pronouncements and teachings about its LGBT members, and I have concluded that the church's public image has been seriously and permanently damaged. In the era of the Internet, doctrines that have always been protected behind the curtain of "Thus saith the Lord" are now revealed in their actual, blemished state. Just as the Wizard of Oz tells Dorothy and her companions to "pay no attention to that man behind the curtain," the leaders now tell members to pay no attention to the factual information behind the myths. But some things are impossible to unsee.

In October 2014, the Supreme Court refused to hear Utah's appeal of a 10th Circuit Court ruling that had invalidated the state's 2004 constitutional amendment. The amendment had established marriage between one man and one woman as the only legally recognizable union in the state. By refusing to hear the case, the Supreme Court made same-sex marriage legal in the state of Utah and several other states under the 10th Circuit Court's jurisdiction. In an ironic twist, Utah's appeal was the catalyst that forced the state to pass out marriage licenses to same-sex couples. But activists on both sides predicted that the Court would revisit the issue.[239]

Just three months later in January 2015, the Supreme Court agreed to hear multiple cases from across the United States in which plaintiffs claimed their fundamental right to marry had been violated because of their sexual orientation. Then on June 26, 2015, much to the dismay of orthodox religious groups, the Court found that same-sex marriage bans were a violation of the Fourteenth Amendment's Due Process and Equal Protection Clauses.[240]

Three days after the Court ruled in favor of same-sex marriage, the First Presidency of the Mormon Church sent a letter to be read to every U.S. congregation on Sunday, July 5, affirming that "changes in the civil law . . . cannot change the moral law that God has established." The letter clarified that local religious leaders should not perform same-sex marriages and that church property could not be used for any activities "associated with same-sex marriages." It was noted, however, that all visitors were welcome on church property if church standards of conduct were respected. This conflict between civil laws and religious mandates remains unbridgeable to this day and has caused all sorts of anguish.[241]

Before marriage equality laws were enacted in the state of Utah, the church had claimed that it was simply following the law of the land in not condoning same-sex unions. However, once such marriages *did* become legal, the Mormon Church acted quickly to create what has since become known colloquially as the *"November 2015 Policy."* Never intended for public viewing, the guidelines on how to discipline gay couples were revised in the church's official *Handbook 1*—a series of instructions for high-ranking male leaders—and were leaked online via social media on Thursday, November 5, 2015. Prior to that, the general membership had been unable to access or read the church's instructions to bishops, stake presidents, and mission presidents, among others. After Handbook 1 appeared online, however, members became aware of a new policy that labeled same-sex married couples as "apostates." The penalties for apostasy are either complete repentance, temporary expulsion, or excommunication.

Even more disturbing, Handbook 1 contained a new and highly controversial requirement that the adopted or natural children of same-sex parents were to be denied infant blessings, baptism, the bestowal of the priesthood (for males), and mission calls until they "specifically disavow[ed] the practice of same-gender cohabitation and marriage," and did not live with a "parent who has lived or currently lives in a same-gender cohabitation relationship or marriage." In practical terms, this meant that children of a gay parent would be unable to live with that parent if they wanted to be officially accepted into the church, potentially leading to custody disruptions and other complications. Opponents of the policy claimed that children were being required to denounce their gay parents in order to obtain good standing in the institution.[242]

According to the church's official news site on November 12, 2015, Elder D. Todd Christofferson, one of the Twelve Apostles, explained that the new rule was "about family . . . about love and especially the love of the Savior." While he and other leaders insisted that the policy's main goal was to protect the children of gay couples from experiencing trauma, it actually increased their trauma. In the same statement in which Christofferson explained that God's love was endless and perfect, he reiterated the belief that same-sex marriage was a "particularly grievous or significant, serious kind of sin that requires Church discipline."[243]

The policy was a public relations fiasco, to say the least. Lauren McNamara, a Mormon woman from Utah, organized a protest near Temple Square in Salt Lake City on November 14 that was attended by up to 2,000 members and former members.[244] When Mormon writer Jana Riess later analyzed the number of resignations that resulted from this policy, she concluded that while it did not lead to a "mass exodus" of active members, it was the "last straw" for those members who already had other questions about church teachings.[245]

The handbook changes occurred under the leadership of Thomas S. Monson, the sixteenth president of the Mormon Church. First, it was soft-pedaled as a "policy" to forestall criticism; later, it was upgraded to doctrinal status as the highest-ranking church officials found themselves in the awkward position of defending the new guidelines that many found to be tone-deaf and needlessly harsh. By 2016, then-head of the Quorum of the Twelve Apostles, Russell M. Nelson, defended the policy as being "the mind of the Lord and the will of the Lord."[246] By a sleight of hand, policy was transmuted into doctrine, and gay Mormons and their allies took notice.

In a February 2016 broadcast during a visit to Chile, Elder David A. Bednar, a member of the Quorum of the Twelve Apostles, went so far as to proclaim that there were *"no homosexual members of the church"* [emphasis added]. Bednar, one of the highest-ranking leaders in the Mormon Church, said this in response to a question from a Chilean member who asked how gay Mormons could be steadfast in their faith. Bednar answered that rather than being *gay* members, they were simply members who were facing "challenge[s] in the flesh," such as "being born with a body that is not fully functional." In describing same-sex orientation as a physical handicap, Bednar and other church leaders have pointedly ignored the most current findings of mental health professionals. Despite claiming that all are worthy of God's love, Bednar emphasized that God's "plan is halted in anything but a marriage between a man and a woman"; he then reminded his listeners that *only* those who "act on the inclination or the attraction" have committed a "sin,"[247] as if that concession could erase the decades of heartache suffered by gay Mormons.

On March 8, 2016, Apostle Jeffrey R. Holland was the featured speaker in the church's first "Face to Face" broadcast event for young single adults. About one hour and thirteen minutes into the broadcast, an audience member asked how to help gay members who felt "scared," "alone," and like they didn't "fit into the Lord's kingdom." Holland responded that the church does not "make any attempt to say why . . . or how [homosexual attractions] happened" and that those with such attractions have "complexities in their makeup" that we don't fully understand. He added that what the church requires "for those inclined to a homosexual feeling is exactly what we ask for those with heterosexual feelings"; he asserted that rather than making gay members "second-class citizens," the church was treating them exactly like single women who hadn't yet found a marriage partner.[248]

The logical fallacy in this statement is one known as "false equivalence," or the argument that two or more things are equivalent in all ways simply because they are equivalent in some ways. A simple example of false equivalence would be labeling cats and dogs as members of the same species since both are mammals with four legs and a tail. To return to

Holland's example, the church has frequently argued that *all* unmarried couples are expected to remain celibate; therefore, they have insisted, unmarried gay couples are held to no higher standard than unmarried straight couples are. Or, as a friend once told me, "Well, there's no difference between your gay son having sex outside of marriage and my straight daughter having sex outside of marriage."

Actually, there *is* a difference, and it's not a minor difference—it's a critical one. For straight couples who "sin" and have sex before marriage, there is always the hope of repentance, church and community acceptance, and temple marriage. For gay couples who "sin" and have sex before marriage, no such possibilities exist. The straight couple has a bright future inside the Mormon Church should they so choose; the gay couple is told that they are "broken" and need to be fixed, or at least banished, so as not to pollute the body of Christ. Claiming that these two groups are equivalent is like claiming that a paper cut and an amputation are equivalent: after all, both involve a sharp edge and a bit of blood.

In September 2017 Elder Dallin H. Oaks stated that the 1995 Family Proclamation's teachings on same-sex marriage were not changeable policies but statements of eternal truth and the will of God. He lamented the increase in public acceptance of same-sex marriage and acknowledged that opposing this acceptance could cause conflicts with family and friends; nonetheless, he reminded church members that they should choose God rather than acquiesce to popular opinion.[249] That same year during a speech to youth in Kansas, Oaks expressed his belief that it was possible for gay members to "cease to have those feelings"; he professed to have letters from people who formerly considered themselves gay but who, after "repent[ing] of some transgressions," were able to successfully marry a member of the opposite sex and produce children.[250]

During the next two years, the harmful teachings continued: church members were told that "same-sex marriage is only a counterfeit . . . [which] cannot bring lasting happiness" and leads to "darkness";[251] that "Satan's lies" would lead astray the children of members who don't properly teach them the true meaning of "marriage as being between a man and woman";[252] and that exaltation with God "can be attained only through an eternal marriage between a man and a woman."[253] Although the state of Utah had been forced to pass out marriage licenses to gay couples, church leaders never backed down on their anti-gay rhetoric.

Dan Reynolds, the lead singer for Imagine Dragons, produced a 2018 HBO documentary entitled *Believer*. In it, the former Mormon claims there is literally *no way out* for gay Mormons because the church has never offered them any feasible options. Gay members haven't been allowed to pursue committed relationships or to marry with the church's blessing; neither have they been able to attend the temple or, in most cases, to worship with their local congregations on Sundays. Historically, the only way out for gay members has been either to leave the church, to cover up their true orientation, or to attempt a lifetime of celibacy, all the while keeping their fingers crossed that they will be resurrected as a straight person, as Mormon leaders have promised.

In fact, being gay has long been so taboo, so unthinkable, that the church leadership has refused to admit that sexual orientation is an inherent part of a person's identity and cannot be changed or wished away. Instead, the church uses the fuzzy term "same-sex attraction," which makes it sound like it's a superficial choice—just an attraction, just a temporary whim—instead of an essential part of someone's nature. Despair can set in early for gay Mormon teens as they come to realize that they are trying to color outside the lines that their family and their church have bequeathed them. Although they are repeatedly told that they are beloved children of God, within that constant reminder there is a hidden yet well-known warning: those who want to earn a place with the righteous and dwell with their families for eternity must avoid the sin of falling in love with the wrong person. Like a snake in the grass, that warning coils behind every sunny proclamation, ready to strike without notice and inflict terrible damage.

On April 4, 2019, during the church's semiannual general conference. Apostle Dallin H. Oaks stunned members worldwide when he announced that the November 2015 "revelation" that had pointedly excluded the children of gay parents from full church participation was being revised. The church rolled back its assertion that same-sex married couples were apostates, while still proclaiming that such relationships were sinful in the eyes of God. In addition, the children of such couples would be allowed to be baptized, after all. Never before had the church made such a public reversal of a policy in such a short time.[254] While church leaders trumpeted this newest revelation as the true, updated doctrine from God, others found it strange that the eternal, unchanging God had changed His mind once again.

Although gay members and their allies welcomed the 2019 revelation rollback, the leaders nonetheless remained firm in their doctrinal stance that same-sex marriage was an affront to God. Speaking at a BYU Hawaii devotional in June of 2019, just two months after announcing the church's reversal of the November 2015 Policy, Oaks made it a point to link a "culture of evil . . . perversions . . . [and] lesbian, gay, and transgender lifestyles and values."[255] That same month, Apostle Jeffrey R. Holland bemoaned the fact that the youth of today see "gay marriage and transgender rights . . . [as] part of everyday life."[256] Then in September of that year, President Russell M. Nelson pointedly reminded BYU students that "God has not changed *His* definition of marriage [emphasis in original]."[257]

Had the church really reversed the November 2015 Policy? Or was the backpedaling simply a smokescreen to deflect the uncomfortably negative gazes from an increasingly interconnected world? Ever since the handbook was leaked in 2015, the church has undertaken regular revisions and announced the updates to the public. Each time a new handbook is published, all earlier versions are rendered obsolete. The handbook essentially functions as an ongoing, revelatory document, which purports to contain God's word to the leaders and members of today's church, and it is not uncommon to see the removal or revision of previously accepted doctrines. One can easily see the danger here: to admit to an error in past prophetic revelations is to admit that leaders are fallible men whose beliefs have been colored by their own biases and the historical milieu in which they have been raised. What, then, is to stop a current prophet's views from being discarded or revised once he is replaced? And if the church is led by fallible men whose declarations can be questioned, why should members be under any obligation to take such declarations seriously?

A family member recently told me, "The problem is *not* the doctrine. It's the culture, and the culture is changing." Because I love her, I didn't argue. But it's quite clear to me that the reverse is actually true: the problem is *not* the culture, i.e., the general membership and many of their beliefs and actions. The problem *is* the doctrine. In few areas have church leaders been as vitriolic as they have been in condemning the gay "lifestyle." Any changes in tone occur on the surface only, usually within earshot of outsiders or the press. But the real message, the one that lies deep within the marrow of the church, is that being gay is, at best, a serious sexual *handicap* that will limit a person's ability to find happiness in this life. At worst, it is a serious sexual *sin* that will possibly condemn them to an eternity without their families.

One of the church's most well-known doctrines of sealing families together for eternity sounds comforting until one scratches beneath the surface; then many disturbing realities beneath the veneer are exposed. For example, during the church's semiannual general conference on Sunday, April 7, 2019, President Russell M. Nelson made troubling remarks about earning the "high privilege of exaltation." He said that members who did not accept the sealing ordinances provided by the church would not be bound to their families in the world hereafter.[258] Many saw this as a direct assault on part-member families or families with gay members.

In 2020, there seemed to be a real shift when Brigham Young University revised the school's Honor Code by removing the word "homosexual" and replacing it with a condemnation of "any sexual misconduct." Gay students assumed that showing romantic behavior, such as handholding and dating, was now acceptable, and there were reports that at least some administrators agreed. The celebration was short-lived, however; merely two weeks later, after much turmoil, the church clarified its position. Elder Paul V. Johnson, the Commissioner of the Church Educational System that oversees all of the church's college campuses, sent out a letter in which he said that "same-sex romantic behavior cannot lead to eternal marriage and is therefore not compatible with the principles included in the Honor Code."[259] Students who had been cheering their newfound freedoms only days before now found themselves in danger of being expelled from the university for practicing the same sorts of romantic behavior that straight couples were freely allowed to engage in.

As the senior member of the Quorum of the Twelve Apostles, Dallin H. Oaks stands next in line to inherit the role of prophet, seer, and revelator when the current prophet, Russell M. Nelson, passes away. Therefore, Oaks's continually harsh rhetoric about same-sex orientation has been duly noted by gay members and their families. In the April 2020 general conference, for example, Oaks warned that any uses of the "procreative power" outside of heterosexual marriages are a "sinful degrading and perversion of the most divine attribute of men and women."[260] Later, during the church's April 2022 general conference, Oaks reiterated that exaltation in the celestial kingdom "can be obtained only through faithfulness to the covenants of an eternal marriage between a man and a woman. That divine doctrine is why we teach that 'gender is an essential characteristic of individual premortal, mortal, and eternal identity and purpose'." He added that "distorting marriage," as in the case of legally gay marriage, was one of Satan's chief goals. Then Oaks tried to assuage his listeners with the thought that the "kingdom of glory we receive in the Final Judgment is determined by the laws we choose to abide by in our Heavenly Father's loving plan."[261] Mormon doctrine teaches that God has prepared multiple kingdoms so that all of His children, even those who have "come short of the glory of God," can still be assigned to an eternal dwelling place (Rom. 3:23, KJV). In other words, even if gay members (or sinful straight members) can't reside in the highest, most glorious realm, they can still be assigned to a lesser realm, or "degree of glory." Rather than being good news, this seems like a half-hearted effort to award a consolation prize to those not deemed worthy enough to attain the church's highest stated goal: life as an eternal, exalted family.

In August 2021, Apostle Jeffrey R. Holland reiterated that the church stance on same-sex marriage had not changed and that professors at Brigham Young University needed to step up their efforts to defend the church's position. In a speech to faculty members that has since become infamous in the post-Mormon world, Holland complained that some of the faculty had become too religiously liberal and that they needed to fully embrace the church's conservative doctrines in order to be true to their "integrity." He reminded his listeners that as professors at BYU, their first obligation was to protect the "doctrine of the family and defending marriage as the union of a man and a woman."

Holland spent a good portion of his talk focusing on the challenges facing LGBT members and students and prayed that *"all* will try to avoid language, symbols, and situations that are more divisive than unifying at the very time we want to show love for all of God's children [emphasis added]." Yet after calling for a careful use of loving language, he repeatedly used war imagery, especially the term "musket fire," as he demanded that faculty members protect the church's doctrines and beliefs from the encroachments of the world's fallen standards of morality. Holland reminded his listeners of former apostle Neal A. Maxwell's comparison of BYU faculty members to the "builders of the temple in Nauvoo, who worked with a trowel in one hand and a musket in the other." He followed this with Dallin H. Oaks's 2017 comments that he would "like to hear a little more musket fire from this temple of learning."

Holland then moved on to criticize Matt Easton, the 2019 BYU political science valedictorian. Easton had announced during his commencement address in 2019 that he was "proud to be a gay son of God."[262] Holland complained that Easton had "commandeer[ed] ... a graduation podium" for an announcement about his sexuality that was inappropriate and undignified. The post-Mormon community found Holland's condemnation of Easton to be especially harsh, given that it was a public denunciation of a student by a much more powerful church leader.

Near the end of his speech, lest anyone in the audience had missed the true intent of his message, Holland emphasized the following: "My brethren have made the case for the metaphor of *musket fire*, which I have *endorsed yet again today* [emphasis added]. There will continue to be those who oppose our teachings and with that will continue the need to define, document, and defend the faith." His use of words with hostile overtones was surely deliberate, especially from a man who has received multiple advanced degrees from well-respected universities. Make no mistake—Elder Holland knows the power of language, and instead of using words to bind up the wounds of those suffering from exclusion, he used words to inflict damage, while ironically calling for healing.[263]

Despite the controversy surrounding Holland's talk, BYU has decided to make a lightly edited version of it required reading for all incoming freshmen at the university beginning fall of 2024. Spokesperson Carri Jenkins recently explained that Holland's speech is one of several that will help new students understand the "unique mission and purpose of BYU." Jenkins then added that campus administrators "want all our students, including our LGBTQ students, to feel both the love of the Savior and the joy associated with living his commandments as part of a covenant-keeping community." But both off-campus and on-campus LGBT support groups fear that rather than promoting acceptance and love for all students, Holland's message will harm gay students and create an "unsafe environment" for them.[264]

Amongst church bishops and stake presidents, there is discordance about how to deal with the gay members in their midst; reportedly, some leaders are much more tolerant and accepting of gay couples. The most well-known case is that of Charlie Bird, who served as the Brigham Young University mascot, Cosmo the Cougar, for two years. Bird and his husband, Ryan Clifford, have been allowed to attend church together, receive the sacrament, and hold church callings. Some have speculated that the couple's high profile has kept them safe: Bird published a best-selling memoir about his experiences as a gay Mormon through Deseret Book, a bookstore owned by the Mormon Church. In addition, both men have a large following on Instagram.

While LGBT members and their allies see the couple's continued inclusion as a hopeful sign, some wonder why that same acceptance has not been extended to others. One explanation is that the geographical location of gay members' wards inside the United States is often the determining factor in how they are treated. There is a wide variance between leaders' styles and personalities, which has led to the coining of a new term—"bishopric roulette." Basically, it means that even though the church has correlated guidelines on how to respond to various issues, there is in practice a wide range of responses that actually occur.[265]

One recent example of a married gay couple being called in for church discipline is that of Douglas and Brennen, who were interviewed on Mormon Stories Podcast. Both men had been raised Mormon, but both eventually stopped attending church and entered into a legally recognized marriage in the state of Idaho. On May 4, 2022, Brennen received a hand-delivered letter from his previous bishop informing him that a membership counsel would be held regarding his "conduct related to church policy on same-sex marriage." The two men were subjected to personal visits and interviews with church leaders who pressured them to submit a "withdrawal of membership," or to leave the church of their own accord.

What made this case even more unusual was that it was originated by Brennen's former bishop, who crossed stake boundary lines to seek out Brennen. A stake is a group of multiple church congregations that join together due to physical proximity, usually consisting of 3,000 – 5,000 members. According to the church's own guidelines, bishops or stake presidents should not cross boundaries to seek out former members; rather, the process explicitly calls for the member's current bishop or stake president to be the one who initiates the disciplinary hearing. Brennen and his husband were able to record all of their phone calls and in-person conversations with local church leaders because the state of Idaho is a "single party consent state," which means that recording conversations is legal even if all parties are not informed. Although the letter that initially called Brennen to meet with church leaders had only mentioned one thing—his conduct regarding "same-sex marriage"—once the meetings started, leaders began to shift their focus to several other items which were never mentioned in the letter, claiming that the men's marriage was *not* the reason for the investigation.[266]

In June 2024, a woman who was a lifelong member and had been attending church with her non-Mormon wife was called in for an interview with her stake president in West Orange, Texas. Janette Petersen was stunned when her leader announced that because she was "married to a woman, she was breaking the faith's law of chastity." She was counseled to seek a divorce immediately or to risk being excommunicated. When Petersen offered to cease all intimate physical relations with her wife, Tammy, in order to preserve her membership, she was told that just by living together, the couple would project an "appearance of sin." Petersen's membership was officially withdrawn, as were the memberships of three other gay women in Texas and Utah.[267]

The church's most recent version of its official handbook says that "The Church *does not take a position on the causes of same-sex attraction.* [emphasis added]." This statement effectively negates decades of previous church teachings that blamed same-sex orientation on masturbation, Satan's influence, inept parenting, or a lack of faith, among other things. The handbook then says, "God's commandments forbid all unchaste behavior, either heterosexual or same-sex. . . . Behavior that is *inconsistent with the law of chastity* may be cause for holding a *Church membership council* [emphasis added]."

What kind of behavior is inconsistent with the law of chastity? For heterosexual members, "adultery [and] fornication" are outlawed, but sexual relations within marriage are approved by God. However, all gay relationships are classified as a sin: "Only a man and a woman who are legally and lawfully wedded as husband and wife should have sexual relations." One can easily see the discrepancy here. Straight couples can have sex inside marriage. Gay couples cannot. A few lines later, the handbook specifies that even a legally sanctioned, "same-sex marriage" may still be grounds for a *membership council*. A "membership council" is the updated name for a disciplinary event (formerly called a disciplinary council) in which members who are accused of violating the church's standards are called in to meet with male leaders, typically to have their membership temporarily suspended or permanently revoked unless they forsake their offending behavior.[268]

The Mormon hierarchy focuses almost exclusively on the "serious sin" of sex between gay couples, as if there were no other components upon which successful relationships must be based. Just like straight couples, gay couples want companionship, emotional and financial support, community acceptance, a part in their extended family, and sexual intimacy. Over the past several decades, however, the church has told its gay members that they are deceived, immoral, unnatural, and perverted. This was the only drumbeat that my contemporaries and I heard as we matured to adulthood and beyond.

Of course, many other churches besides the Mormon Church have had to come to terms with the existence of gay individuals in their midst. Over time, some have stumbled their way towards a more inclusive embrace. For example, in September 2013, Pope Francis said, "Tell me: when God looks at a gay person, does he endorse the existence of this person with love, or reject and condemn this person? We have to find a new balance; otherwise even the moral edifice of the church is likely to fall like a house of cards, losing the freshness and fragrance of the Gospel."[269] In 2014 and 2017, the Pew Research Center conducted interviews and released data showing that a majority of both American Buddhists (88 percent)[270] and Muslims (52 percent)[271] believed that persons with same-sex orientation should be accepted by society.

The Mormon Church hierarchy, however, along with those of other orthodox faiths like the Southern Baptist Church,[272] stubbornly holds on to its belief that gay relationships are and always will be an offense to God. I have asked a few straight men if they thought that their sexual attractions to women were reversible or if they believed they could "pray the straight away" if their salvation depended on it. Their looks of utter horror and incomprehension would be comical if it weren't for the fact that for decades the church has told its gay members to do exactly that. Here's an analogy I once heard: "Imagine that you really, really hated broccoli. Then somebody told you that you had to eat it, no matter what, if you wanted to go to heaven. You might be able to gag it down, but it doesn't mean you would like it." Imagine eating broccoli for all eternity, trying to choke down its pungent greenness as it threatens to work its way back up. This analogy illuminates the dilemma that gay Mormons have always faced: neither in heaven nor on earth will they ever be completely accepted.

CHAPTER 40

The Mormon Moment?

In the 2010s, the Mormon Church experienced a wave of positive attention in what has since been dubbed "The Mormon Moment." Republican Mitt Romney, a prominent, wealthy Mormon who had previously served as the governor of Massachusetts, announced his 2012 presidential campaign. Mormon Harry Reid was a powerful Democratic senator for twenty years, culminating with his service as the Senate Majority Leader from 2007 to 2015. Mormon convert Glenn Beck was taking over the airwaves as a popular, although controversial, political commentator. The "I'm a Mormon" campaign, which was started in 2011 under the direction of sixteenth church president Thomas S. Monson, portrayed Mormons as approachable, friendly people: celebrities and lay members alike were featured in ads that appeared on billboards in Times Square and around the world.[273] But fourteen years later, the Mormon Church is facing the stark reality of a moment lost, most likely never to return.

Mormonism has held a monopoly over Utah families, neighborhoods, schools, and local government ever since the arrival of the pioneers in 1847. When I was growing up in Davis County during the 1960s, I did not know a single "non-Mormon." By the time I attended high school during the 1970s, Mormons still comprised the vast majority in the state, but there was a slight increase of non-Mormon migrants due to population growth in the United States, the ease of modern travel, and economic forces. Dr. Ryan T. Cragun, a professor in the Department of Sociology at the University of Tampa, recently explained in a Mormon Stories Podcast interview that the 1960s–1980s were the decades of the most rapid growth in the church's membership inside the state; his information corresponds with my personal experience.[274] Since that time, there has been a downward trend, with Mormons reportedly comprising nearly 77 percent of the state's population in 1992[275] and about 61 percent in 2024, at least according to some estimates.[276] In 2020, the *Salt Lake Tribune* reported that the state was about 61 percent Mormon.[277]

However, a study recently published in the *Journal of Religion and Demography* upends the membership statistics that have been reported by the Mormon Church. Dr. Ryan T. Cragun, along with two colleagues, utilized "self-reported religious identification from surveys collected in Utah" to determine that "Mormons are no longer a majority in Utah." Cragun explained in his Mormon Stories interview that self-reported religious identification is the commonly preferred method of "sociologists and social scientists around the world."[278] Their research found that the state is less than 50 percent Mormon; in fact, using a "99.9% confidence interval," they found the lower limit to be 38.3 percent and the upper limit to be 45.7 percent.

In his article, Cragun demonstrates that the sizable discrepancy between the church's reported numbers and those found in his study are due to the Mormon Church's methods of defining membership: after a person is baptized and confirmed a member of the church, their names remain on the rolls until they die, they are excommunicated, they officially resign, or until their "110th birthday if their whereabouts are unknown." One can easily see how such methods could be misleading, whether intentionally or not. For example, I personally know at least thirty people who no longer attend church or consider themselves believers but are still officially counted as members on the church's rolls because they have not formally resigned. Indeed, Cragun has found that in the last twenty years, there has been a "rapid, substantial change in Utah's religious demography fueled primarily by Mormon defections." Because such defections have rendered the Mormon Church statistics "unreliable and unsuitable for social science research," Cragun argues that their continued use suggests that the Mormon hierarchy is focused more on "public relations and propaganda" than on an accurate accounting of the church's membership numbers.[279]

It is worth pointing out that even as the state's Mormon population has dwindled, as of 2024 Mormons still constitute nearly 75 percent of the population in my hometown of Farmington, Utah, which is located within Davis County.[280] The Association of Religion Data Archives shows that as of 2020, 70.5 percent of Davis County was Mormon.[281] Davis County is the third largest county in Utah, making it a powerful force in the state's financial, political, and educational decisions; in fact, the persistence of the Mormon hegemony in Utah has long stood out as notable.[282] Columnist Robert Gehrke raised the question of whether the redistricting maps approved by the Utah State Legislature in 2022 might have been purposely drawn to "effectively disenfranchise voters who are not members of The Church of Jesus Christ of Latter-day Saints." He explained that although nearly 40 percent of Utah (and 53 percent of Salt Lake County) was *not* Mormon in 2020, 86 percent of the legislature *was* Mormon. The discrepancy between the religious affiliations of voters in the state and those of the legislature is therefore worrisome because the question of religious discrimination arises.[283]

And even as the state becomes more religiously diverse, Mormons have long made up a "commanding majority in many parts of the state" and have influenced many statewide policy decisions. In 2005, University of Utah's Pam Perlich said that the LDS Church would continue to be an important player in Utah's social and religious milieu: "For as long as that church is vibrant, Utah culture will always be tied to it."[284] In addition, Dr. Cragun has explained that even as the percentage of Mormons drops throughout the state, people with similar religious affiliations often tend to vote in similar ways, which could account for the over-preponderance of Mormons in government positions.[285]

When it comes to membership throughout the United States, however, thirty-four states had a drop in their percentage of Mormon Church members from 2019 to 2021.[286] Nonetheless, according to Mormon writer Jana Riess, there is both good news and bad news about the church's membership trends. The good news is that despite a much slower growth rate than occurred in the past, in 2021 a small amount of growth (.85 percent) still occurred. This distinguished Mormonism from other "Christian churches," which are actually losing members.

The bad news is that in the United States, "growth [in new members] has essentially been cut in half." In addition, the numbers of young men and women serving Mormon missions dropped 18.6 percent from 2019 to 2021.[287] Furthermore, Riess reported in 2016 that a "leaked video of a behind-closed-doors 2008 meeting of the LDS Church's top leaders" revealed that the "overall worldwide activity rate" of Young Single Adults was only 25 percent. Riess openly admits that while this information is now multiple years "out of date," that if there is anything to be learned from earlier "Mormon retention" surveys, it's that things are continuing to get worse, so Riess believes it's more likely that the activity rate figures reported for young adults are actually too low, especially in the United States.[288]

While it is true that other religious groups are also seeing a substantial decline in new members, Mormon Church "growth in terms of raw numbers" in 2021 was the lowest since the 1970s.[289] Significantly, young adults and teens are leaving in droves,[290] and even older, previously stalwart believers are disappearing. Although numerous church leaders still claim that the church is now stronger than ever, Riess says that such a claim is "just not statistically true, at least in the United States, and it wasn't even true five years ago."[291]

Notably, although a 2022 survey showed that Mormons in the United States were more religious than the general population (in terms of praying, attending church, and talking to religious leaders), they also "ranked first among members of different faiths" when it came to thinking about leaving their religion. One in four Mormons admitted that they had thought about leaving the church, which came as a "major surprise" of the study.[292]

Internationally, membership is also stagnating. While the church claims to have approximately seventeen million members worldwide in 2024, estimates show that only 35 percent of those members are currently active. Independent researcher Matt Martinich analyzed figures from 2021 to 2024 that showed some surprising trends. First, there has been a "significant slowdown in membership growth" in countries that were previously considered strongholds, such as the United States, Mexico, Brazil, the Philippines, Peru, and Chile.[293] Second, "most of the missions in Europe that have closed in the past 25 years have been in Russia, Germany, the United Kingdom, France, Switzerland, and Spain."[294] Finally, figures released in 2022 showed that Africa is the top world region for the most "rapid membership growth."[295]

In a 2023 Mormon Stories Podcast episode, the misleading nature of the church's reported membership statistics in countries outside the United States was analyzed. For example, according to official church statistics, Mexico has the second largest number of members, coming in second behind the United States with 1,234,545 members in 2010 and 1,498,296 members in 2021. But according to the Mexican census for those years, which includes questions about a person's religious affiliation, there were 314,932 members in 2010 and 337,998 members in 2020. Comparing these much lower census numbers to the church's reported numbers shows that only 26 percent of the people whom the church claimed as members in 2010 self-identified as Mormon; likewise, for 2021, only 23 percent of those identified as members by church statistics self-identified as Mormon. One possible reason could be that even though the church is continuing to baptize new members at a rapid rate, those members are either no longer participating, or no longer consider themselves Mormon.

The census numbers are based on how an individual self-identifies, which is significant because it shows a person's current religious affiliation rather than reflecting previous religious affiliations. Each household is asked, "What is your religion? What religion are you practicing?" According to a currently serving Mormon bishop who resides in Mexico, the census methodology has improved and now includes an "equivalency table" so that answers ranging from "Mormon" to "Latter-day Saint" to "Church of Jesus Christ of Latter-day Saints" are all coded as the same church for statistical purposes. Census figures are considered to be more reliable since 2010 when the updated coding procedures led government officials to announce that the census "accurately reflect[s] religious affiliation of citizens."[296]

And it's not only happening in Mexico; the Brazil 2010 census showed the same trends. According to the *Salt Lake Tribune*, the 2010 Brazilian census showed that 225,695 people self-identified as Mormon while the church reported 1,138,740 members. Independent Mormon researcher Matt Martinich says that means that those who self-identified as Mormons account for "only 20 percent of total membership officially reported by the church in Brazil."[297] These statistics illustrate a massive discrepancy between the robust numbers the church claims and what the country's own census shows.

When asked about possibly misleading membership statistics in 2022 at the National Press Club, Apostle David A. Bednar claimed that he had "no idea what the real numbers are." Then, inexplicably, he said, "We have numbers, and I believe the numbers, but there is some uncertainty in the numbers."[298] What the numbers actually show, according to the best estimates, are that the exodus has begun and shows no signs of stopping.

However, despite a nearly flat level of membership growth and a significant increase in the number of people who no longer self-identify as Mormon, the church's wealth has continued to increase at an astonishing rate. As of May 2024, the Mormon Church (officially known as The Church of Jesus Christ of Latter-day Saints) ranks as the wealthiest church on the planet, with approximately "$265 billion in wealth," according to The Widow's Mite, an independent, watchdog website established in 2021.[299] As a reference point, the second wealthiest church, the Catholic Church, has approximately $77 billion from its combined holdings in Italy, Australia, France, and Germany. The third wealthiest church, Hinduism, has $35 billion worth of assets in India.[300]

The Mormon Church has multiple real estate, business, and portfolio investments, but because of its non-profit status, it has been "exempted in the United States from paying taxes on . . . [its] income." It has also closely guarded the extent and details of its wealth. But according to a complaint filed with the IRS in 2019 by David A. Nielsen, a former senior portfolio manager at church-owned Ensign Peak Advisors, the church has illegally "stockpile[ed] their surplus donations instead of using them for charitable works"; in addition, member-donated tithing funds, which are tax-exempt, have been used to "bail out a church-run insurance company and a shopping mall in Salt Lake City."[301]

After Ensign Peak and the Mormon Church paid a $5 million settlement to the U.S. Securities and Exchange Commission in 2023, the church announced that it "regretted its 'mistakes'" [and] considered the matter 'closed.'"[302] However, The Widow's Mite website, which has been tracking and providing links to "all known public sources of information about Church finances,"[303] recently announced that they have since found "additional alleged violations of securities laws" in which Ensign Peak did not file the legally required forms with the SEC. The website's analysts, which include anonymous "current and former church members" with professional backgrounds in "finance, law, real estate" and other related fields, have accused the church of a purposeful "failure to report to regulators." In addition, they claim that much of the church's wealth has been housed in shell companies which were created to hide the true extent of the church's holdings. As of May 2024, the Mormon Church had not responded to this latest round of troubling allegations.[304]

Thus, digital technology and its steady stream of information continues to upend the church's carefully controlled narrative. By the year 2000, "almost half of the population" in the United States had Internet access; by 2016 that number had expanded to 76 percent of the population.[305] As of 2024, nearly "94 percent" of the American population uses the Internet.[306] And the Internet is still relatively young. Who knows where the digital highway will travel next? No doubt it will take us to currently unimaginable destinations, creating worldwide connections and complications that will continue to reverberate throughout our children's and grandchildren's lives and far beyond.

Will the Mormon Church survive this unprecedented access to information? If it does, it will likely be a different church in many aspects, perhaps transforming into something smaller and less dogmatic, while also becoming more flexible and transparent in essential ways. For those of us who came of age during the heyday of the church's growth, there will always be a sense of nostalgia—even a sense of loss—as the religious myths that nurtured us to adulthood gradually erode and then finally disappear. There will be no more small-town complaisance about uniformly accepted views of the meaning of life in this world or in the next. But along with that loss, there will arise something better: a kinder, gentler church that can bind up the wounds of those whom it previously rejected, enfolding them at last in a loving embrace instead of keeping them at arms' length. When that occurs, the Mormon pioneers' belief that "all is well" will finally have arrived.

CHAPTER 41

The Prodigal Returns

Joy and despair are the two faces of the coin called parenting; once minted, these opposing forces are inextricably linked. When I first held the coin in my hand, it felt heavy and substantial—its size belying its weight. Indeed, the tiny bodies and fragile limbs of our infant children carry enough weight to irretrievably break us, as every parent knows. We bring them into a dangerous world without their consent, and as such we are required to protect them for the rest of their lives—to do anything less would be to abrogate a responsibility as deep and inescapable as breathing itself. The child exists because of us; in return, we exist to protect the child. In losing ourselves to them, we find ourselves. Such is the paradox of parenthood.

Growing up in the 1960s and '70s in Farmington, Utah, I attended many funerals. Funerals were a big event in our small religious community—a chance to mourn, to preach repentance, and to send our deceased loved ones off to heaven with one final prayer for good luck. I often heard family members speak in hushed whispers about how their loved ones were better off, in a much happier place. But I resisted that thought. Death, I thought, would be the most horrible thing of all: the last catch of breath in the throat, the slow expiration of the final sigh, the headlong plunge into the unknown on the other side. I trembled at the thought of being entombed in a casket and lowered into the dark, musty earth where all manner of corruption would embrace me.

In the false bravado of children coming to terms with something unthinkable, we used to sing on the school playground during recess:

> Did you ever think when a hearse goes by,
> that you might be the next to die?
> They cover you up with a big white sheet,
> and bury you down 'bout six feet deep.
> The worms crawl in, the worms crawl out,
> the ants play pinochle on your snout.
> And big green bugs with big green eyes
> crawl in your liver and out your eyes.

Even as I sang along with my companions, I decided that I would somehow find a way to avoid death itself, which, after all, only happened to the very old or the very unlucky. Like all heedless young to whom the future seems a far-off destination, I determined that death was something so remote that it would have no relevance in my life.

It wasn't until the fifth decade of my life, however, after our son's life-and-death battle with substance abuse, that I realized that *living* was actually the most frightening thing. In dying I saw only two alternatives—either we continued on in some state, or we didn't. But in living—that's where I came to understand that the forks in the road and the dead ends were truly dangerous. Each day I could stumble upon a hundred ways to hurt someone I loved or to be hurt by them in turn. Each day I risked losing those I loved. And despite the cheery admonitions of well-intentioned mourners, some wounds never heal. A heart that is shared with others is a heart that can be shattered with a single blow. Living was definitely the riskier thing. Living was the brief moment between the unknown before and the unknowable after.

Unpacking my religious life after five decades was much like unpacking a suitcase after a long-desired vacation. The anticipation was gone, the adventure was over, and now it was time to empty the suitcase and face the facts: I packed all the wrong clothes, I took too many shoes, and my shampoo exploded in the interior of my suitcase sometime after takeoff. I berated myself over the side excursions I missed and the streetside vendor whose questionable cuisine had me sprinting to the toilet for three days afterwards. I realized that others had found better flights than mine, stayed in better hotels, and somehow spent less money. I questioned whether going on this particular voyage had ever been in my best interest, even though it was insisted upon by well-intentioned family members.

As I unpacked my own particular brand of religion—Mormonism—I kept coming across things that should have pointed me in a different direction sooner. There were the nagging questions about polygamy, women's roles, racist doctrines, and, of course, the church's disastrous responses to the LGBT issue. There were also the disturbing historical realities that many of Joseph Smith's contemporaries viewed him as a charismatic con artist and that Brigham Young was, by many accounts, a cruel, albeit consummate, leader.

To the true believer, these things were and still are explained away with questionable logic: If Joseph Smith and Brigham Young were inspired by God, then *anything* they did must be righteous; likewise, their era was so different from ours that to assume that we from a modern viewpoint can understand the social mores of their time is naive. In fact, to the dedicated believer, to consider for even a brief moment that one's entire system of beliefs might be a sophisticated farce is a terrifying prospect. When I thought about such things, my heart pounded in dread. I felt dizzy, nauseous, and unmoored—a small boat adrift on a vast ocean of doubts with no port in sight.

The only thing that could ever have forced me to detach myself from the safety of that inland port was the belief that my child's physical and emotional health was at risk. After our son came out at age eighteen, I eventually came to realize that his survival and our family's happiness would necessitate a departure from the church in which I had spent the formative years of my life. And still, I hesitated. The roots of Mormonism had grown so deeply into my soul that uprooting them seemed an impossible task—a task that I once believed might destroy my eternal family.

In the Biblical parable, the prodigal son story had a happy ending. However, I am convinced that *before* that happy ending, while the prodigal was out starving and sleeping with swine, his parents were locked in an agony of waiting, their eyes forever focused on the distant horizon where they hoped to catch a glimpse of their lost son. Although the mother in the parable remains voiceless, she knew something that no father can ever completely understand—that carrying a child inside your body for nine months, beneath your heart, means that a piece of your heart is never reclaimed, for it resides within your child.

When Eric returned from the wilderness, poorer but wiser, we were there to meet him. We welcomed him, embraced him, rejoiced with him, and then shut the door on the Mormon Church forever. There was no other way to live, love, or go forward. There was no other way to find balance or peace. The church of my ancestors had driven all of us to despair. How could I, in good conscience, continue to be part of such an organization? It was time to say goodbye to the spiritual home that had nurtured me for so long and had kept me safe during my growing-up years, all the while offering hopeful answers to many of life's difficult questions. The church had given me invaluable support during my husband's twenty-year submarine career, which had rendered me a single parent in many ways. I had loved the church, I had given it my all, and, finally, I had outgrown it. I find it ironic that the highest ideal in all of Christianity—charity—flowered fully only after I turned my back on my religious inheritance and my ancestors' expectations. In loving my son above all else, in rashly leaving my spiritual roots behind, I became a fellow wanderer—a prodigal mother.

The transition out of Mormonism was both terrifying and liberating. I now understand the fear of "gazing into the abyss," as Nietzsche so memorably wrote. Even more terrifying, instead of simply gazing over the edge of our previously stable lives, Jason and I had to jump into the bottomless chasm that yawned before us. But we had no choice. The ancient imperative that drove our cavemen ancestors to protect their tribe at all costs was awakened. And so, holding hands, trembling yet resolute, we jumped together.

Instead of destruction, however, we found something entirely unexpected. Once the trauma of leaving had passed, we found ourselves viewing the world with new eyes. My vision no longer obstructed by fear, I saw intriguing paths, previously untraveled roads, and more destinations than I had ever imagined possible. When I stopped dividing people into two simplified categories—saints or sinners—I began to see them more clearly. I felt greater compassion for humanity's weaknesses and strengths, its failings and strivings, its fears and triumphs.

In following the surest impulse of my heart and embracing my son unconditionally, I learned in the deepest part of my soul that I was the only one who had the right to choose my path through life; no outside authority or organization would ever be given that power again. Finally, after years of turmoil and the fear that our family had somehow fallen short of some eternal decree, I knew the truth: rather than wasting my spiritual birthright, my wanderings in the wilderness had multiplied my inheritance a thousand times over.

SPECIALIZED TERMS USED IN THE PRODIGAL MORMON MOTHER

(After each term, the chapter in which it first appeared is noted.)

FOOTNOTES

[1] Pseudonyms are used throughout this book for all private individuals; public figures are identified by their actual names.

[2] Throughout this book, I use the term *Mormon* to refer to the Church of Jesus Christ of Latter-day Saints. Although current-prophet Russell M. Nelson has called upon church members to avoid using this common nickname, it retains its historical and cultural significance and is the term that all of my contemporaries and I grew up using. All specialized Mormon vocabulary will be italicized the first time it appears, along with a brief definition or explanatory footnote. Subsequent occurrences of that term will appear in regular font.

[3] Mark Henshaw, "How Wilford Woodruff and Brigham Young Entered the Salt Lake Valley Together—a Driver, and a Bedridden Passenger," *LDS Living*, July 24, 2020, https://www.ldsliving.com/how-wilford-woodruff-and-brigham-young-entered-the-salt-lake-valley-together-a-driver-and-a-bedridden-passenger/s/93060.

[4] Early members of the Church of Jesus Christ of Latter-day Saints (or Mormons) were commonly known as *Saints* because they claimed to follow Jesus's teachings as did the early Christians. Today the term "Latter-day Saints" is used more often.

[5] "Bamberger Railroad," UtahRails, May 16, 2024, https://utahrails.net/utahrails/bamberger.php.

[6] Glen M. Leonard, "Suburbia and the Freeway," History to Go, accessed July 6, 2024, https://historytogo.utah.gov/suburbia-freeway/.

[7] Kay Beal and Robert Beal, eds., *Seasons of North Farmington* (Bountiful, UT: Carr Printing Company, 1992), 9.

[8] A *ward* is a local church unit comprising one or more neighborhoods.

[9] The *priesthood* is a formal position bestowed upon all "worthy" males at age twelve. It confers the power and authority to act in the name of God to carry out the work of the salvation of mankind.

[10] *Sunday School* meetings teach the basic principles of the gospel to all family members.

[11] A *bishopric* is a group of three adult male members who have been assigned to run each of the local church units.

[12] *Sister* is a respectful term of address that members use to address adult women.

[13] *Ordinances* are Mormon rites such as baptism, confirmation, temple endowments (blessings and solemn commitments) and temple marriage, all of which are believed to be essential to eternal exaltation.

[14] The *Thirteen Articles of Faith* were written by the Prophet Joseph Smith in 1842 when he was asked to summarize the beliefs of the church. Considered inspired revelations, they are contained within the Pearl of Great Price, one of Mormonism's canonized books of scripture.

[15] *Primary* is a special group of classes held for children ages eighteen months through eleven years. Although Primary is now held on Sundays, from its establishment in 1878 until 1980 it was held midweek after school.

[16] A *stake* is the organizational level directly above that of a local ward. A stake usually contains three- to five-thousand members living in geographically close wards that join together on occasion for wider-based instruction and activities.

[17] Temple Square is a five-block area that surrounds the Salt Lake Temple in the middle of downtown Salt Lake City. The historic and cultural center of the city, it houses the Salt Lake Temple, the Salt Lake Tabernacle, and several other historic sites from the church's earliest Utah years.

[18] "Salt Lake Tabernacle," Church of Jesus Christ, last modified

Apr. 17, 2024, https://www.churchofjesuschrist.org/learn/salt-lake-tabernacle-temple-square?lang=eng.

[19] *Temple clothing* is special, ceremonial clothing that is worn only inside temples by both men and women who are getting married or performing other types of temple work.

[20] A *Relief Society president* is the highest-level female leader in the local ward who, with her two female counselors, oversees many of the physical and spiritual needs of any women who live within the ward boundaries.

[21] This scripture contains a central Mormon tenet. It occurs in the first book of the Doctrine and Covenants, a canonized collection of revelations believed to have been received by Joseph Smith. While the church says other Christian faiths may contain important truths and may be peopled by genuine followers of Christ, they still insist that the fulness of the gospel can only be obtained in the saving ordinances found exclusively in the Mormon Church.

[22] After baptism (usually at age eight for children born in the church), people are *confirmed*, or blessed, to be an official church member after a male priesthood holder gives them a blessing and commands them to "receive the Holy Ghost."

[23] *Junior Sunday School* was a Sunday worship and teaching service for children up until their twelfth birthday. Meetings usually lasted for about ninety minutes.

[24] A *polygamist* is person (usually a man) who is married to more than one person of the opposite sex at the same time. While polygamy is currently illegal under the Utah State Constitution, in 2020 the Utah State Legislature decriminalized polygamy and reduced the punishment to a minor infraction among consenting adults.

[25] A marriage is *sealed* when a husband and wife are eternally linked in the temple by a male who holds the priesthood. Likewise, children can be *sealed* to their parents.

[26] *D&C* is the common abbreviation for the Doctrine and Covenants, a collection of writings by Joseph Smith that church members consider to be revelations. Smith wrote

almost all of the book, with only four later prophets adding small additions.

[27] Todd Compton, *In Sacred Loneliness: The Plural Wives of Joseph Smith* (Salt Lake City: Signature Books, 1997), 1, 12-13, 21, 25-42.

[28] Brigham Young, "Beneficial Effects of Polygamy," *Journal of Discourses* 11, (August 19, 1866): 269.

[29] "Brigham Young: Family Life," Church of Jesus Christ, accessed July 12, 2024, https://www.churchofjesuschrist.org/study/history/topics/brigham-young?lang=eng.

[30] Compton, *In Sacred Loneliness*, xiii.

[31]Compton, xiv-xv; Ann Eliza Young, *Wife No. 19: The Story of Ann Eliza Young* (Hartford, CT: Dustin, Gilman & Co., 1876). While Ann Eliza Young's autobiography is sometimes criticized as polemical, she nonetheless had intimate, firsthand knowledge of how polygamy affected her mother's life, her own life, and the lives of many women who lived in Utah at the time.

[32] Records obtained on https://www.familysearch.org and from personal, unpublished family records.

[33] A *bishop* is the highest-ranking male leader in a local ward.

[34] Joseph Fielding Smith, *Doctrines of Salvation,* ed. Bruce R. McConkie, vol. 1 (Salt Lake City: Bookcraft, 195), 56.

[35] Compton, *In Sacred Loneliness*, 33.

[36] Compton, 19.

[37] Compton, 464.

[38] All faithful members are expected to *tithe* 10 percent of their income annually to the Mormon Church, no matter their financial circumstances. In the nineteenth century, members could make "in-kind" donations, such as grain, vegetables, lumber, farm animals, etc.

[39] Family journals, letters, and records in possession of the author.

[40] Thomas G. Alexander, "The Odyssey of a Latter-Day Prophet: Wilford Woodruff and the Manifesto of 1890," *Journal of Mormon History* 17 (1991): 176, 192.

[41] "Official Statement by President Joseph F. Smith," *Deseret Evening News*, April 6, 1904, 1.

[42] Joseph F. Smith, "Plural Marriage for the Righteous Only," *Journal of Discourses* 20 (July 7, 1878): 28-31.

[43] *Temple divorce* is the colloquial term for a "cancellation of sealing." It must be approved by the First Presidency of the church.

[44] "To the Point: If My Parents Were Sealed in the Temple and Then Got Divorced, Which One am I Sealed To?" *New Era*, Aug. 2015, https://www.churchofjesuschrist.org/study/new-era/2015/08/recipe-for-a-happy-family?lang=eng.

[45] See Doctrine and Covenants 132.

[46] David J. Whittaker, "The Bone in the Throat: Orson Pratt and the Public Announcement of Plural Marriage," *Western Historical Quarterly* 18, no. 3 (1987): 293, 305-06, 312-314.

[47] Casey Paul Griffiths, Mary Jane Woodger, and Susan Easton Black, "The Myth About Brigham Young's 'This Is the Place' Quote," *LDS Living*, July 24, 2017, https://www.ldsliving.com/the-myth-about-brigham-youngs-this-is-the-place-quote/s/85936.

[48] The *First Presidency* is the highest governing body of the entire church, consisting of the prophet and his two male counselors.

[49] The *Quorum of the Twelve Apostles* is the second highest governing body of the church, consisting of twelve men.

[50] *Excommunication* (recently renamed "Withdrawal of Membership") is the harshest form of church discipline. A person is no longer considered a member of the church, and any of his/her previously received blessings are revoked. A person who is excommunicated can join the church again after a period of repentance.

[51] Peggy Fletcher Stack, "Mormon Critic John Dehlin is Excommunicated," *Salt Lake Tribune*, March 12, 2015, https://www.sltrib.com/news/mormon/2015/03/12/mormon-critic-john-dehlin-is-excommunicated/.

[52] An *LDS (or Latter-Day Saint or Mormon) missionary* is usually

a young-adult male or female member who dedicates twelve to twenty-four months in preaching the gospel around the world. Retired, married couples can also serve.

[53] Taylor Stevens, "Mormon Church Excommunicates Sam Young, a Former Bishop Who Has Been Protesting Sometimes Sexually Explicit One-on-One Interviews Between Clergy and Youths," *Salt Lake Tribune*, September 16, 2018, https://www.sltrib.com/religion/2018/09/16/mormon-church/.

[54] Doug Robinson, "Neleh—From TV's 'Survivor' to Motherhood," *Deseret News*, April 28, 2014, https://www.deseret.com/2014/4/28/20540301/neleh-from-tv-s-survivor-to-motherhood/.

[55] "President Russell M. Nelson: 'The Correct Name of the Church,'" *Church News*, October 7, 2018, https://www.thechurchnews.com/2018/10/7/23221287/president-russell-m-nelson-the-correct-name-of-the-church/.

[56] "Mormon.org 'I'm a Mormon' Effort Launches in New York City," Church of Jesus Christ, June 16, 2011, https://newsroom.churchofjesuschrist.org/article/mormon-ads-new-york-city.

[57] Nelson, "The Correct Name."

[58] Michael R. Cope, "You Don't Know Jack: The Dynamics of Mormon Religious/Ethnic Identity," (master's thesis, Brigham Young University, 2009), https://scholarsarchive.byu.edu/etd/1939/.

[59] An *active* Mormon is one who regularly participates in all church meetings and activities and is generally considered to be a sincere believer.

[60] Dallin H. Oaks, "Pornography," *Ensign*, May 2005, 90.

[61] Jane Ridley, "Julianne Hough: From Mormon to Wild Child," *New York Post*, October 12, 2013, https://nypost.com/2013/10/12/former-mormon-julianne-hough-has-come-a-long-way/.

[62] Russell M. Nelson, "Face the Future with Faith," *Ensign*, April 2011, 34.

[63] Tad Walch, "President Nelson Makes Impassioned Plea

for all to 'Come unto Christ,'" *Deseret News*, April 7, 2019, https://www.deseret.com/2019/4/7/20670476/president-nelson-makes-impassioned-plea-for-all-to-come-unto-christ/.

[64] Russell M. Nelson, "Think Celestial!" *Liahona*, October 2023, 118.

[65] "Millennium," Church of Jesus Christ, July 30, 2024, https://www.churchofjesuschrist.org/study/manual/gospel-topics/millennium?lang=eng.

[66] Russell M. Nelson, "Rejoice in the Gift of Priesthood Keys," Church of Jesus Christ, April 2024, https://www.churchofjesuschrist.org/study/general-conference/2024/04/57nelson?lang=eng.

[67] The *Relief Society* is the church's official organization for all women ages eighteen and up; it focuses on gospel study, personal betterment, and philanthropic service.

[68] Fawn M. Brodie, *No Man Knows My History: The Life of Joseph Smith*, (New York: Alfred A. Knopf, 1945).

[69] James Reston, Jr., "The Mormon Excommunication of Fawn Brodie: Why Banishing the Famous Biographer Reverberates 65 Years," Washington Independent Review of Books, July 30, 2012, https://www.washingtonindependentreviewofbooks.com/index.php/features/the-mormon-excommunication-of-fawn-brodie-why-banishing-the-famous-biograph.

[70] Curt Bench, "Reviews: Fifty Important Mormon Books," *Sunstone*, October 1990, 57, https://sunstone.org/wp-content/uploads/sbi/articles/079-54-58.pdf.

[71] All names of private individuals are pseudonyms.

[72] "1914 Whooping Cough," Mayo Clinic, accessed July 17, 2024, https://www.mayoclinic.org/diseases-conditions/history-disease-outbreaks-vaccine-timeline/whooping-cough.

[73] Personal history in possession of the author.

[74] Anne M. Butler and Wendy Wolff, *United States Senate Election, Expulsion and Censure Cases, 1793-1990*, ed. Sheila P.

Burke, (Washington: U.S. Government Printing Office, 1995), 272-274.

[75] "The Manifesto and the End of Plural Marriage," Church of Jesus Christ, accessed August 2, 2024, https://www.churchofjesuschrist.org/study/manual/gospel-topics-essays/the-manifesto-and-the-end-of-plural-marriage?lang=eng.

[76] "Racial Segregation in the Church," Equal Justice Initiative, January 1, 2016. https://eji.org/news/history-racial-injustice-racial-segregation-in-church/.

[77] Barbara Jones Brown, Naomi Watkins, and Katherine Kitterman, "Gaining, Losing and Winning Back the Vote: The Story of Utah Women's Suffrage," Utah Women's History, accessed July 18, 2024, https://utahwomenshistory.org/2018/02/receiving-losing-and-winning-back-the-vote-the-story-of-utah-womens-suffrage/.

[78] Jonathan Edwards, "Sinners in the Hands of an Angry God," July 8, 1741.

[79] Proselyting *missions* have long been considered obligatory for all single young men in the church. In addition, young women and older married couples are also encouraged to serve, but there is not nearly as much pressure put upon them as there is on the young men.

[80] Hannah Wheelwright, "Mormons, Sex, and Not So Hilarious Consequences," Young Mormon Feminists, August 29, 2015, https://youngmormonfeminists.org/2015/08/29/mormons-sex-and-not-so-hilarious-consequences/.

[81] *Married student wards* are segregated from student wards that serve unmarried students.

[82] Gabriel Lopez-Garrido, "Locus of Control Theory in Psychology: Definition and Examples," Simply Psychology, August 3, 2024, https://www.simplypsychology.org/locus-of-control.html.

[83] John Dart, "Mormons Modify Temple Rites: Ceremony: Woman's vow to obey husband is dropped. Changes

are called most significant since 1978," *Los Angeles Times*, May 5, 1990, https://www.latimes.com/archives/la-xpm-1990-05-05-vw-353-story.html.

[84] Jana Riess, "Major Changes to Mormon Temple Ceremony, Especially for Women," Religion News Service, January 3, 2019, https://religionnews.com/2019/01/03/major-changes-to-mormon-temple-ceremony-especially-for-women/.

[85] Lou Cannon, "Ronald Reagan: Impact and Legacy," University of Virginia Miller Center, accessed July 18, 2024, https://millercenter.org/president/reagan/impact-and-legacy.

[86] Members in good standing are expected to pay a 10 percent *tithe* on all of their income to the church each month. Most young children start this practice after turning eight and being baptized.

[87] Laura Williamson, "Is Caffeine a Friend or Foe?" American Heart Association News, August 8, 2022, https://www.heart.org/en/news/2022/08/08/is-caffeine-a-friend-or-foe.

[88] Michael McGrath, "Nancy Reagan and the Negative Impact of the 'Just Say No' Anti-Drug Campaign," The Guardian, March 8, 2016, https://www.theguardian.com/society/2016/mar/08/nancy-reagan-drugs-just-say-no-dare-program-opioid-epidemic.

[89] Markus Heilig et al., "Addiction as a Brain Disease Revised: Why it Still Matters, and the Need for Consilience," *Neuropsychopharmacology* 46, no. 10 (February 22, 2021): 1715, 1717, 1719, 1720, https://doi.org/10.1038/s41386-020-00950-y.

[90] "Genomics and Your Health: Epigenetics, Health, and Disease," Centers for Disease Control and Prevention, May 15, 2024, https://www.cdc.gov/genomics-and-health/about/epigenetic-impacts-on-health.html.

[91] Maria Angeliki S. Pavlou and Tiago Fleming Outeiro, "Epigenetics in Parkinson's Disease," *Advances in Experimental Medicine and Biology* 978 (2017), 363-90, https://doi:

10.1007/978-3-319-53889-1_19.

[92] Lindsy Liu, Diana N. Pei, and Pela Soto, "History of the Opioid Epidemic: How Did We Get Here?" National Capital Poison Center, accessed January 13, 2023, https://www.poison.org/articles/opioid-epidemic-history-and-prescribing-patterns-182.

[93] A *priesthood blessing* is one in which a male church member who holds the priesthood can lay his hands upon the head of any person in his family or circle of acquaintances who require special help or power from God. Blessings are pronounced, and often advice is given.

[94] Leslie Waghorn, "Surge in Heroin Use Tied to Prescription Opioid Abuse, According to CDC," Vital Record, August 17, 2015, https://vitalrecord.tamhsc.edu/surge-in-heroin-use-tied-to-prescription-opioid-abuse-according-to-cdc/.

[95] "CDC's Efforts to Prevent Overdoses and Substance Use-Related Harms 2022-2024," Centers for Disease Control and Prevention, last modified October 3, 2023, https://www.cdc.gov/ore/search/pages/cdc-efforts-to-prevent-overdoses_2022-2024.html.

[96] J. Reuben Clark, "First Presidency Message of October 1942," in *Messages of the First Presidency,* ed. James R. Clark, vol. 6, (Salt Lake City: Bookcraft, Inc., 1935-1951), https://josephsmithfoundation.org/first-presidency-message-of-october-1942/.

[97] Jeffrey R. Holland, "Of Souls, Symbols, and Sacraments," *Brigham Young University 1987-88 Speeches* 4, (January 12, 1988), https://speeches.byu.edu/talks/jeffrey-r-holland/souls-symbols-sacraments/.

[98] After 105 years of being associated with the Boy Scouts of America, the Mormon Church severed contact with the organization on December 31, 2019. Reportedly, the Boy Scouts ran afoul of the church when they decided to admit openly gay and transgender youths and adult volunteers and also opened the association to girls. See Gary Fields and Brady McCombs, "Mormon Leader: We Didn't Leave Boy Scouts, They

Left Us," AP News, November 15, 2019, https://apnews.com/article/us-news-ap-top-news-ut-state-wire-medical-marijuana-reinventing-faith-bd0129a803df40f08e0240d75dd66f2b.

[99] *Seminary classes* are daily gospel study sessions for teens held during the school day in Utah and other western states. Some states hold the classes in the early morning hours in nearby churches before school starts.

[100] Spencer W. Kimball, "A Counseling Problem in the Church," BYU Devotional for LDS Seminary & Institute Instructors, July 10, 1964.

[101] Victor L. Brown, "Two Views of Sexuality," Church of Jesus Christ, July 1975, https://www.churchofjesuschrist.org/study/ensign/1975/07/two-views-of-sexuality?lang=eng.

[102] Amber B. Raley and Jennifer L. Lucas, "Stereotype or Success?"
Journal of Homosexuality 51, no. 2 (October 17, 2008): 23, https://doi:10.1300/J082v51n02_02.

[103] APA, *Diagnostic and Statistical Manual: Mental Disorders-1* (Washington, D. C.: American Psychiatric Association, 1952), 38-9.

[104] Jeremy W. Peters, "The Decline and Fall of the 'H' Word," *New York Times*, March 21, 2014, https://www.nytimes.com/2014/03/23/fashion/gays-lesbians-the-term-homosexual.html.

[105] Bruce Chadwick, "Midnight for New York's 1960s Gay Community?" History News Network, October 12, 2018, https://www.historynewsnetwork.org/article/midnight-for-new-yorks-1960s-gay-community.

[106] *Elder* is a term of respect used to identify male members ages eighteen and older who have shown themselves worthy to receive the Melchizedek Priesthood, or higher-level priesthood.

[107] "5 Attitudes Jesus Condemned in the Pharisees," Jesus Film Project, May 31, 2021, https://www.jesusfilm.org/blog/5-attitudes-jesus-condemned-in-pharisees/.

[108] "Interview with Elder Dallin H. Oaks and Elder Lance B. Wickman: 'Same-Gender Attraction',' Church of Jesus Christ, accessed April 13, 2021, https://newsroom.churchofjesuschrist.org/article/interview-oaks-wickman-same-gender-attraction.

[109] Peggy Fletcher Stack, "Landmark 'Mormon Doctrine' Goes Out of Print," *Salt Lake Tribune*, May 21, 2010, https://archive.sltrib.com/story.php?ref=/ci_15137409.

[110] McConkie was called to serve as a member of the First Council of Seventy in 1946, when he was only thirty-one years old. He then served as a member of the Quorum of the Twelve Apostles from 1972 until his death in 1985. His decades of service in the highest levels of leadership added weight to his pronouncements in *Mormon Doctrine*.

[111] Bruce R. McConkie, *Mormon Doctrine* (Salt Lake City: Deseret Book Company, 1966), 496.

[112] "Utah LGBTQ+ Suicide Prevention Plan: 2020 - 2023," Utah Suicide Prevention Coalition, accessed January 14, 2023, 6, https://sumh.utah.gov/wp-content/uploads/LGBTQ-Strategic-Plan-2020.pdf.

[113] "List of U.S. States by Elevation," The Fact File, April 19, 2024, https://thefactfile.org/50-states-elevation/.

[114] "Utah Suicide Prevention State Plan 2022-2026," Utah Suicide Prevention Coalition, accessed March 18, 2023, 34, 32, http://sumh.utah.gov/wp-content/uploads/Utah-Suicide-Prevention-State-Plan-2022-2026-FOR-IMMEDIATE-RELEASE.pdf.

[115] Adam G. Horwitz et al., "Risk and Protective Factors for Suicide among Sexual Minority Youth Seeking Emergency Medical Services," *Journal of Affective Disorders* 279, (January 15, 2021), 274-281, https://doi.org/10.1016/j.jad.2020.10.015.

[116] "What's the Difference Between Passive and Active Suicidal Thoughts?"
Salt Lake Behavioral Health, January 5, 2022, https://saltlakebehavioralhealth.com/blog/whats-the-difference-

between-passive-and-active-suicidal-thoughts/.

[117] Jennifer Tzeses, "Tell Me Everything I Need to Know about Cognitive Dissonance," Health Central, November 30, 2020, https://www.healthcentral.com/mental-health/cognitive-dissonance.

[118] D. Michael Quinn, "Male-Male Intimacy Among Nineteenth-Century Mormons: A Case Study," *Dialogue: A Journal of Mormon Thought* 28, no. 4 (Winter 1995): 106.

[119] Peter Gay, *The Bourgeois Experience: Victoria to Freud*, vol. 2, The Tender Passion (New York: Oxford University Press, 1986), 217.

[120] George Painter, "The Sensibilities of Our Forefathers: The History of Sodomy Laws in the United States," Gay and Lesbian Archives of the Pacific Northwest, August 10, 2004, https://www.glapn.org/sodomylaws/sensibilities/utah.htm.

[121] D. Michael Quinn, *Same-Sex Dynamics Among Nineteenth-Century Americans: A Mormon Example*, (Chicago: University of Illinois Press, 1996), 40-41.

[122] Quinn, *Same-Sex Dynamics*, 276.

[123] *Sixty-Eighth Semi-Annual Conference of The Church of Jesus Christ of Latter-Day Saints* (Salt Lake City: Deseret News Publishing Company, 1897), 53.

[124] *One-Hundred Twenty-fifth Semi-Annual Conference of The Church of Jesus Christ of Latter-day Saints* (Salt Lake City: Deseret Book Company, 1954), 79.

[125] Bruce R. McConkie, *Mormon Doctrine*, 2nd ed. (Salt Lake City: Bookcraft, 1966), 709.

[126] D&C 132:27.

[127] *General authorities* are the highest-ranking male leaders in the church, composed of the First Presidency, the Quorum of the Twelve Apostles, General Authority Seventies, and the Presiding Bishopric.

[128] Ernest L. Wilkinson, private journal, May 21, 1959, quoted in Connell O'Donovan, "The Abominable & Detestable Crime Against Nature," accessed August 14, 2024, http://www.connellodonovan.com/lgbtmormons.html.

[129] Ernest L. Wilkinson, "Make Honor Your Standard," in *Brigham Young University Speeches of the Year*, September 23, 1965, 8, https://lattergaystories.org/wp-content/uploads/2020/03/Make-Honor-Your-Standard-Ernest-Wilkinson.pdf.

[130] Spencer W. Kimball, *The Miracle of Forgiveness* (Salt Lake City: Bookcraft, Inc., 1969), 34.

[131] Kimball, *Miracle*, 36.

[132] Kimball, *Miracle*, 34.

[133] Kimball, *Miracle*, 13, 34-6.

[134] Kimball, Miracle, 37.

[135] Jack Drescher, "Out of DSM: Depathologizing Homosexuality," *Behavioral Sciences* 5, no. 4 (December 4, 2015): 565-75, https://doi.org/10.3390/bs5040565.

[136] "Electroshock Therapy Shock Program | Brigham Young University," On the Record, accessed August 15, 2024, https://lattergaystories.org/?s=On+the+Record.

[137] Spencer W. Kimball, "A Counseling Problem in the Church: Address to Seminary and Institute of Religion Faculty," (lecture, Brigham Young University, Provo, UT, (July 10, 1964), 15. archive.org/details/PresidentKimballACounselingProblemInTheChurch/mode/2up.

[138] Peggy Fletcher Stack, "Dallin Oaks Says Shock Therapy of Gays Didn't Happen at BYU While He Was President. Records Show Otherwise," *Salt Lake Tribune*, November 16, 2021, https://www.sltrib.com/religion/2021/11/16/dallin-oaks-says-shock/.

[139] Allen E. Bergin, "Toward a Theory of Human Agency," *New Era*, July 1973, 33.

[140] Allen E. Bergin, "An Apology," On the Record, accessed August 16, 2024, https://lattergaystories.org/bergin/.

[141] Boyd K. Packer, quoted in On the Record, accessed August 16, 2024, https://lattergaystories.org/wp-content/uploads/2020/02/To-Young-Men-Only.mp4.

[142] Vaughn J. Featherstone, "Charity Never Faileth," *BYU*

Speeches, February 27, 1979, https://speeches.byu.edu/talks/vaughn-j-featherstone/charity-never-faileth/.

[143] Gordon B. Hinckley, "Reverence and Morality," *Ensign,* April 1987, 47, https://www.churchofjesuschrist.org/study/general-conference/1987/04/reverence-and-morality?lang=eng.

[144] Spencer J. Condie, "A Mighty Change of Heart," *Ensign,* October 1993, 16-17, https://www.churchofjesuschrist.org/study/general-conference/1993/10/a-mighty-change-of-heart?lang=eng.

[145] On rare occasions, the First Presidency or the Quorum of the Twelve Apostles issue formal proclamations. There have been only six proclamations issued since the church's founding in 1830.

[146] Gordon B. Hinckley, "Stand Strong against the Wiles of the World," *Ensign,* November 1995, 101, https://www.churchofjesuschrist.org/study/general-conference/1995/10/stand-strong-against-the-wiles-of-the-world?lang=eng.

[147] James Brooke, "To be Young, Gay, and Going to High School in Utah," *New York Times,* February 28, 1996, https://www.nytimes.com/1996/02/28/us/to-be-young-gay-and-going-to-high-school-in-utah.html.

[148] As of 2024, the Mormon Church ranks as the richest church in the world based upon its net worth. In 2023, their "total wealth reached an estimated $265 billion." See https://www.vanguardngr.com/2024/08/top-5-richest-churches-in-the-world-2024/.

[149] Gordon B. Hinckley, quoted in Don Lattin, "Mormon Church: The Powerful Force Behind Proposition 22," SFGate, February 6, 2000, https://www.sfgate.com/news/article/Mormon-Church-The-Powerful-Force-Behind-2778116.php.

[150] Mark Miller, "To be Gay—and Mormon," *Newsweek,* May 7, 2000, https://www.newsweek.com/be-gay-and-mormon-159959.

[151] A stake center is a church meetinghouse where multiple

local congregations can meet together.

[152] Miller, "To be Gay."

[153] Fred Karger, quoted in Stephanie Mencimer, "Of Mormons and (Gay) Marriage," Mother Jones, March/April 2010, https://www.motherjones.com/politics/2010/04/fred-karger-save-gay-marriage/.

[154] Stephanie Mencimer, "Mormon Church Abandons Its Crusade Against Gay Marriage," Mother Jones, April 12, 2013, https://www.motherjones.com/politics/2013/04/prop-8-mormons-gay-marriage-shift/.

[155] "President Packer's Speech Prompts National Controversy, Revisions," Sunstone, December 2010, 68, https://sunstone.org/wp-content/uploads/sbi/articles/161-68-70.pdf.

[156] Rosemary Winters, "Mormon Apostle's Words About Gays Spark Protest," Salt Lake Tribune, October 19, 2010, https://archive.sltrib.com/article.php?id=50434583&itype=CMSID.

[157] Carly M. Springer, "30 Things You Might Not Know About the Conference Center," LDS Living, September 30, 2016, https://www.ldsliving.com/30-things-you-didnt-know-about-the-conference-center/s/76671.

[158] Gordon B. Hinckley, "To All the World in Testimony," ChurchofJesusChrist.org, April 2000, https://www.churchofjesuschrist.org/study/general-conference/2000/04/to-all-the-world-in-testimony?lang=eng.

[159] Carol Lynn Pearson, No More Goodbyes: Circling the Wagons Around Our Gay Loved Ones (Brigham City: Brigham Distributing, 2007), xii.

[160]Pearson, No More, 59, 61.

[161] Ray Parker, "Groups Team Up to Reach Out to Homeless LGBT Mormon Youths," Salt Lake Tribune, January 25, 2013, https://archive.sltrib.com/article.php?id=55659498&itype=cmsid.

[162] "Mama Dragons History Timeline," Mama Dragons, accessed February 6, 2024, https://www.mamadragons.org/

history-of-mama-dragons.

[163] Peggy Fletcher Stack, "Mama Dragons Lead the Fight for Their Gay Mormon Kids," *Salt Lake Tribune*, May 6, 2015, https://www.sltrib.com/news/mormon/2015/05/27/mama-dragons-lead-the-fight-for-their-gay-mormon-kids/.

[164] The Young Men's organization is the official church program for young males between the ages of twelve and eighteen in each ward.

[165] Ryan J. Hallstrom, "Granite Mountain Records Vault," Intermountain Histories, accessed August 2, 2024, https://www.intermountainhistories.org/items/show/422.

[166] Benjamin Knoll, Ph.D., "Many Mormons are Unaware of the Messy Details of LDS Church History," HuffPost, last modified January 24, 2015, https://www.huffpost.com/entry/many-mormons-are-unaware_b_6195784.

[167] Jeremy T. Runnells, *CES Letter: My Search for Answers to Mormon Doubts*, last modified October 2017, https://read.cesletter.org/.

[168] Charles Seife, *Virtual Unreality: Just Because the Internet Told You So, How Do You Know It's True?* (New York: Viking Penguin, 2014).

[169] "President Nelson Challenges Youth to Participate in 'Greatest Cause' on Earth," Newsroom, Church of Jesus Christ, June 3, 2018, https://newsroom.churchofjesuschrist.org/article/president-nelson-challenges-youth-greatest-cause-on-earth.

[170] Church News Staff, "President Russell M. Nelson: 'Sisters' Participation in the Gathering of Israel,'" Church News, October 6, 2018, https://www.thechurchnews.com/2018/10/6/23264577/president-russell-m-nelson-sisters-participation-in-the-gathering-of-israel/.

[171] An *Area Seventy* is a male church member who is called to lead the church in various geographic areas throughout the world, depending upon his home country.

[172] Sandra Tanner, ed., "Apostasy in Sweden! Their 15

Unanswered Questions," *Salt Lake City Messenger* 121 (October 2013), http://www.utlm.org/newsletters/no121.htm.

[173] Hans Mattsson, *Truth Seeking*, with Christina Hanke (Eugene, Oregon: Andersson & Isacson AB, 2018), 154, 161.

[174] Tanner, "Apostasy."

[175] Jeffrey R. Holland, "Lord, I Believe," Church of Jesus Christ, April 2013, https://www.churchofjesuschrist.org/study/general-conference/2013/04/lord-i-believe?lang=eng.

[176] Laurie Goodstein, "Some Mormons Search the Web and Find Doubt," *New York Times*, July 20, 2013, https://www.nytimes.com/2013/07/21/us/some-mormons-search-the-web-and-find-doubt.html.

[177] Mattsson, *Truth Seeking*, 217.

[178] Mattsson, *Truth Seeking*, 179.

[179] The *Gospel Topics Essays* were quietly introduced on the church website in 2013. They were written by a group of faithful Mormon scholars who were attempting to answer some of the members' "thorniest historical and theological questions" about their faith.

[180] Jana Riess, "For Mormons in a Faith Crisis, the Gospel Topics Essays Try to Answer the Hard Questions," Religion News Service, October 27, 2020, https://religionnews.com/2020/10/27/for-mormons-in-a-faith-crisis-the-gospel-topics-essays-try-to-answer-the-hard-questions/.

[181] "Are the Gospel Topics Essays Helping or Hurting LDS Membership?" Mormonism Research Ministry, accessed July 21, 2024, https://www.mrm.org/essays-reaction.

[182] Gina Colvin, "A Former Bishop's Doctrinal Dilemmas," Kiwi Mormon, February 12, 2014, https://www.patheos.com/blogs/kiwimormon/2014/02/a-former-bishops-doctrinal-dilemmas/.

[183] "Race and the Priesthood," Church of Jesus Christ, accessed March 19, 2024, https://www.churchofjesuschrist.org/study/manual/gospel-topics-essays/race-and-the-priesthood?lang=eng.

[184] Joseph F. Smith, Jr., letter to Alfred M. Nelson, January 13, 1907, Salt Lake City, microfilm of original typescript, MS 14591, LDS Church Archives.

[185] Joseph Fielding Smith, "The Negro and the Priesthood," *Improvement Era*, April 1924, 565.

[186] Joseph Fielding Smith, *The Way to Perfection*, (Salt Lake City, Genealogical Society of Utah, 1931), 43.

[187] Matthew L. Harris, *Second-Class Saints: Black Mormons and the Struggle for Racial Equality* (New York: Oxford University Press, 2024).

[188] Bruce R. McConkie, *Mormon Doctrine*, (Salt Lake City: Bookcraft, Inc., 1958), 476-77. In Mormon theology, the *first estate* is the premortal life. In pre-1978 Mormon theology, those who were "less valiant" during the pre-existence came to earth as "negroes."

[189] "Race and the Priesthood."

[190] "New Policy Occasions Church Comment," *Times-News*, June 9, 1988. https://www.newspapers.com/article/the-times-news-partial-transcript-of-ap/21138508/.

[191] A stake president is the male leader of a stake, which is a group of wards that are linked due to geographical proximity. Stakes usually consist of five to ten wards, or 3,000 to 5,000 members.

[192] A visiting teacher was a woman who was assigned to visit a group of women in her ward, usually monthly, providing service, encouragement, and a short gospel lesson. This calling was eliminated in 2018 and has since been replaced by a call for members to be "ministers" instead.

[193] A pseudonym

[194] Mormons believe in an afterlife in which persons will be assigned to one of three eternal *kingdoms*: the celestial kingdom (the highest degree of glory), the terrestrial kingdom (the middle kingdom of glory), and the telestial kingdom (the lowest kingdom of glory). Assignments will be made based upon a person's faithfulness and obedience to the testimony of Jesus.

[195] Lewis Carroll, *Alice's Adventures in Wonderland* (London: McMillan & Co., 1865), 9-12.

[196] Laurie Goodstein, "Some Mormons Search the Web and Find Doubt," *New York Times*, July 20, 2013, https://www.nytimes.com/2013/07/21/us/some-mormons-search-the-web-and-find-doubt.html.

[197] *Temple prayer rolls* are paper lists kept in the temples of those needing special blessings. Patrons are invited to write the names of any family members or friends whom they are especially concerned about.

[198] Peter L. Berger, *The Heretical Imperative: Contemporary Possibilities of Religious Affirmation* (New York City: Anchor Press/Doubleday, 1979), 58.

[199] Berger, 58.

[200] Berger, 33.

[201] "Pope Francis: 'I Prefer a Church Which is Bruised, Hurting, and Dirty,'" *USA Today*, November 26, 2013, https://www.usatoday.com/story/news/world/2013/11/26/pope-francis-poverty/3759005/.

[202] Molly Schnell, "The Opioid Crisis: Tragedy, Treatments, and Trade-offs," Stanford Institute for Economic Policy Research (SIEPR), February 2019, https://drive.google.com/file/d/1TSJybQjOHQSwKsh9-0jFJ1JZSHF47FW0/view.

[203] "Facts about Fentanyl," United States Drug Enforcement Agency, accessed September 3, 2024, https://www.dea.gov/resources/facts-about-fentanyl.

[204] "One Pill Can Kill," United States Drug Enforcement Agency, accessed September 3, 2024, https://www.dea.gov/onepill.

[205] "The 'Speedball': Risks of Mixing Heroin and Cocaine," Delphi Behavioral Health Group, Accessed Nov. 27, 2022, delphihealthgroup.com.

[206] "Thousands of U.S. communities to receive opioid recovery funds from $26 billion global settlements as soon as May 2022," National Opioid Settlement, accessed September 3,

2024, https://nationalopioidsettlement.com/wp-content/uploads/2022/02/Opioids_release_20220225.pdf.

[207] "National Opioid Settlement," Brown Greer, accessed September 3, 2024, https://www.browngreer.com/case-studies/national-opioid-settlement-administration/.

[208] Lewis Carroll, *Alice's Adventures in Wonderland*, (London: Macmillan & Co., 1865), 60, 155.

[209] Markus Heilig et al., "Addiction as a Brain Disease Revised: Why it Still Matters, and the Need for Consilience," *Neuropsychopharmacology* 46, no. 10 (September 2021): 1715-23, https://pubmed.ncbi.nlm.nih.gov/33619327/.

[210] Amanda Ruggeri, "How Bedlam Became London's Most Iconic Symbol," BBC, December 15, 2016, https://www.bbc.com/culture/article/20161213-how-bedlam-became-a-palace-for-lunatics.

[211] Joseph Curtis, "Faces of Bedlam: How a Victorian Photographer's Haunting Portraits of Patients Sent to the Notorious Bethlem Asylum Were Used to Examine Them for Evidence of Mental Health Conditions," Daily Mail, July 29, 2019, https://www.dailymail.co.uk/news/article-7296751/Faces-patients-notorious-Bedlam-Asylum.html.

[212] A pseudonym

[213] "What We Investigate: Bank Robbery," FBI Federal Bureau of Investigation, Accessed December 10, 2022, https://www.fbi.gov/investigate/violent-crime/bank-robbery.

[214] Edwards, "New Jail is Just Right."

[215] Alan Edwards, "New Jail is Just Right—Ugly" *Deseret News*, July 22, 1998, https://www.deseret.com/1998/7/22/19392528/new-jail-is-just-right-ugly/.

[216] "Oxbow Jail Set to Fully Reopen After Nearly a Decade," ABC4, October 25, 2017, https://www.abc4.com/news/local-news/oxbow-jail-set-to-fully-reopen-after-nearly-a-decade/.

[217] Clayton Norlen, "Prisoners Again Populate Oxbow Jail," *Deseret News*, July 19, 2009, https://www.deseret.com/2009/7/19/20329743/

prisoners-again-populate-oxbow-jail/.

[218] John Seaman, "Commentary: Harsh Conditions Define Life at the Salt Lake County Jail," *Salt Lake Tribune*, September 23, 2018, https://www.sltrib.com/opinion/commentary/2018/09/23/commentary-harsh/.

[219] "ACLU: Statewide, Independent Utah Jail Inspections Needed," Associated Press, May 30, 2017, https://apnews.com/article/aa8c118b58444a22bf51258ce4c267d0.

[220] Taylor W. Anderson, "In a Reversal that Will End Years of Secrecy, Utah's County Jail Guidelines Will Be Made Public," *Salt Lake Tribune*, January 28, 2018, https://www.sltrib.com/news/politics/2018/01/26/in-a-reversal-that-will-end-years-of-secrecy-utahs-county-jail-guidelines-will-be-made-public/.

[221] Taylor W. Anderson, "Two Dozen People Died in Utah Jails Last Year. Now a Legislator Wants More Transparency on Inmate Deaths and Jail Rules to Prevent More," *Salt Lake Tribune*, November 29, 2017, https://www.sltrib.com/news/politics/2017/11/29/two-dozen-people-died-in-utah-jails-last-year-now-a-legislator-wants-more-transparency-on-inmate-deaths-and-jail-rules-to-prevent-more/.

[222] Taylor W. Anderson, "In a reversal," *Salt Lake Tribune*.

[223] Paighten Harkins, "Years After a Spate of Questionable Utah In-Custody Deaths, Utah Jail Operating Standards Are Now Public Records," *Salt Lake Tribune*, April 2, 2021, https://www.sltrib.com/news/2021/04/02/years-after-spate/.

[224] Taylor W. Anderson, "Two Dozen People Died," *Salt Lake Tribune*.

[225] Marcos Ortiz, "The Justice files: New Hope for Madison Jensen's Family," ABC4, February 25, 2020, https://www.abc4.com/new/justice-files/the-justice-files-new-hope-for-madison-jensens-family/.

[226] Taylor W. Anderson, "Duchesne County Nurse Charged with Negligent Homicide Nine Months After 21-Year-Old Inmate Died from Dehydration," *Salt Lake Tribune*, September 25, 2017, https://www.sltrib.com/news/

politics/2017/09/25/duchesne-county-nurse-charged-with-negligent-homicide-nine-months-after-21-year-old-inmate-died-from-dehydration/.

[227] Taylor W. Anderson, "Records Indicate Inmate Begged for Help Before Dying in Duchesne County Jail," *Salt Lake Tribune*, May 1, 2017, https://archive.sltrib.com/article.php?id=5230597&itype=CMSID.

[228] Marcos Ortiz, "The Justice Files," abc4.com.

[229] Kate Belcher, "District Judge Vacates Summary Judgment in Madison Jensen Civil Trial," *Uintah Basin Standard*, September 5, 2023, https://www.uintahbasinstandard.com/news/2023/09/05/district-judge-vacates-summary-judgment-in-madison-jensen-civil-trial/.

[230]Alisa Roth, *Insane: America's Criminal Treatment of Mental Illness* (New York: Basic Books, 2020), 99, 106, 111.

[231] Pat Reavy, "Utah Officials Hope New State Prison Offers Opportunities, Not a 'Dead End'," KSL.com, June 22, 2022, https://www.ksl.com/article/50427702/utah-officials-hope-new-state-prison-offers-opportunities-not-a-dead-end.

[232] Pat Reavy, "Too Nice for Inmates or Redefined? Why New Prison Is Much Different than at Point of the Mountain," KSL.com, July 25, 2022, https://www.ksl.com/article/50442238/too-nice-for-inmates-or-redefined-why-new-prison-is-much-different-than-at-point-of-the-mountain.

[233] Kaitlyn Bancroft, "Advocates, Families Say There's a Lack of Medical Care, Humane Treatment at New Utah Prison," KSL.com, September 7, 2022, https://www.ksl.com/article/50471105/advocates-families-say-theres-a-lack-of-medical-care-humane-treatment-at-new-utah-prison.

[234] Sean Higgins, "Advocates See Significant Improvements at the Utah State Correctional Facility," KUER, April 11, 2024, https://www.kuer.org/race-religion-social-justice/2024-04-11/advocates-see-significant-improvements-at-the-utah-state-correctional-facility.

[235] Reavy, "Too nice for inmates."

[236] "Utah Justice Reinvestment: Improving Public Safety, Addressing Treatment Needs," Crime and Justice Institute, December 2020, https://www.cjinstitute.org/publication/utahjri2020/.

[237] Daniel Soucy, Makenna Janes, and Andrew Hall, "State of Homelessness: 2024 Edition," National Alliance to End Homelessness, 2024, https://endhomelessness.org/homelessness-in-america/homelessness-statistics/state-of-homelessness/#why-do-people-experience-homelessness.

[238] "Drugs, Brains, and Behavior: The Science of Addiction," National Institute on Drug Abuse, accessed June 29, 2024, https://nida.nih.gov/publications/drugs-brains-behavior-science-addiction/treatment-recovery.

[239] Dennis Romboy, "Same-Sex Marriage Legal in Utah After Supreme Court Rejects Case," KSL, October 6, 2014, https://www.ksl.com/article/31845612/same-sex-marriage-legal-in-utah-after-supreme-court-rejects-case.

[240] "US: Supreme Court Upholds Same-Sex Marriage," Human Rights Watch, June 26, 2015, https://www.hrw.org/news/2015/06/26/us-supreme-court-upholds-same-sex-marriage.

[241] "Church Leaders Counsel Members After Supreme Court Same-Sex Marriage Decision," Church of Jesus Christ, June 30, 2015, https://newsroom.churchofjesuschrist.org/article/top-church-leaders-counsel-members-after-supreme-court-same-sex-marriage-decision.

[242] Jennifer Dobner, "New Mormon Policy Makes Apostates of Married Same-Sex Couples, Bars Children from Rites," *Salt Lake Tribune*, November 6, 2015, https://archive.sltrib.com/article.php?id=3144035&itype=CMSID.

[243] Sarah Jane Weaver, "Elder Christofferson Says Handbook Changes Regarding Same-Sex Marriages Help Protect Children," *Church News*, November 12, 2015, https://www.churchofjesuschrist.org/church/news/elder-christofferson-says-handbook-changes-regarding-same-sex-marriages-help-protect-children?lang=eng.

[244] Rich Kane, "Hundreds Rally Against New Mormon Policy; Many File Forms to Quit the Faith," *Salt Lake Tribune*, December 5, 2015, https://archive.sltrib.com/article.php?id=3178894&itype=CMSID.

[245] Jana Riess and Benjamin Knoll, "Commentary: Did the 2015 LGBTQ Policy Drive a Mass Exodus from the LDS Church? No, but for Many it Was the 'Last Straw'," *Salt Lake Tribune*, May 29, 2019, https://www.sltrib.com/religion/2019/05/29/commentary-did-lgbtq/.

[246] Russell M. Nelson, "Becoming True Millennials," Worldwide Devotional for Young Adults, Brigham Young University-Hawaii, January 10, 2016, https://www.churchofjesuschrist.org/study/broadcasts/article/worldwide-devotionals/2016/01/becoming-true-millennials?lang=eng.

[247] "There Are No Homosexual Members of the Church,'" MormonThink, accessed September 12, 2024, http://www.mormonthink.com/responses/bednar-no-homosexuals.htm.

[248] Jon A., "Elder Holland on Same-Gender Attraction, but Really Just Chastity," Out of Obscurity, March 9, 2016, https://outofobscurity.org/2016/03/09/elder-holland-on-same-gender-attraction-but-really-just-chastity/#more-5468.

[249] Dallin H. Oaks, "The Plan and the Proclamation," Church of Jesus Christ, October 2017, https://www.churchofjesuschrist.org/study/general-conference/2017/10/the-plan-and-the-proclamation?lang=eng.

[250] Dallin H. Oaks, "Youth and YSA Conference," (lecture, Wichita, KS, August 26, 2017), https://www.youtube.com/watch?v=JhADf8fHOBQ.

[251] Larry R. Lawrence, "The War Goes On," Church of Jesus Christ, April 2017, https://www.churchofjesuschrist.org/study/ensign/2017/04/the-war-goes-on?lang=eng.

[252] Bonnie L. Oscarson, "Rise Up in Strength, Sisters in Zion," Church of Jesus Christ, October 2016, https://

www.churchofjesuschrist.org/study/general-conference/2016/10/rise-up-in-strength-sisters-in-zion?lang=eng.

[253] Dallin H. Oaks, "Truth and the Plan," Church of Jesus Christ, October 2018, https://www.churchofjesuschrist.org/study/general-conference/2018/10/truth-and-the-plan?lang=eng.

[254] Peggy Fletcher Stack, "LDS Church Dumps Its Controversial LGBTQ Policy, Cites 'Continuing Revelation' from God," *Salt Lake Tribune*, April 5, 2019, https://www.sltrib.com/religion/2019/04/04/lds-church-dumps-its/.

[255] Dallin H. Oaks, "Anxiety in Stressful Times," Brigham Young University Hawaii, June 11, 2019, https://speeches.byuh.edu/devotional/anxiety-in-stressful-times.

[256] Jeffrey R. Holland, "Angels and Astonishment," Seminary & Institute Annual Training Broadcast, June 12, 2019, https://www.churchofjesuschrist.org/study/broadcasts/miscellaneous-events/2019/06/14holland?lang=eng#title1.

[257] Russell M. Nelson, "The Love and Laws of God," BYU Speeches, September 17, 2019, https://speeches.byu.edu/talks/russell-m-nelson/love-laws-god/.

[258] Tad Walch, "President Nelson Makes Impassioned Plea for All to 'Come Unto Christ,'" Deseret News, April 7, 2019, https://www.deseret.com/2019/4/7/20670476/president-nelson-makes-impassioned-plea-for-all-to-come-unto-christ/.

[259] Courtney Tanner, Erin Alberty, and Peggy Fletcher Stack, "After BYU Honor Code Change, LDS Church Now Says Same-Sex Relationships Are 'Not Compatible' with the Faith's Rules," last modified May 27, 2022, *Salt Lake Tribune*, https://www.sltrib.com/news/education/2020/03/04/after-byu-honor-code/.

[260] Dallin H. Oaks, "The Great Plan," Church of Jesus Christ, April 2020, https://www.churchofjesuschrist.org/study/general-conference/2020/04/51oaks?lang=eng.

[261] Dallin H. Oaks, "Divine Love in the Father's Plan," Church of

Jesus Christ, April 2022, https://www.churchofjesuschrist.org/study/general-conference/2022/04/51oaks?lang=eng.

[262] Jenna Alton, "BYU Valedictorian Comes out as Gay in Viral Convocation Speech," *Daily Universe*, April 29, 2019, https://universe.byu.edu/2019/04/29/byu-valedictorian-comes-out-as-gay-in-viral-convocation-speech/.

[263] Jeffrey R. Holland, "'We Must Have the Will to Stand Alone' — Read LDS Apostle Jeffrey R. Holland's Talk at BYU," August 26, 2021, *Salt Lake Tribune*, https://www.sltrib.com/religion/2021/08/23/we-must-have-will-stand/.

[264] Peggy Fletcher Stack, "BYU Will Require Incoming Students to Read Apostle Jeffrey Holland's Controversial 'Musket Speech,'" *Salt Lake Tribune*, March 15, 2024. https://www.sltrib.com/religion/2024/03/15/byu-will-require-incoming-students/.

[265] Tamarra Kemsley, "LDS Church Withdrawing Memberships of Some Saints in Same-Sex Marriages. But Not All." *Salt Lake Tribune*, June 16, 2024. https://www.sltrib.com/religion/2024/06/16/leadership-roulette-leaves-same/.

[266] John Dehlin, "Episode 1613/Persecuted by the Mormon Church—A Modern Case of Lying for the Lord," *Mormon Stories Podcast*, June 21, 2022, https://www.mormonstories.org/lying-for-the-lord-douglas-brennen/.

[267] Tamarra Kemsley, "LDS Church Withdrawing Memberships."

[268] "Repentance and Church Membership Councils (Section 32); Church Policies and Guidelines (Section 38)," Church of Jesus Christ, accessed September 16, 2024, https://www.churchofjesuschrist.org/study/manual/general-handbook?lang=eng.

[269] "Faith Leaders Respond to Pope Francis Comments on LGBT People," National LGBTQ Task Force, September 19, 2013, https://www.thetaskforce.org/news/faith-leaders-respond-to-pope-franciss-comments-on-lgbt-people/.

[270] "Views about homosexuality among Buddhists," Pew

Research Center, accessed November 20, 2023, https://www.pewresearch.org/religious-landscape-study/database/religious-tradition/buddhist/views-about-homosexuality/#demographic-information.

[271] "U.S. Muslims concerned about their place in society, but continue to believe in the American Dream," Pew Research Center, accessed November 20, 2023, https://www.pewresearch.org/religion/2017/07/26/findings-from-pew-research-centers-2017-survey-of-us-muslims/.

[272] "Letters to the Southern Baptist Church," Tyler Clementi Foundation, accessed September 16, 2024, https://tylerclementi.org/letters-to-the-southern-baptist-church/.

[273] Walter Kirn, "The Mormon Moment," *Newsweek*, last modified July 14, 2011, https://www.newsweek.com/mormon-moment-67951.

[274] John Dehlin, "Episode 1847/ Mormon Church in Decline in Utah? w/Dr. Ryan Cragun," *Mormon Stories Podcast*, January 4, 2024, https://www.mormonstories.org/mormon-church-in-decline-in-utah/.

[275] Lowell C. Bennion and Lawrence A. Young, "The Uncertain Dynamics of LDS Expansion, 1950-2020," *Dialogue: A Journal of Mormon Thought* 29, no. 1 (1996): 11, https://www.dialoguejournal.com/wp-content/uploads/sbi/articles/Dialogue_V29N01_14.pdf.

[276] "Utah Population 2024," World Population Review, accessed September 16, 2024, https://worldpopulationreview.com/states/utah.

[277] Matt Canham, "Utah Sees Latter-day Saint Slowdown and Membership Numbers Drop in Salt Lake County," *Salt Lake Tribune*, January 5, 2020, https://www.sltrib.com/religion/2020/01/05/utah-sees-latter-day/.

[278] Dehlin, "Episode 1847."

[279] Ryan T. Cragun, Bethany Gull, and Rick Phillips, "Mormons Are No Longer a Majority in Utah: Causes, Consequences, and Implications for the Sociology of Religion," *Journal of Religion and Demography* 10 (December 19, 2023): 162, 163, 165, 168,

177, 178, https://www.ryantcragun.com/mormons-are-no-longer-a-majority-in-utah-causes-consequences-and-implications-for-the-sociology-of-religion/.

[280] "Community Demographics in Farmington, Utah," Dwellics, accessed September 17, 2024, https://dwellics.com/state/utah/community-in-farmington.

[281] "Davis County, Utah – County Membership Report (2020)," The Association of Religion Data Archives, accessed September 17, 2024, https://www.thearda.com/us-religion/census/congregational-membership?y=2020&y2=0&t=0&c=49011.

[282] Michael B. Toney, Carol McKewen Stinner, and Stephen Kan, "Mormon and Nonmormon Migration In and Out of Utah," *Review of Religious Research* 25, no. 2, (December 1983): 124. https://doi.org/10.2307/3511489.

[283] Robert Gehrke, "Gerrymandering Utah's Non-LDS Voters Into Quarters Virtually Guarantees All-LDS Representation, Robert Gehrke Contends," *Salt Lake Tribune*, January 2, 2022, https://www.sltrib.com/religion/local/2022/01/02/gerrymandering-utahs-non/.

[284] Pam Perlich, quoted in Matt Canham, "Mormon Portion of Utah Population Steadily Shrinking," *Salt Lake Tribune*, July 24, 2005. https://archive.sltrib.com/article.php?id=2886596&itype=NGPSID.

[285] Dehlin, "Episode 1847."

[286] Andy Larsen, "The LDS Church is Losing Member Share in Most of the U.S.—and Other Things I learned When Researching the Rolls," *Salt Lake Tribune*, May 23, 2022, https://www.sltrib.com/religion/2022/05/23/andy-larsen-lds-church-is/.

[287] Jana Riess, "Is Mormonism Still Growing? Five Facts about Latter-day Saint Growth and Decline," Religion News Service, April 7, 2022, https://religionnews.com/2022/04/07/is-mormonism-still-growing-five-facts-about-latter-day-saint-growth-and-decline/.

[288] Jana Riess, "Worldwide, Only 25 Percent of Young

Single Mormons are Active in the LDS Church," *Religion News Service*, October 5, 2016, https://religionnews.com/2016/10/05/leaked-worldwide-only-25-of-young-single-mormons-are-active-in-the-lds-church/.

[289] Christian Anderson, quoted in Riess, "Is Mormonism Still Growing?"

[290] Madisan Hinkhouse, "WATCH: Leaked Videos Show LDS Leadership Meetings," KUTV, October 3, 2016, https://kutv.com/news/local/watch-leaked-videos-show-briefings-of-lds-leadership.

[291] Jana Riess, "Jana Riess: Dear LDS Parents, It's Not Just Your Children Who Are Leaving Church," *Salt Lake Tribune*, June 30, 2020, https://www.sltrib.com/religion/2020/06/30/jana-riess-dear-lds/.

[292] Jana Riess, "One in 4 US Mormons Has Thought About Leaving the LDS Church, Study Shows," Religion News Service, May 19, 2023, https://religionnews.com/2023/05/19/one-in-four-us-mormons-has-thought-about-leaving-the-lds-church-study-shows/.

[293] Matt Martinich, "Growth of The Church of Jesus Christ of Latter-day Saints (LDS Church)," LDS Church Growth, April 5, 2022, https://ldschurchgrowth.blogspot.com/2022/04/country-by-country-membership.html.

[294] Matt Martinich, "Growth of The Church of Jesus Christ of Latter-day Saints (LDS Church)," LDS Church Growth, December 10, 2022, https://ldschurchgrowth.blogspot.com/search?q=December+10%2C+2022.

[295] Matt Martinich, "Growth of The Church of Jesus Christ of Latter-day Saints (LDS Church)," LDS Church Growth, May 14, 2023, https://ldschurchgrowth.blogspot.com/2023/05/country-by-country-membership.html.

[296] John Dehlin, "Episode 1733/Mormon Bishop in Mexico Blows Whistle on Misleading Church Statistics," *Mormon Stories Podcast*, February 23, 2023, https://www.youtube.com/live/NnrIy8qhcwI.

[297] Matt Martinich, quoted in Peggy Fletcher Stack, "Brazil

Mystery: Case of the Missing Mormons (913,045 of Them, to be Exact)," *Salt Lake Tribune*, July 16, 2012, https://archive.sltrib.com/article.php?id=54497395&itype=cmsid.

[298] David Bednar, quoted in Jen Judson, "NPC Headliner Luncheon: Elder David A. Bednar, The Church of Jesus Christ of Latter-day Saints," National Press Club Live, May 26, 2022, https://www.youtube.com/watch?v=vAx1LRSB9kU.

[299] Tony Semerad, "New Allegations Surface of Federal Violations in LDS Church's Stock Portfolio," *Salt Lake Tribune*, May 2, 2024, https://www.sltrib.com/religion/2024/05/02/new-allegations-surface-federal/.

[300] Michelle Nati and Jessie Fetterling, "Richest Religious Organizations in the World," MSN updated June 18, 2024, https://www.msn.com/en-us/news/world/richest-religious-organizations-in-the-world/ar-BB1r5C9r.

[301] Jon Swaine, Douglas MacMillan, and Michelle Boorstein, "Mormon Church Has Misled Members on $100 Billion Tax-Exempt Investment Fund, Whistleblower Alleges," *Washington Post*, December 17, 2109, https://www.washingtonpost.com/investigations/mormon-church-has-misled-members-on-100-billion-tax-exempt-investment-fund-whistleblower-alleges/2019/12/16/e3619bd2-2004-11ea-86f3-3b5019d451db_story.html.

[302] Semerad, "New Allegations Surface."

[303] "The Widow's Mite, A Report on the State of Wealth in The Church of Jesus Christ of Latter-day Saints," The Widow's Mite, accessed July 1, 2024, https://thewidowsmite.org/2023update/.

[304] Semerad, "New Allegations Surface."

[305] Max Roser, "The Internet's History Has Just Begun" Our World in Data, October 3, 2018, https://ourworldindata.org/internet-history-just-begun.

[306] Ani Petrosyan, "Internet Usage in the United States—Statistics & Facts," Statista, March 13, 2024, https://www.statista.com/topics/2237/internet-usage-in-the-united-states/.

Made in the USA
Las Vegas, NV
11 December 2024

13813042R00193